WILD
ADVENTURES
OF THE NEW AVIATORS

WILD
ADVENTURES
OF THE NEW AVIATORS

CHALLENGES AND THRILLS OF HANG-GLIDING,
PARAGLIDING, PARAMOTORING AND
MICROLIGHTING

BRIAN MILTON

WILD ADVENTURES OF THE NEW AVIATORS
Challenges and Thrills of Hang-gliding, Paragliding, Paramotoring and Microlighting

First published in Great Britain in 2024 by
Air World
An imprint of
Pen & Sword Books Ltd
Yorkshire – Philadelphia

Copyright © Brian Milton, 2024

ISBN 978 1 39904 863 7

The right of Brian Milton to be identified as Author of this work has been asserted by him in accordance with the Copyright, Designs and Patents Act 1988.

A CIP catalogue record for this book is available from the British Library.

All rights reserved. No part of this book may be reproduced or transmitted in any form or by any means, electronic or mechanical including photocopying, recording or by any information storage and retrieval system, without permission from the Publisher in writing.

Typeset by SJmagic DESIGN SERVICES, India.

Printed and bound in the UK by CPI Group (UK) Ltd.

Pen & Sword Books Limited incorporates the imprints of After the Battle, Atlas, Archaeology, Aviation, Discovery, Family History, Fiction, History, Maritime, Military, Military Classics, Politics, Select, Transport, True Crime, Air World, Frontline Publishing, Leo Cooper, Remember When, Seaforth Publishing, The Praetorian Press, Wharncliffe Local History, Wharncliffe Transport, Wharncliffe True Crime and White Owl.

For a complete list of Pen & Sword titles please contact

PEN & SWORD BOOKS LIMITED
George House, Units 12 & 13, Beevor Street, Off Pontefract Road,
Barnsley, South Yorkshire, S71 1HN, England
E-mail: enquiries@pen-and-sword.co.uk
Website: www.pen-and-sword.co.uk

or
PEN AND SWORD BOOKS
1950 Lawrence Rd, Havertown, PA 19083, USA
E-mail: uspen-and-sword@casematepublishers.com
Website: www.penandswordbooks.com

Contents

Introduction vi

Chapter 1   Characters and Other Holy Lunatics 1
Chapter 2   Distances and Heights After 1981 44
Chapter 3   Birds and the New Aviation 55
Chapter 4   Paragliding 72
Chapter 5   Women and the New Aviation 98
Chapter 6   Events After 1980 141
Chapter 7   Deaths, and All That 179
Chapter 8   Migration 216
Chapter 9   Didier Favre – Vagabond of the Skies 237

Sources 267

Introduction

I think the idea of a second history of aviation, focused on foot-launched flight, is true and potent. It is a noble story, worth telling, of courage, daring, stoicism and sacrifice. When I completed the first draft of this book, all the New Aviation pioneers were either still alive, and even if some are dead, there are recordings on video and film, and sound recordings of their experiments. Most of us in the New Aviation do not know our own past. This is a comprehensive attempt to come to terms with it.

I was not certain when I started to write *The History of the New Aviation* where I would focus at the end. But it is now obvious, years from where we started, that a small group of flyers in France and Switzerland mark out the New Aviation as wholly different from the Mainstream. They practise 'vagabonding' or what is called bivouac flying, living with a foot-launched wing, either hang glider or paraglider, and making a way through the weather either by foot or foot-launched flight. This is the deepest of all the dreams of man. To stand on a hill, the wind in your face, unfold your wings and be carried aloft by them, who does not wish to have the power to do that? Now we can do it. The Knights Templar among us, Hubert Aupetit, Pierre Bouilloux, Mike and Caroline de Glanville and the great Didier Favre, have done it; there is no reason why you could not too.

Chapter 1

Rich Pfieffer provoking Chris Price to collide with him at 1,500ft, Pfieffer faces 104,000 counts of assault with a deadly weapon over Rose Bowl. Elsinore pilots soar forest fires, moonlight flying in the

INTRODUCTION

Pennines Knock Out distance event in 50mph winds, Lester Cruse blows wing apart at 300ft in Alps without parachute. the experiences of four OAPs, 'thanks to those who threw me off Beachy Head when I lost my bottle', mad aerobatics at American Cup, woman climbs through hole in wing at 6,000ft and jumps off. Swiss bungee jumps off paraglider for 30th birthday, Dangerous Sports Club jumps off Kilimanjaro, cliff jumping from 5,000ft, clash between New Aviation ideas and *Daily Telegraph*.

Chapter 2

225lb English pilot climbs to 10,400ft over Yorkshire Dales in 'wave', crossing the Pyrenees in one flight, South African flies 314km in 'dust devils', Jim Lee's ethics of 'dust devil flying', Kevin Christopherson's 287m flight off Whisky Peak chased by Mom, Larry Tudor's 300-mile world record in dinosaur country, Liavan Mallin's witty 'flutter over the back' in Ireland.

Chapter 3

Judy Leden and the besotted vultures of India, eagle attacks on competitors in the 1988 Worlds in Australia, Jo Bathmann's once-friendly eagle called Maximillian in the Austrian Alps only seen off by pollution, hitch-hiking Mam Tor Crow in the Pennines, two Canadians teach a bunch of geese to see a microlight as their mother, teaching them how to migrate.

Chapter 4

Origins and development of paragliding, hang gliding teaches them to foot launch, a jump off Everest, explosion of growth (80,000 in Japan, 20 per cent women), tumbling distance and height-gain records, Swiss accident study, record flight in South Africa in storms, first 100-mile flight in England, Hubert Aupetit tours Scotland by foot and paraglider as aerial vagabond.

Chapter 5

Early sexist battles, Paige Pfieffer's 51-mile record, sick Japanese girl sung to by Larry Tudor as they create world record in Owens Valley, Kay Simpson and a proposal of marriage flying dual at 500ft. Liavan Mallin ('Little Irish me') creates world record in Owens before amazing accident, Eve Jackson flies first microlight to Australia, Katherine Yardley beats Leden's six-year record, Kari Castle breaks 200 miles wearing adult nappies, Judy Leden – giant of the sport – champion of Britain, Europe and the world, dropping off a balloon in a hang glider over Jordan at 40,000ft, her eyes frozen shut.

Chapter 6

How the British established competition dominance for twelve years, emergence of 1985 World Champion John Pendry, whinges at media disinterest, my downfall as British competitions boss, leading American teams twice against Britain, Royal honours, the killer 1989 World Championships and how they were won by 20-year old Robbie Whittall.

Chapter 7

Debate on death vs growing old, statistics covering twenty years of US hang gliding deaths, examination of why they died, details of all 1991 US deaths, stories about Bob Wills before we lost him to a helicopter. How George Worthington won all world records aged 60 and died two years later because of hubris. Some English deaths and why they happened, the 'Great Italian Killer Storm of 1989', famous pilots die, John Hudson's poetic view of wave before his death, plea to understand why deaths happen, Keith Cockroft dies as he lived.

Chapter 8

Milton's Migration Rules, origins of the 444, bivouac-flying like the birds, Mike and Caroline de Glanville's first migration flight, band of

INTRODUCTION

Knights Templar dream of living daily on the wing, Pierre Bouilloux does 385km over twelve days in a paraglider, France's Hubert Aupetit lays down ethics of bivouac flying for ordinary mortals.

Chapter 9

Pilot comment on Swiss champion Didier Favre, throws over business and tries for 444 on a hang glider, years of attempts, agony of living with self-imposed ideals. Didier's account of a 1991 success in the Alps, shepherd dubs him 'Vagabond of the Skies', gear needed for bivouac flying. Didier tries for 1,111km flight over Alps from Monaco to Slovenia, fails because he 'betrayed the ideal', 1993 success after three months' living on his wing with the eagles, champions new type of wing, killed at 47 testing it.

Chapter 1

Characters and Other Holy Lunatics

However much it is denied, a key element of the New Aviation is its attraction to holy lunatics. Mainstream Aviation had a similar attraction before the regulators cleaned its act up in the 1930s. I am rather partial to holy lunatics; they all share the quality I admire most, individual courage, moral and physical. Courage is the one quality that crosses all culture barriers. It is the existential quality, and the New Aviation was seen, early on, as a playground of courage.

I once heard a British Army bomb-disposal officer called Chris Hunter interviewed on BBC Radio 4's *Today* programme about the nature of the courage he had to find within himself to do his terrifying job. Unusually – because there was no special reaction from the BBC presenters to his answer – he was asked where he found such courage. He said, with him, it had three elements.

The first was *atonement*, the second was *duty*, the third was *exhilaration*.

The interview moved on without comment!

On my part I was so electrified I leapt out of bed and tore down the stairs to find a pen and paper to note the details. I had never heard such an exact description of the qualities I aspired to, and still aspire to in life, but especially within the New Aviation. Compare such an answer to the whiny cries for *safe spaces* and *no platforming* we hear from our modern university-based, so-called officer classes.

Bill Moyes is now a revered pioneer of hang gliding, but at heart he is a holy lunatic. He has broken virtually every bone in his body one way or another giving flying shows, and only started flying because barefoot water-skiing became too tame. Bill Bennett was hardly an academic when he went off to America to bring them the word. Jack Lambie, Richard Miller, Nick Regan, George Worthington … holy lunatics to a man.

One such character is America's Rich Pfieffer, who came into hang gliding in 1978 after being a champion skydiver. Rich is not very tall, not terribly beautiful, but bright and certainly aggressive. His book, *Hang Gliding According to Pfieffer*, is the best raw guide to competing in the New Aviation, quite outstanding among a series of worthy guides about how to fly. Pfieffer thinks all the time ... about winning. He very quickly learned to fly and went off to Owens Valley, listened sceptically to George Worthington putting him down for his inexperience, and in short order notched up two competition wins, one year after the other.

I remember Rich Pfieffer as a noise off stage during the 1980 American Cup in Tennessee, when we were finally beaten by the American hang gliding team. 'Is that guy Milton a lawyer?' he asked, after a row over ballast left the Americans wrong-footed. But I first really noticed him in the final of the US Nationals in 1981, when he beat one of my heroes, another American called Jeff Burnett, with as brilliant a piece of flying as I have ever seen.

During that period of US competition, pilots flew one-on-one tasks around a pylon course, first man around the last pylon the winner. You would see pairs of hang gliders all over the sky, like male birds about to mate with desperately unwilling females, in a tactical game that was fascinating to watch if you knew what was happening. In general, the pilot who stayed highest in the pair won, for coming up to the pylon he had the choice to pull in the bar and speed around it first before going back to 'sit' on his opponent.

In the Nationals, Burnett had Pfieffer pinned in the air, flying above him with a glider just as fast and was odds-on to win. Yet in a ten-second decision Pfieffer got away to complete the course and left Burnett on the ground. I was the public commentator at the competition, and hope I was able to convey – despite my British accent, I had been a BBC Radio journalist for ten years by then – the sheer excitement at such a superb exhibition of flying skills.

In a thermal, one competition pilot has to out-climb the other. Pfieffer favoured winding up his opponents on the ground first, going up and glaring at them (difficult when you only reach the chest of some pilots, but Rich persisted), telling them to stay out of his thermal ... or else. The 'or else' resolved itself into Pfieffer flying under his opponent, throwing the bar out, screaming and looking the other way. The general effect was to frighten the opponent into leaving the thermal, even 360ing the wrong way out of it so that Pfieffer ended up on top, where he stuck like glue. Pfieffer did not worry about being bellowed at when they both landed, so long as he won.

He tried this tactic with Chris Price in one competition, a tall experienced pilot with a mind and a unique pedigree, former best friend of Bob Wills. Price did not take kindly to being threatened on the ground by this small ferocious man, and secondly, to looking down at Pfieffer below him in the air as Pfieffer grinned and pushed the bar out. Pfieffer's glider reared right up in front of Price, who was forced to turn one way or the other. Mad as a rattlesnake, Price did a fast 360 and stuffed the nose of his hang glider right up Pfieffer's bum!

The two wings, locked together, started spinning out of the sky from about 1,500ft, while the pilots 'had words with each other'. They kicked the wreckage apart and both threw their parachutes, which worked, lowering them and their wings to the ground. The competition organisers disqualified both pilots for that flight, so Pfieffer learned how to modify his tactics, especially against Price. After all, if you end up with a zero, it is not worth doing it.

It was an ambition of Californian pilots ever since learning how to soar, to try and fly a hang glider over the Rose Bowl American football match in Pasadena. The Rose Bowl is an annual competition between the two best college football teams in the US, and has a status somewhere between Ascot, the Oxford vs Cambridge rugby match at Twickenham, and a garden party at Buckingham Palace. The cream of American society has to be there. Year after year a small dedicated band of hang glider pilots gathered on nearby Mount Wilson and prayed for the right flying conditions to fly over the Bowl. For years they failed. Finally, on 1 January 1981, Rich Pfieffer, now US National Champion, took off, got over the park in the middle of the match, did three 360s and then flew away to land.

Boy, was Pasadena mad! At the time Pfieffer made the flight there was nothing specifically illegal in what he had done, so he was initially facing charges of 104,000 counts of assault with a deadly weapon! One would like to attribute this to a delicious American sense of humour, but in fact, the charges were serious. Though Pfieffer had harmed no one he faced thirty days in jail. He took his case to law – he subsequently went on in life to become a lawyer – and was cleared of these amazing charges. But I understand new laws have been drafted that make it illegal even to *possess* a hang glider within the limits of the City of Pasadena. The outrage chuntered on for months. The Old Farts Tendency in hang gliding wanted to crucify Pfieffer for that flight, and certainly to take away his title.

Joe Bostik, Czech-born 1988 US hang gliding champion, once topped the international ratings as the best competition pilot in the world. In the brush fire season in California in September–October 1988, the Sylmar area burst into flames, including the hang gliding take-off area and parts of Elsinore, where the local club sports a skull and crossbones and members cheer ironically when a pilot crashes in the landing area. Five local pilots, including Bostik, thought the brush fires would produce some interesting lift and took off to soar the burning hills and houses. One said later that he climbed above the flames at between 2,000 and 3,000ft a minute, that is, the height of the Empire State Building in thirty seconds, but he thought at one time his wings would catch fire. It was felt this activity got in the way of the helicopters and aircraft mobilised to put out the flames, and a number of predatory American lawyers became interested. Bostik, unusually, was first to land, and as a result was first to carry the blame for the flight. He was barred from competitions for six months.

In 1977, Phil Robinson in Lancashire took off on Thursday and landed on Friday:

> Bob Calvert and I were returning home from our local pub one night (The Last Drop) when I discovered that if I turned off the headlamps of my car, I could see to drive OK by the reflection of the moonlight on the snow. This sparked a conversation between Bob and myself along the lines of 'if we could see to drive without lights then it could be possible to go flying!' After checking wind strength and direction, and finding it to our liking, we decided to have a go. I stopped on the way to ring Graham Hobson, asking if he was coming along. It was about 10.45pm and Graham, not convinced, decided to go back to bed, and teddy!
>
> Eventually we arrived at the bottom of the ridge, got out and found the wind across the slope. Not easily deterred, we set off and up. Approaching the top we were pleasantly surprised to find the wind coming right up the face, and would you believe it? 16 mph!

CHARACTERS AND OTHER HOLY LUNATICS

Without further ado Bob rigged, clipped in, and took off into the deep black sky and soared upwards. I soon lost sight of him as he merged into space and I began to get a little worried. Minutes later, he came back into view and yelled down to me that it was absolutely smooth and that the view was fantastic! (visibility was no problem).

Looking up at Bob, it was difficult to see him from the ground except when he 360'd and I caught sight of the moonlight shining on the ice formed on the sail. After 15 minutes, Bob landed back on top and then it was my turn. A few ecstatic words were exchanged and then it was 'click', four steps, and away and up to about 150ft above the top.

It was amazing how bright the land below was, and the air was perfectly smooth. The view was beautiful, I could see the surrounding towns and villages lit up and twinkling, just like the stars above. To the west, the coast was visible. I could see Blackpool and the tower. I relaxed in the smooth air and floated from one end of the ridge to the other, barely needing to initiate the turn at the end of each beat. Bob's Cloudbase hang glider was flying as wonderfully as ever.

What a view! Looking down at all the white below and watching my shadow follow me as I floated high above the land, and then looking up into the deep black of space at all the stars resembling the lights of the towns below. After 15 minutes I reluctantly landed on top, settling down into the snow, light as a feather and a little bit pleased with myself. It was a flight I will never forget, as at one point in the air I flew through midnight to the next morning.

Dunstan Hadley, the BHGA's doctor, always a man to look for a way to let holy lunatics get on with it, wrote mildly about making sure pilots had night vision in the air when they flew at night, and brought down a hail of abuse from a couple of OFTs. Freddy de Frias from the CAA also commented, rather kindly, on the flight, but shuddered at the thought of ice forming on a hang glider's wing:

> I do not deny that night flying is potentially more dangerous than daytime flying. It most certainly is. Perhaps the risks

inherent in our sport anyway are enough. Nights fit for flying are few and far between and have to be selected with care. If you consider yourself a safe and responsible pilot, if you take double the care you normally take, if you obey the law, night flying under a full moon and snow can be absolute magic.

Sometimes holy lunacy just happens. You are on your own, and a deep feeling of the 'go-for-its' fills you so that horizons are blinkered and you are consumed with longing to fly. Other times, it is a collective decision. In the first ten years of hang gliding when it was almost exclusively a male sport, otherwise sensible pilots would gather on a hill and together, without actually discussing it, decide to go bonkers. One such event was the short-lived but memorable Welsh Knock-Out Distance Event at Rhossili in 1978. There was no money to be won, just a cup and a title not worth a tremendous amount because, by this time, everyone was going XC. And yet ... put competition pilots together and they will compete. Trevor Birkbeck, who made that lovely flight on Winter Hill with John Hudson, established his reputation as a blowed-in-the-glass animal here, to use a Jack London quotation. Bob 'Spitfire' McKay was Meet Director, and wrote about it:

> A huge wave hits the backside of the Worms Head Hotel and the spume rises 200ft in the rotor to be whipped off the top away to the North. 'It's blowin' a hooley!' says the coastguard, relaying a forecast, south-south-west, Force 5/7, increasing to Storm Force 9. Not much point in going to the top of Rhossili, but we do. We gather on the ridge. The wind is almost south, straight off the Pimple. I start to walk over to Rectory Ridge around the back of the Bowl. Nobody follows. Nobody believes we are going to fly. I arrive to find Tony 'Bullet' Fletcher, our wind-dummy, already rigging his brand-new Gryphon. The ventimeter reads 26-30-28-34-16 mph ...
>
> The wind is about 10 degrees off Rectory Ridge which faces south-west, but away goes Tony (like a ruddy bullet), climbing steadily but not penetrating much, sliding away sideways to get over the beach, no lift once he's out there,

CHARACTERS AND OTHER HOLY LUNATICS

'orrible turbulence over the ledge and he drops about 100ft, smooths it out and turns into wind over the sand, lands, kneels and gives thanks!

A couple of pilots detach themselves from the bunch on Rhossili Ridge and start to carry across. It is tough to make a ruling so we leave it like this: if both competitors in a one-on-one distance event agree to postpone, OK. If one is prepared to fly and the other not, he must withdraw and let any willing reserve take his place (I know, I know, 'Bob McKay's a bastard') but nobody has to fly if they don't want to.

Two Gryphons go up for a five-minute soar, several more pilots detach themselves from the bunch gathered on the ridge, like a scene from 'Apache Pass'. The beach party set the mark so that the first leg is cross-wind due west to about 100 yards out from the ledge next to the beach, then turn left straight into wind along the beach. It's blowing! Never below 25 mph at the top, never below 18 along the beach. Bob Calvert and Jo Binns are ready.

Steve Hunt's Hiway have brought seven prototypes ('Yor bloody competitions cost me two hundred parnds in overtoim last week!') and it speak volumes for the design ability of him and his team that their flyers are ready to go in these conditions with only one, or at most two previous flights on their latest machine. Each pilot is allowed 5 minutes in the air. Jo Binns is away first. His wing flexes a bit as he is whipped up from take-off but he turns away a little too soon and is losing a lot of height getting to the mark. The turbulence has increased, the wind has shifted a little further to the south.

Bob Calvert is in the air, staying with the lift a bit longer than Jo, penetrating more forward across the bowl and gaining height before breaking for the mark. It is obvious halfway down he has got it won and when he turns his penetration is better. He wins by a 'cricket pitch'. The distance is foreshortened by the strong wind. In still air this would have been considerably longer. Groundspeeds are about 5/10 mph in the final leg.

We just haven't enough marshals or time to make full notes, and we are too busy to see the whole of each flight. The wind is shifting further south but not getting any stronger. Turbulence is increasing.

Lester Cruise beats Bob Bailey by a good few yards and puts up the longest distance so far. The Wasp Gryphons are demonstrating their undoubted superiority, a brilliant design and the full year's development is paying off.

Brian Wood withdraws and in goes Heinz Dorler (Gryphon) to beat Simon Wooton (Chargus) after a very hairy ride.

We are all confident it is going to ease off as the day goes on. It doesn't. The wind is inching around to dead south, on a west-facing slope. Jim Pedroza (Gryphon) makes it look easy penetrating well into the bowl and never allowing himself to get downwind of the mark. Rob Lewis-Evans (Birdman) does get downwind and loses to Jim.

Miles Handley gives his place to Trevor Birkbeck, who wins in fine style, putting up the longest flight of the day, even passing Lester's mark.

Ashley Doubtfire, the ace distance flyer, does it again and brings his Moonraker down to beat one of the Gryphons flown by Mick Evans, who hit bad turbulence and got downwind of the turning mark.

Dale Clothier and Bob Wiseley postpone, so do Chris Johnson and Tom Knight. The wind shifts east of south, we can't really go on much longer but we do, pilots are still coming to the line.

Paddy Munroe (Hiway Prototype) hits such bad turbulence with the wind scrubbing right along the ridge and screwing into the bowl that his 'droop tips' partially retract with each buffet, and he ornithopts to victory over Mark Southall (Birdman Moonraker). Mark has made a fair recovery from his recent accident but says he still feels it a bit in one shoulder.

Nobody gets far along the beach after turning the mark. Only Lester and Trevor approach the 200-yard mark.

CHARACTERS AND OTHER HOLY LUNATICS

Well, that's all who are going today, gone! The wind is still 25–30 but almost south-east. It is too bad we have to call it off for the day, and we hope we can get through the rest of the competition tomorrow. It cannot be any worse than today.

It is! Sunday morning on Rectory Ridge finds us all cowering in a hollow. It's south-south-west, 40 mph on the crest, and 25 mph on the beach where the sand is streaming along like ice crystals in Scott of the Antarctic.

OK, says I, we will keep the course open until 4pm. Anyone left in the competition can go at their own discretion. Longest flight wins.

The day drags on. Nobody rigs – wrong, Trevor Birkbeck rigs, he's going to try it. Down the face it's about 25–30 mph. He lies in prone, the nose is raised a 'smidge' and he hurtles into the sky. Working hard but seemingly relaxed he is torn away from the ridge and downwind. He's not going to make the mark but is steady. He lands about 20 yards short but a little further out. We accept it as a 'distance'.

Nobody rigs. A gust is recorded at 45 mph. We adjourned to the pub for a glass of lemonade (ho-ho-ho) and a pie. Back on top at 2pm it is still 40+ and 'heather-lobbing' competitions are the order of the day. Down on the beach it is 22/26. Ashley Doubtfire rigs and leers at everybody. Lester Cruise rigs and carries down for a take-off halfway. A speed of 50 mph is registered at the top. Trevor's solitary marker stands unchallenged. The deadline is 4pm and it is now 3.45pm. The beach party are writing something in the sand. In big letters, 'Merry Christmas, Trevor'. We get the message. Ashley de-rigs. Lester de-rigs. The tide comes in and gently washes away the greeting. It's over!

Well, it may not have been much of a distance competition but it was a magnificent testimony to the design and construction of British hang gliders, and the skill and discretion of our leading pilots. Do you ever get the feeling that nobody loves you?

One of my favourite lunatics is Lester Cruise, an original among the fifty-six names in the British National League of Hang Gliding, and subsequently a member of the southern 'Rat Pack'. Other Rat Pack members were Keith Reynolds, Mick Maher, Mick Evans, Brian Wood and Alan Weekes. They were superb pilots, and all except Weekes represented Britain in A-Team competitions like the Europeans or the American Cup. I remember during the early League going around waking pilots up for a briefing, and pulling open the door of Mick Maher's London taxi; two or three bodies, half asleep and groaning, the worse for drink, would fall out. It never seemed to affect their flying.

Lester was due to fly in the first League competition, and was desperate for a place in British teams. But he also had a burning ambition, back in 1976, to loop his hang glider. The loop may be commonplace now among specialised aerobatic pilots, some of whom carry two parachutes as back-up. Back then, looping was considered a lunatic ambition, especially as we had no parachutes at all. Sure enough, when Lester went for it, it went wrong:

> I have been asked to write about what happened in Austria on 30 January, 1977. Before I begin I would like to thank all those people who asked after me when I was in hospital, especially those who wrote and particularly those who took the trouble to telephone. It was nice to hear from you all.
>
> There were many wild rumours going around, including one that I had expired and much speculation as to how it happened.
>
> It is common knowledge that I fly radical manoeuvres and that I am particularly interested in the loop. Since the World Championships in Kossen last September where I was pushing unsuitable machinery to its limits, I have been waiting for the right equipment and opportunity.
>
> The equipment was a hot-rod glider we called the Super Nova, a lovely little prototype that I was really getting together, with 118 degree nose angle, 175 sq ft sail, fully cambered, and a 32 ft span. Nice design work by Terry Haynes and potentially the best wing I have ever flown.
>
> I work full-time for Waspair, largely on development work, building, testing, and demonstrating hang gliders. I also accompany Robin Haynes on promotional trips abroad, and this is where the opportunity came in. A trip was proposed in

January taking us through Luxembourg, Germany and then into Austria and the mountains of the Tyrol. The mountains often provide the necessary altitude in the still air conditions I find useful for assessing a wing's performance.

The glider was strong, already with 3mm rigging, 19 ft leading edges and triple steel deflexers. It really felt stiff and I was into 130 degree wingovers on the Sussex Downs as it was. However, in view of the proposals I had for the glider, it was decided to make it even stronger using 1-inch tube to build the control bar. At this stage I must point out that Terry was helping me reluctantly as he was very much against my radical manoeuvres, stating that the stresses couldn't be accurately calculated. And in fact I undertook not to loop until we knew more, particularly as efforts were made to provide a parachute, but a suitable one was not available at short notice.

Anyway, after the usual disorganised departure we made tracks in my little Escort van. First stop across the water was Luxembourg; there are few hills in this tiny country so they mostly fly in France.

Germany next, around Lake Tegernsee in the Tyrol. Beautiful. They usually fly the Wallberg here but the ski lift was out of action so we went to the small training slope called Bookhiem. Here I had a go on a Sun Swift (nice kite) before having a squirt on the Nova which was the first since its Charles Atlas course. My flight here revealed slight differences with the handling. The centre of gravity seemed back a shade, and directional stability was not as good, but it was still air and most of my flying on Super Nova had been in soaring conditions. So I had to wait until the next flight to clarify the problems and it was this flight in Austria that turned out nearly fatal for me.

We moved on that afternoon to stay with a friend and colleague, Heinz Dorler in Kirchberg, Austria, where there are a number of mountains to fly, all with ski lifts or roads to the top.

After a good night's sleep and a little business in the morning, we joined forces with two other flyers, Austrian

Helmut Lorenzoni and Australian Wally Reeves. Wally worked at Heinz Dorler's school and has since worked at the Wasp factory. We set off for the Guisberg, a local mountain below which a horse race was taking place, and we had been asked to do some exhibition flying and land on the course.

Flying into the race course would have used up all the useful altitude so I decided not to participate in this activity. Instead, I would fly over the usual landing area at the bottom of the ski lift and evaluate the glider some more.

I informed the lads of my intention and explained that I would probably do some wingovers, but would not be attempting the loop at this stage.

Heinz was particularly interested in our latest design, so he wanted to take off after me and watch it from the air. Wally went first and made for the race course.

I launched next, the deep snow making running difficult and the wearing of snow boots essential, but I was cleanly into the air settling down on a different course from Wally.

The glider felt fine, obviously trimmed a little differently as it wasn't quite 'hands off' but not as bad as I had thought after the flight in Germany.

By the time I was vertically over the landing area Heinz had taken off and was observing me. I was happy enough with Super Nova to wing it over so ... here we go ... stall out, then bar way back to a steep, fast but controlled dive ... now bar out to pop it over, rolling off at 90 degrees ... that went well, so I thought I'd go over the 90 this time. I was not anticipating any problems, I'd been over lots of times before and I had plenty of inertia coming out of the first wingover so ... accelerate by pulling on even though already in a steep dive, then bar out applying less bank and timing it perfectly so it doesn't roll off before winging over, peachy 120/130 degree but a little slow over the top. The steeper the wingover, the more inertia builds up and things were really buzzing at this moment.

Doing a double continuous wingover should have provided enough speed and so I decided coming fast out of the second to go again. I made sure of the speed by going right through the trapeze bar and holding for at least 3 more seconds than previously, then ... pow! up it went, the rate of conversion from speed to height was always amazing, but 'Oh Gawd! What have I done?' The glider was going over at about 160 degrees and had already pitched over the 90 so pulling the bar back at that time would have put me into an horrific keel-slide and a possible forward tuck. Apart from being too steep, Super Nova was slowing down and I had no choice but to go with it.

She crept over the top and 'parked' upside down, too far over to roll off, and instead stabilised inverted. I had actually prepared for this by fitting catch rigging on the back wires which I dropped into, and holding tightly on to the control frame I was fully supported off the keel. I was looking down on the nose of the glider and I could see land below me, so I was almost over but the sail had turned inside out and it began to free-fall upside down. Now at this point I wasn't too worried because the king post was holding out and I knew that it would pull out sooner or later because my weight had to transfer to below the glider somewhere, but what followed was quite disturbing.

It was inverted for only a few seconds, but during that time it was falling, and built up a dangerous speed. It was just beginning to oscillate when it flipped, rotating around the cross-boom.

This action was so fierce that I don't remember the transition period between being wrong and being right side up, only being squashed into my harness by the centrifugal force and the control bar tearing out of my hands. I was totally disorientated by the speed and I didn't hear the noise of the sail whip-lashing to the fully-inflated position, which according to Heinz was very loud.

Super Nova simply blew apart. Both leading edges broke, one side before and after the cross-boom, bending steel deflexers in the process. The keel broke, making the control-bar fly away due to loss of cable tension, but amazingly, the cross-booms survived.

WILD ADVENTURES OF THE NEW AVIATORS

The 4.7oz sail burst both sides of the keel, one side in the stitching and the other in the fabric itself. For the latter to happen, the manufacturers of the sail cloth calculated that the force generated by the whiplash was in excess of 100Gs. The force I experienced has been estimated at about 10G.

This all happened rather quickly at about 300ft, and I wouldn't accept that it had broken until I was falling vertically with no trapeze bar around me, and growing sail noise coming from above. I confirmed this by looking up and seeing a lot of sky, ragged sail, broken leading edges and not one part of the glider appeared intact.

You can probably imagine the rest.

I seemed to fall slowly at first, looking down on pine woods and fields, but I got rapidly lower and faster until I was merging with the landscape at a terrifying speed. Death seemed imminent and I tried not to be conscious over the last 50ft. Obvious thoughts and feelings went through my head but the fall lasted only six or so seconds and I hit the ground so hard that I still don't know how I survived, but I did.

I became progressively conscious of me still being alive, light to my eyes, movement to my head, arms, etc. I had landed feet first in the middle of a downhill ski racecourse, and punched a hole in the well-compacted snow up to my waist. The wreckage, luckily, had missed me. My first reaction was to get up and walk away from the glider and pretend it never happened, but all I could manage was to crawl away spitting blood and gasping for breath.

Heinz, who saw everything from the air, came circling over and landed as quickly and as near as possible. He helped me a lot interpreting and escorting me to the hospital. They discovered I had compression fractures on two vertebrae and a broken ankle, together with temporarily paralysed insides due to shock and a lot of pain for a few days.

They plastered me up and I was walking in a week and a half, and back home in just over two. But I won't forget the lovely Austrian nurses, corridor-racing on crutches, playing hookey to the pubs every night also on crutches, and the farewell booze-up in the hospital reception.

CHARACTERS AND OTHER HOLY LUNATICS

I was flying again the day after the removal of my leg plaster seven weeks after the accident. Nobody knows how fortunate I was more than I do, and whilst I wish it hadn't happened, I have become rather more experienced in the way in which I intend to carry on flying, and a newly-acquired parachute improves the safety aspect a great deal.

I was one of those who telephoned Lester in hospital, wondering if he was going to make the first League competition. He couldn't fly then because of his injuries, but he pleaded urgently down the phone that I had to keep a place open for him. He would be back, he said, I shouldn't worry, and I can imagine him wrestling with a 'lovely Austrian nurse' as he was speaking.

Later that year, Lester broke his leg again and turned up at the fifth League with the offending leg in plaster. On one still-air day he couldn't get up enough speed to take off in a competitive round so four fellow pilots picked him and his glider up like a gigantic dart and launched him into the task. He came tenth overall for the year, and I believe he won that task.

Lester Cruise went to the 1978 European Championships as a member of the British Team, and during one task was nowhere to be found. The rest of the team rigged his glider and set up his harness. Then someone more knowing that the rest found him in urgent discussions of a horizontal nature in a nearby bush with a lady called Petra. The team pulled him out just in time to set him up, before he was called to fly. He kept saying in an injured tone, 'I would have got here on time, fellas.' And, of course, one day he did his beloved loop. He's happily married now and running a windsurfing centre in the West Country. But he had an exotic youth.

I have had aspirations, myself, from time to time, to holy lunacy. In 1977 we were having dinner one night at home in St Albans, 25 miles north of London, and I was feeling a few pangs of conscience about hang gliding. All the holiday my wife Fiona had had in the past two years was spent on windy hills. Fiona had produced a terrific dinner, and drink had been taken.

'Why don't I take you to Norfolk for a canal cruise on the Broads for a week?' I said, after about three bottles of wine.

'Why don't you have a crack at hang gliding across the English Channel?' she said. 'Wouldn't you rather do that?'

As she was the mother of my 2-year-old son James at the time, this was a very sporting proposition, if it was actually true. It turned out, she wasn't joking. Fortified by the wine, I phoned Ken Messenger, the first conqueror of Snowdon, and said, 'How high must you go, and what glide angle would you need?'

'– to cross the Channel, 'he said. 'Yes, I've always wanted to do that.'

The big problem was organisation. We split the jobs that night. Ken made the hang gliders and drop gear, I looked after official permissions, Met reports and publicity, and Fiona used her newly formed Flight Promotions company to get sponsorship. Ken had his own favourite balloonist, a Wiltshire farmer called David Liddiard, and I got the OK from Phillip Hutchins, a Buckinghamshire solicitor, who had dropped Graham Driscoll and me from a balloon from 13,770ft the previous November in Shropshire for a new world record.

We all thought it could work.

That was about the middle of March. We set the permissions to come into operation by 20 May, and began building a most extraordinary and co-ordinated organisation to cope with getting everything together on sixteen hours' notice when the weather came right. It was easy to decide what was ideal weather; a northwester wind, light on the surface, strong at 20,000ft, with clear skies, and those conditions had to occur between dawn and 6.30 in the morning. If we went any later, we would have Concorde sniffing around our back rigging. The wind had to be a *deep* northwester, and we called off some early alerts because, while the surface wind was in the right direction, upper winds were not. It was a given that, not only would the hang gliders – which could be steered – have to cross the Channel, but by their very nature, the balloons had to make the crossing as well.

The Civil Aviation Authority approved the attempt, provided CATO 6 – the Civil Air Traffic Organisation – agreed, and after talks with Mr Tony Slow we began to get the letters into the post for the right permissions. The French proved to be odd to cope with; six weeks after we asked them for permission to land near Calais we had a letter back with a long list of demands. But a lovely set of Frenchmen we discovered through Phillip Hutchins, who often ballooned in France, said go ahead. 'If everything goes right,' said one French count, 'the authorities will be happy. Just make sure you don't have an accident.'

CHARACTERS AND OTHER HOLY LUNATICS

Ken and his crew at the Birdman factory began experimenting with balloon releases, and working on figures to discover what height we needed in different winds to cover the 27 miles between Dover Castle – where the great French aviator Louis Blériot crash-landed in 1909 – and Blériot Plage, where he had taken off from. A visit to France by Fiona's sister Jeanie (fluent in French) fixed a landing area, right next to the village of Sangatte, just south of Calais. Phillip Hutchins got his sponsors, J&B Whisky, interested in the idea, while David Liddiard, who is a sort of classical Tory squire with all the qualities that make one understand why people vote Tory, chose a 5-year-old balloon called Beatrice to get Ken up there.

Fiona was a wonder with the sponsors. There was a magical week in which she succeeded in getting Long John Whisky interested in the British Hang Gliding Open at Mere, in Wiltshire, against all the odds, when budgets had already been allocated for the year. At the same time she found two sponsors for the Channel flight. I paired up with Phillip to fly for J&B Whisky, while Ken got Olympic Holidays, and we had enough money to put the whole exercise together. All of that came down to Fiona, because deep down, none of us actually believed she would succeed. Flight Promotions also organised the whole thing.

We had to get oxygen for seven people, with no precedent to work on; transponders for the balloons, to clear heights so that aircraft could start flying again on the blocked airways between Paris, Brussels and London; a helicopter for the film crew; a stills photographic agency; two more balloons as camera platforms; huge banners for the sponsors (we found another David Liddiard type of man in Harold Lessey, from the Royal Temple Yacht Club) ... there were a hundred things to organise. From my point of view, I also had to cope with getting the National Hang Gliding League off the ground and through a bit of flak, suffer a good carve-up at the AGM standing against Pat King for the Chairmanship, try and finish my long-suffering book on hang gliding, and hold down a freelance reporting job at the BBC.

In the middle of all this, we discovered that an ace American pilot called Wayne Mulgrew had also gone through the complicated permissions process, swearing everyone to secrecy, and was going to fly *our* Channel, in *our* Jubilee year, to the eternal shame (if he succeeded) of the whole British hang gliding community. We were determined to beat him, and so kept everything under wraps as long as possible.

Wayne was unfortunate enough to ask Phillip Hutchins to fly him, so that's where his secrecy broke down.

We had a false alarm on 21 June, when conditions looked like they would be right the following day. The massive phone-around began and we all assembled at a hotel – the Bramling House – near Canterbury for take-off the next day. The one sour note was the farmer who owned the take-off field who, on learning we were sponsored, demanded £1,000 for the use of his field for two hours, and would not go down below £100. Everything worked, except the weather. The four balloonists turned up, the helicopter went on standby, we had an aircraft waiting for the film crew to rush them to France, and stills photographers turned up. There were ground crews for Ken and I (Roy Hill, Dave Raymond, Johnny Carr, Dave Weedon, Mark Southall); we all piled into a party at Olympic Holidays' expense, and at three o'clock in the morning, I had the agony of calling the whole thing off. The weather trough that was due through with north-westerlies behind it had been delayed, and it came past us on our way back to London at 6.30 in the morning, too late to try within our permissions window.

When conditions began to look right again, around 19/20 July, the pulling together operation was not so smooth. All the principals made it to the hotel, but we could not get hold of Don Cameron for his camera balloon, and went without him. The film crew we had originally used was not available (the Queen was visiting Birmingham, and they were covering that), so we pulled one together at really short notice. This time, though, the weather was nearly right, and we went off at 3am to the new take-off field near Pelham and began to set up.

I had always been confident that I would get across, so long as I had the right height. There was some amicable arguing with Phillip, with me saying, 'I'll negotiate down reluctantly from 20,000ft,' and him worrying about the fuel he would use getting above 15,000ft. He was very conscious that he, too, had to cross the Channel after I had dropped away from him on my own flight. What none of us brought into our calculations was the extraordinary sink over the Channel. We boast of sink rates of 250ft/min, so what do you think of 1,000ft/min? That is what I had, all the way. Ken fared better, but he got a lot closer to the English coast when his real flying began.

As the sky began to get light, we saw a bit more cloud around than we were happy with, but enough blue sky to keep us cheerful. The wind was the right speed and direction, and the preparations on the ground went perfectly. Three balloons were inflated, two fitted with transponders (which tell radar the identity and height of the aircraft), and the helicopter arrived on schedule. Both the kites were rigged, and we all dressed in thermal underwear, ski suits, double gloves, thick socks, and various bits and pieces like cameras and tape recorders. The take-off went smoothly, but we began to split up early on. David Liddiard was so loaded with gas bottles that Phillip shot up past him, and I remember looking down on Ken as we drifted towards Dover. The camera balloon just went further and further away from us, and we never really got near to it.

Ken said he watched me go for it when he was at 10,000ft, 3 miles short of the coast, and he climbed steadily to 18,000ft with just a few scares. David was burning gas furiously, so that a warning device – set to drop when the top of his balloon reached 220°F – fell on to Ken's hang glider on the way up, and was carried across to France on the king post. Every time David stopped burning, he asked Ken if he wanted more height, and when Ken shouted back, 'Yes, please', he carried on climbing until they saw the coast go past beneath them.

Ken's drop was rather vertical in the thin air. His nose in the oxygen mask was clogged up, and as he swung towards France before pulling the release, he was very cold indeed. But he shot away smoothly, having lost sight of me, and set off just to the right of the sun, with a sink rate of around 600ft/min, well clear of the cloud. The trip across was very fast, because about twelve minutes later, he looked through a hole in the cloud and saw land – France! Picking his way through thin cloud, he in fact passed over the landing area and found himself over Calais, and dropping through cloud at 4,000ft, he could see the landing area 2 miles or so – up-wind! – behind him. The landing, on a small road just 200 yards short of where he wanted to go, was smooth and easy, but the intense cold had got through to Ken's bones, and for a while he suffered. The lucky man was right there, though, when the champagne and whisky were opened, and the celebrations began as soon as the hovercraft deposited all the ground crew and cameramen in France. But Fiona began to get a bit worried, even though Ken was convinced I was on my way to Paris.

The balloon crossing of the Channel, a rare event, had never been done before by a gang of three. Phillip, who had dropped me from J&B, had been very worried about his fuel, and Harold Lessey was following him in a motor boat with spare gas cylinders on board for a mid-Channel refuelling if it was needed. In the event, Phillip landed near Boulogne with ample fuel to spare, more than two full gas cylinders left of the six he had started with. The camera balloon continued on its merry way with its makers – the Thunder manufacturers Tom Donnelly and Dick Wirth – thoroughly enjoying fulfilling their ambition to make the Channel crossing. David, in Beatrice, had a nice moment when it came out of cloud with David facing the wrong way, not able to see France and wondering if he ever would. He landed in a reed bank and was passed up an escalating scale of French coppers until someone actually believed he had crossed the Channel. It was unfortunate that all the ground-crew gannets had consumed the champagne by the time the balloonists eventually arrived at the landing site. It was, after all, a first for them, too (though Phillip had actually made a solo crossing a year earlier).

As I say, the celebrations were in full swing. Fiona could not find me, and when Phillip phoned in to say that he had dropped me at 14,000ft instead of the agreed on height of 20,000ft, it dawned on some of those drunkards that I might, just might, be in the drink. I had been, as it happened, for an hour and a half. So what happened to me?

I was higher than Ken and about a mile in front of him, as we approached the coast. But my communication with Phillip was not good, what with him having to cope with the radio as well, and things began to go wrong. I did not know at the time that Phillip had approached Ken Messenger the previous evening, and asked him confidentially what was a safe height to drop me, below my requested height of 20,000ft. I heard later that Ken had told him that I could safely be dropped at 14,000ft. It would have been helpful if he had talked to me about this, because dangling 30ft below a balloon at 14,000ft is not a time or place to begin a debate. At 500ft above that height, Phillip told me he was going to descend, and I should be ready to drop off. We were still a mile and a half short of the coast.

Listening to the tape of the conversation later, I note I asked him to go on a bit, as we were not at the coast and we were too low. I assumed he had fuel problems – he had warned me I could not argue with balloon pilots about their fuel – so I did not argue when he started to descend. I gave him a warning I was going to go on a count of fifteen (to tell the cameramen), struggled into the budgie position on the bar, counted, and released.

CHARACTERS AND OTHER HOLY LUNATICS

I had not been, and I am surprised at this, at all nervous, though I was not happy about the low height I was being dropped from, because it left no room at all for miscalculations. The drop was easy, I turned out towards the sea, and was shattered to discover my sink rate was really high. The tape says I crossed Dover harbour at 13,000ft and with that sink rate I only had 13 minutes left to fly. All the way down I had a continuous debate with myself, passing through wisps of cloud, wondering if that solid lump I could see up front was France, catching sight of land once on my right and then discovering it was England. I was too far south of my intended track, but heading for Cap Gris Nez, the nearest point in France to England. But I was comfortable, not at all cold, a bit irritated with the compass, which was playing roundabouts, and aiming, like Ken, just to the right of the sun when I could see it. Despite the constant horrific sink rate, which no amount of bar pulling and pushing could change, I was actually very calm in my head. If I don't actually make it to France, I thought, I can always land on a boat.

Breaking through cloud at 4,500ft, I saw France, and just a few seconds' calculation showed it was too far to get to. There were five ships that looked, in the air, quite close, but proved, in the water, to be a couple of miles away. Maybe I should have 360'd down so my sail would show up, but I didn't, maintaining a steady course, just puffing up my water wings a minute before I hit the water. That nearly killed me, because we settled easily on to the sea, without a nose-in dive, the sail forced me down and the life jacket forced me up, and I found I couldn't unclip. Christ! I thought, I could drown here, and that thought gave me the extra effort. I got out and heaved myself on to the rigging at the back of the kite, swam around to the nose, and began an easy backstroke towards France, towing the Moonraker hang glider behind me.

Over on the right I could see the balloons making the crossing; they were in sight for more than an hour, being followed by Harold Lessey in the rescue boats. After ten minutes the kite fell away slowly into the deep, despite efforts to keep it up, so I began swimming in earnest. I remembered a piece of advice I had had; don't take your helmet off, it keeps the heat in, so I took nothing else off and just swam. Yet again, I say it as shouldn't, I was not frightened. I could see the coast when I wasn't swallowing water – the Channel tastes of diesel, which doesn't improve a delicate palate – and on tops of waves, I could see ships in the distance on the Channel one-way system, passing from right to left, making for Europe. Our helicopter was, I thought, out looking for me (it wasn't, in fact, until later, and then it looked inland). I could hail a passing ship when I got close enough, and if all else failed, I could swim to France.

An hour of steady swimming went by – I had been school swimming champion at Harrow County Grammar in 1960 – and the French coast looked nearer. I told myself to keep swimming, and thought that, twenty-four hours from now, I would be wrapped up in a warm bed and this would just be a memory. On top of one wave, after a particularly bad bout of Channel-swallowing, I saw a ship coming towards me, and another behind it, so I trod water until it came level.

'M'Aidez! M'Aidez!' I bellowed – in a surreal way, please notice the culture here, in that I refused absolutely to shout 'Mayday' – and I blew on my little red whistle when it was clear of water.

The ship, a Russian freighter called *Kargopol*, had half a dozen crewmen on deck, who suddenly began running around and telling others there was a bloke in the sea in a yellow ski suit, waving at them. The ship blew three great blasts – meaning man overboard – and went off into the distance, slowing down. Meanwhile, the second ship went by in front of me with not a soul in sight, and thundered off towards the horizon. I watched the *Kargopol* turn and come back and began to allow myself to feel the cold. They were a long time lowering the rowing boat – I have since worked out they were looking for a big enough jar for the vodka they were bringing to me – and then it rowed towards me, I grabbed a rope and that was it, I was safe. It was 9.30 Moscow time, 7.30 our time.

Three men hauled me into the boat, and a lady member of the crew handed me a huge vodka. Contrary to tabloid media reports – the *Daily Mail* and the *Daily Express* really went to town on the story – they described her as a beautiful Russian, but she didn't hug me – I was very wet – and nor did she do anything else to me. I was taken back to the ship, climbed on board, and another huge vodka was thrust into my hand, which I slung back. I slipped out of the harness and was sort of half-carried to a cabin, stripped, and then half-carried to a hot shower and sauna, which was marvellous. Dressing in dry clothes that were too big for me, and given yet another huge vodka in a jam jar, I met the captain with one hand in my pocket – to keep the trousers up – and we set about trying to phone the celebration party.

CHARACTERS AND OTHER HOLY LUNATICS

Fiona, by this time, was worried sick. She had been told by Phillip Hutchins about the height at which he had dropped me, and realised I was in the water. She called for air-sea rescue, but was being pestered by a young man from the charity, Save the Children, who was on his first important job. I was carrying fifty letters on my flight wrapped in plastic – which later sold for twice the price of the fifty letters Ken carried – and when this youngster heard I had fallen into the sea, began berating Fiona about the fate of the letters.

Fiona's reply was more robust than he was expecting.

'F**k your letters! What about my husband?'

When I finally got through to Fiona by radio phone, the vodka had done its good work, and I was very cheerful and made light of what had happened to me. French media comment later concentrated on my sangfroid, but it was the vodka really rather than English cold-bloodedness. I had a difficult time explaining to the Russians what I was doing in the sea, despite efforts with drawings on bits of paper. There was a long, excited conversation between a number of them, until one Russian turned to me and said, 'Excuse me, but are you a sporting man?' When I said that I was a sporting man, that seemed a sufficient explanation for finding an Englishman in a yellow ski suit and a pair of water wings in the middle of the English Channel on a summer morning. They had all read their Ivan Turgenev, and knew that was what sporting Englishmen did.

Luckily for me, the *Kargopol* was on its way from Siberia to Boulogne and not going the other way. The rest of the day was spent coping with the media, and the photographs went to forty-seven countries. The longer-term effects of that adventure are still with us; Fiona gave birth to our daughter Jade nine months later, almost to the day.

The New Aviation, *pace* George Worthington, is often thought of as a young man's game, but to some old-age pensioners it also has appeal. At one time there was talk of forming an OAPs' club. For Bob Robinson, of Darlington in County Durham, flying hang gliders had a lot to do with spending part of the Second World War in a prisoner of war camp:

> It was May 16, 1979. My 65th birthday. My wife and I were about to enjoy our first week of retirement in our caravan, hidden away in the Lake District. All my life I have been

obsessed with jumping or flying over fences. It goes back to 1942. I used to sit and gaze through tangled masses of barbed wire and elevated boxes around my temporary home, the prisoner of war camp Stalag IVB, Mullberg on Elbe. I had an American GI friend there to whom I am still writing, and I remember asking him one day why the brainy guys in the camp, who were able to build a receiving set and hear the news from London, were not able to build something to fly over the perimeter wire. It was only 15ft high.

The day I retired, and to my wife's astonishment, I joined Roger Middleton's Cumbrian Hang Gliding School near Keswick. My wife thought I was a nut-case.

The fun began when I tried to convince my wife and myself that I would make the grade as Pilot 1 by the end of the week. Big deal. I was in for a shock.

The first day went well. We spent the morning doing blackboard work under Roger's watchful eye. Afternoon, site conditions ideal, OK, we all go on tether ropes. A pupil on each wing, Roger holding the nose tether, and up we go. I really leave the ground. I'm actually flying, all of 20ft in the air. I am five feet higher than that impenetrable wire all those years ago, and it's marvellous.

I am not sure how long these thoughts lasted but I came back to earth with a bump. Someone was yelling – 'move that bar to the left! now pull in! push out slowly! NOT TOO MUCH!' Bang! I must have clouted the only bunch of rocks in the whole of the Saddleback range.

The following day the weather was hopeless, and the day after that wasn't much better. By the end of the week Roger was sadly repaying most of his school fees to those pupils who had to return home.

I was one of the lucky ones, able to make use of my van at weekends until I was able to complete the course. It was almost six months to the day after I started. By November, the school closed altogether. I was privileged to buy the school glider I was trained on. Being a novice, I've still got my wheels on the bottom bar. I hope to gain further experience from the North Yorks Sailwing Club.

CHARACTERS AND OTHER HOLY LUNATICS

A second old-age pensioner, Jack Donaldson from Croydon in Surrey, could not stand the thought of spending his old age playing golf. He came into hang gliding by way of the chairmanship of the Surrey Land Yachting Club:

> A few years ago when hang gliding became more generally known and was occasionally seen on television, I eyed the sport with envy and regret. I was approaching senior citizenship, which was a good excuse, and thought there was no fool like an old fool, though a future of old man's golf really stuck in my gut.
>
> A year or so later I went on a land yachting course. The decision, I must admit, was affected by the fact that they also taught hang gliding, not, of course, that I would ever contemplate hang gliding at my age.
>
> Following the land yachting I did try three tethered flights on a hang glider, frightened myself half to death and confirmed I would never do it again.
>
> Still mumbling excuses, with aches and pains and bad weather, it took over a year to get my Pilot 1, by which time I was an official OAP, but very pleased with myself.
>
> I would like to thank all those kind people who helped me up the hills. I would also like to issue a warning that if you see me trying to top land in a clean-looking Harrier, Keep Clear! Remember, there's no fool like an old fool ... enjoying himself.

Four years later, at the age of 70, Jack Donaldson wrote the following letter:

> I would like to say thank you to those in the sport who helped and encouraged me through Pilot One stage, via 'prone harness' and 13 control-bar uprights to Pilot Two. Those who collected me after my blackout and saw me, kite and car safely into hospital. Judy Leden, who nursed me and my fever during that terrible 14-hour bus journey to Delhi. Those who virtually threw me off the cliffs at Beachy Head when my bottle was gone, and many more whose kindness to an old man are too numerous to mention.

I have always considered it a privilege to be involved in hang gliding and to share its secrets. To be among the young flyers who wouldn't know how much they resemble the war-time air crews. Twice in my life I have been fortunate enough to mingle with the Gods.

It was at a veterans Meet in Italy that I 'stuck it in' for the last time. No doubt influenced by the blood pouring from my nose, and the chatter in German from my helpers, I decided 'Jack ist kaput!' I have many photos and memories to comfort me when I get REALLY old … very best wishes to you all.

There are old-age pensioners all over the world who fly hang gliders. Among the best, as a pilot, was Dick Newton, 70 years old, who took up hang gliding after four years' service as a US Marine pilot in the Second World War, and thirty years in the CIA. What turned him on was sharing the same air as pilots who could be his sons or grandsons (or daughters). This is part of an account of his experiences:

During a flight at High Rock on an excitingly great thermal day, I suddenly realised I could not penetrate. The wind had picked up to 45 mph. I was 1,500ft above all the others when I noticed several other gliders encountering a rotor and landing in the trees. I headed north down the ridge, hoping to land at a military base, but the minimal size of the fields, as well as a myriad of wires, compelled me to seek other opportunities. In a WWII charged-up attitude I said to myself, 'what the hell!' and did a 'peel-off' downwind, finally landing in a 100-foot long field bordered by trees, a chicken coop, gardens and fences. It was an elevator straight down to a stand-up landing. An elderly woman stopped 100 yards away in her car and offered a ride back to launch. As in so many cases, the Gods were with me.

The close of another day at High Rock found me about 800ft above everyone else as they headed for the LZ – Landing Zone – one by one. But as I approached 200ft over launch I noticed 'magic lift' taking effect. Silky-smooth non-sink air some 30ft over the ridge allowed me to stay aloft half an hour after the hotshot, younger pilots had landed. Oh, such satisfaction!

On another thrilling day at High Rock, I set the then-altitude record of 8,750ft over launch. I nearly froze to death and recalled with amusement how I had scoffed at pilots who told me that there had been times when they 'couldn't get out of the lift'. That day I had to work at it to get out of lift! Then twice on my landing approach I encountered a strong thermal that carried me back up over launch!

My first cross-country – XC – flight of about 40 miles was a thrill but entirely unplanned. I had never gone XC intentionally, being totally satisfied with local challenges, and wanting to get home (two hours away) before dark so my wife didn't worry. This day, however, the cloud streets were phenomenal, and as my vario seemed to stay pegged I said out loud, 'OK, Mr Thermal Maker, give me 4,000ft over launch and I'll go over the back to the school.' The lift continued and once over the school I circled, saw no one had landed there and again said aloud, 'Thermal Maker, give me 6,000ft and I'll keep going.' Soon I was on my way up again, and was so enraptured I just kept circling, climbing and enjoying the thrill of new vistas below. After playing around for several hours I found the lift was subsiding and I managed a perfect stand-up landing in one of the many possible landing areas. While folding up my glider a young couple in a pickup truck stopped and offered a ride. It was 75 miles back to the launch by road and worth every penny of my $10 tip. Of course, this was the day that Jerry Nielson set the then-record of 60 miles in our area.

Once, when Jerry was on launch contemplating take-off, I kidded him to get going because there were 16 of us waiting. Some 30 to 40 wuffos started booing me when Jerry replied ... 'Please Dad! Don't make me go!'

In the early days of Owens Valley flying, a local pilot called Garland Rhoades crashed and broke his neck. He managed to make it to his truck to drive himself to the hospital. But, in what he now recounts as a funny story, his truck ran out of gas a mile down the remote dirt road. When his flying partners landed hours later, they found him sitting very stiffly behind the wheel. 'What's going on, Garland?' they asked. 'I broke my neck and ran out of gas, but other than that, it's been a good day,' was his answer.

At the 1980 American Cup in Tennessee, a special trophy was offered to please the crowd, the Bob Wills Trophy for the best aerobatic pilot at the Meet. All the AmCup pilots would be the judges, and vote at the end of the competition. Two West Coast pilots with high reputations came to Tennessee for the competition: Dan Racanelli and Rob Kells, both of whom flew the Wills Wing Harrier. Racanelli was the subject of numerous articles in magazines, with great photographs showing past 90 degree wingovers. He turned out to be burly, bearded, wearing a crash helmet that looked like a Nazi wartime leftover, and was thoroughly modest. Rob Kells, winner of the 1980 Grouse Mountain Meet in Vancouver, British Columbia, was president of Wills Wing, and looked like the typical California golden surfin' boy. Both were charming men.

A third entrant was Dave Ledford, one of the final squad of nine pilots competing for a place in the six-man American team, who failed to make it. He flew a Moyes Mega 2, and with Racanelli and Kells, each competition day they filled in the gaps between tasks with aerobatic flying, watched with great interest by the rest of us.

Going off Lookout Mountain, 1,350ft high, there is a mile to fly before you get to the landing area, with perhaps a thousand feet in hand when you're there to put on your display. Obviously, pilots wanted smooth air before they started their manoeuvres, which tend to begin with a steep dive, whack the bar out and away they go ….

I did not actually see the beginning of Dave Ledford's famous flight, though most of it was followed by a good stills cameraman. I was behind take-off when a deep groan came from the assembly on the ramp who had been watching Ledford's routine. Like everyone else, I joined them to see the parachute deploy. Ledford had been trying for a true loop, which is possible these days, and though he had come close with more than 160 degree wingovers, he had not actually made it. On this particular flight he parked upside down, like Lester Cruise, then tail-slid and started tumbling. After three tumbles he got his parachute out and threw it. It opened, and he and the kite floated to the ground, upside down.

In all the tumbling the Moyes Mega wing remained intact, breaking nothing, and it was only when Ledford landed – off the spot, as the more competitive pilots noted – that a small piece on top of the king post broke, being the actual point of impact with the ground. Ledford walked away unharmed, and flew the same kite – cautiously at first – the next day, before settling back again to his routine aerobatics to try and win the Bob Wills Trophy.

There was no doubt Ledford's was a tough act to follow. There were three schools of thought on the subject. One was that Ledford had won outright and everyone should now stop. A second was that Rob Kells, who had been doing more and more outrageous aerobatics and was obviously trying hardest, should get the vote. The third was that Dan Racanelli was keeping his flying beautifully controlled, and not taking needless risks, and in the interests of safety, he should get the vote.

Matters were taken out of our hands because Rob Kells obviously had a good think about Ledford's 'tough act', and came to his own startling conclusions ...

We were all lined up for the presentation of the American Cup. The winning Americans were modest, laid-back and joking. We were shattered. The French were thinking of a last joke to play. The Australians were in mourning for Peter 'The Black Death' Brown, and the Canadians had their little mascot holding the flag. In general, the whole game was over and we were thinking of the partying that evening ... when out from the hill flew a lone black Harrier wing. I think the Canadians were being feted by the commentators as Rob Kells flew over the landing area and then over us, but most of us were looking up, wondering what was going to happen. Right above us, Kells dropped his parachute, and his glider slowly and gracefully went into the vertical. He told me later that he wanted to hang there for a second or two, then pull a quick release, fly free of the open chute in a vertical dive and then execute a genuine loop.

The problem was, when he pulled the quick release, nothing happened, and he kept descending toward us.

We all watched, appalled yet fascinated, as Rob tugged and tugged to release his chute, and nothing continued to happen. He let go of the control bar, put his feet on the bar, and began pulling with two hands, all the time descending vertically at us. It looked like five more seconds and he would crash, nose-down, on the road behind us, and he was close enough you felt you could touch him. Then, the kite waggling from side to side, suddenly the release worked. Rob dived for the control bar and pushed out, and the Harrier went into an enormous wingover right over the tents and the crowd. He had no height left to do anything but land. The parachute drifted down a few yards away, and then, absurdly, so did the deployment bag.

One wonders how Dave Ledford would have followed that if there had been a few more days left. Rob Kells won, of course, and took away the trophy.

There are a number of people in Europe who dream up lovely daft ideas to thrill people, and then video them. Two of the more imaginative are Patrice Genand, a hang gliding and microlight instructor, and a tough young woman called Françoise Mocellin. They had a presentation package incorporating all the new aviation sports, but they wanted something different. Genand wrote about what conclusion they came to:

> Since I was continually releasing parachutists from my wing (they dropped off a double harness), I began to imagine all sorts of different release techniques. Why not from the top of the hang glider wing? A parachutist could climb up through a hole in the sail on to the outer surface and make a jump from there. After all, a parachutist doesn't have to worry about falling!
>
> So the idea was formed. Then we needed some work on the wing, a Tecma tandem wing, the schooling tool I knew best. I began to tackle the major problems:
>
> Due to the air currents that detach themselves from the outer surface before reaching the trailing edge, the hole had to be situated behind the king post.
>
> In order to keep the wing from destabilising, there had to be symmetry, a hole of equal size on either side of the king post.
>
> The hole had to be large enough to allow the passage of a person equipped with a parachute.
>
> I began by fabricating a large hole in an old sail. It was winter, and the snow was an important psychological factor for our tests since take-off and landing on skis is easier. Our first attempt took place on a gentle slope. All went well and the wing apparently didn't lose any of its flying characteristics.

CHARACTERS AND OTHER HOLY LUNATICS

The second launch was from a 300m high hill. We made a few turns and still there were no problems, a brief stall ... everything was in order. Now it was time to try climbing through the hole on to the top of the wing. Françoise, an instructor at my Jonathan school, is extremely courageous and daring. Air is truly her element.

We set off for the Jura mountains where Jean François Putod has a microlight school. After a short huddle, briefing each other on procedure, Françoise and I were towed tandem behind a microlight piloted by Jean François. We released at 1,500m (4,921ft). I stabilised the wing while Françoise began to climb through the hole to the left of the king post. The wing veered to the left. I had to counter the movement with all my weight to get it back on a normal course.

'Are you OK?' I screamed into the air.

The answer was a cry of joy, 'It's super!'

She was already standing on the wing with her arms stretched out. I was able to stay on course for another 10 seconds before engaging a few turns. There was a slight pitch instability but nothing catastrophic. She climbed back down through the hole and clipped her harness in again. We were ready for the next stage. Françoise had never done any parachuting, so she was sent to Royan where her instructors were stupefied by her rapid progress.

During this time I continued tinkering with the wing and concocted a sort of platform from which Françoise could jump from the sail. Something fairly light was needed. Two pieces of stiff polystyrene glued to the keel were sufficient to keep her from sinking into the soft sail and losing her balance before leaping into the air.

When the big day arrived, Jean François and I decided it was better to tow up to 2,000m (6,500ft) for safety reasons. The last metres seemed very slow. Then at 1,900m, a split second of inattention on my part resulted in a lock-out and a quick release.

It wasn't in the bag yet!

We re-coordinated the movements we had repeated a hundred times before, so as to lose no time. During the moments that Françoise walked on top of the wing I was naturally blind to what she was doing but imagined all sorts of things.

When the wing stabilised I gave the 'go!' sign. At her first step the wing tipped slightly. On the second, the keel began to bend and the front cables slackened a bit ... 'gads, what next?'

Phew! I caught a glimpse of Françoise passing before my eyes. I followed her every movement. She spun in the air. 'Has she lost her balance?'

All at once the parachute opened. Phew! I was spared a heart attack. She told me later that in order to relax a bit she allowed herself a few free-fall figures.

The feat was accomplished. Our joy and relief were indescribable. But it was not over. We had to repeat the whole experience at least a dozen more times for a photo and video documentary – and sometimes with great big technical problems to solve!

Another Continental European, Alain Zoller, despite heading the safety organisation in Switzerland, obviously has holy lunatic tendencies, because he celebrated his 30th birthday by bungee jumping from a tandem paraglider. Think about his landing yoyoing three hundred feet underneath his wing!

His pilot was fellow-Swiss Roger Oehler, and they decided Lake Geneva was the best site. The director of a nearby bungee jump centre, Claude Alain Aellen, and his technician Debus Wiss contributed a homespun 400 latex-band bungee cord, specially woven and protected by a latex sheet. At rest the cord was 20m long, and at full stretch 90m.

The flight took place from Villeneuve with a launch from the 1,000m (3,280ft) Sonchaux on 22 August 1993. There was a great deal of tension among paragliding experts, and heated discussion about the behaviour of the canopy subjected to the strains of a bungee jump. Take-off was the most delicate part of the operation, because the bungee cord weighed 25kg, and was placed between the pilot's legs. But they had a good launch and Zoller soon dropped off to begin yo-yoing head first towards the water over the welcoming lake 3,000ft below, looking, as some lakeside farmers remarked, 'perfectly silly'.

Zoller made his descent into the water first and was quickly retrieved by a rescue boat, while Oehler and the paraglider splashed down 28m away. Zoller thought it a perfect way to mark his thirtieth year.

On the subject of bungee jumps, really a cadet branch of the New Aviation, the Englishman David Kirke started the current craze after a rip-roaring party in a Georgian flat near the Bristol Gorge on 1 April 1979. Kirke was a founder and is now chairman of Oxford University's Dangerous Sports Club, which seems to be a reaction against the current mania for wokeness and safety and 'safe spaces'. The club tie is all black, and features a man in a wheelchair. On the night before their first bungee jump an enormous amount of champagne was consumed, and those who chose to test the then-theory of bungee jumping wore tails and top hats. I have seen the photograph of David Kirke a split second after he leapt, clutching his champagne bottle as he cast himself into the void off the 196ft-high Clifton Suspension Bridge. He was very disappointed that he dropped the bottle at the first bounce; he and his colleagues spent the rest of that day in police cells.

Kirke and his merry men bungee-jumped their way across the world. I remember at the 1979 hang gliding American Cup in Chattanooga, Tennessee what a fillip it was to British morale to hear that Kirke and his upper-class hooligans, including an English girl called Janey Wilmot, had gone off the San Francisco Golden Gate Bridge. Kirke was once asked if he could commercialise bungee jumping and sell the jumps for money, and dismissed the idea airily; how much richer a man he would be if he had.

Safety is built into commercial bungee jumping, but a DSC jump is rather different. The jumper, having weighed himself and discussed all the pros and cons, then chooses a length of bungee to either get his feet wet or see the whites of his eyes in the water. I saw the first really successful such jump after a phone call one Sunday from John Fack in Bristol.

'If you want to see a bungee jump, be at the Clifton Gorge Hotel at 1pm,' said John. 'It's the best place for a view. This one's a bit special. There's a microlight involved. I think Mark Southall is flying it, dressed as a gorilla.'

Fiona and I went to lunch on the terrace of the hotel, and waited in the sunlight with a bottle of white wine while three young men proceeded casually across the bridge. One was in a wheelchair, one was pushing, and one seemed to act as a lookout. The appointed time came and passed; no microlight appeared, we carried on drinking, and the three men lurked on the bridge, which had been designed by the legendary Isambard Kingdom Brunel in the nineteenth century. It was apparent after a while that more than a hundred people had come to watch, because every now and again a figure would rise out of the scrub on either side of the gorge, wave a camera about, and sink down again.

Finally, more than an hour late, we saw a microlight in the distance over Ashton Court, heading north-west, obviously going for the sea mouth of the Gorge. The young man in the wheelchair also saw the microlight, got up and clipped an elastic rope that he had been sitting on to a harness he revealed he had been wearing. All three men looked west, awaiting the microlight, which then appeared quite low over the river, flown by a couple of chaps in gorilla suits. The jumper stepped over the railings and looked down, and as the microlight passed underneath and slightly to one side, he jumped. All the cameramen rose out of the brush in unison and clicked away furiously.

The microlight passed by underneath us and flew away to the east again, after a brief wave from one of the gorillas. I understand it was the same microlight, without registration letters, and one of the same gorilla suits that Alan Weston of the DSC flew briefly over the Houses of Parliament earlier that summer. The cameramen in the gorge carried on clicking. Meanwhile, the jumper achieved a 'First' for the DSC. On his very first jump he had so chosen his length of bungee that he was wet up to the knees! He yoyoed up and down a couple of times, fiddled with his harness, produced a rope, unclipped and climbed down the rope to jump into the river. He swam to the side and climbed to the road where a Mini suddenly swerved out of the flow of traffic and stopped. The jumper got in and was driven away. Up above, one of the young men reeled in the elastic and hemp rope, coiled them up, dropped them into a false seat on the wheelchair, sat in it and was pushed off the bridge. It was a slick operation.

Five minutes later three young policemen came out on to the bridge and looked everywhere, underneath and along both sides of the river, found nothing and walked off again. All this time people on the terrace carried on talking, and hardly anyone noticed what was happening, even though my wife and I clapped politely as the jump occurred, joined by a few others in the know. The jumper was so turned on by the experience that he went back the following weekend and repeated it.

Then there was the time Kirke and other DSC members went to Pamplona in Spain, which Ernest Hemingway had made famous for the running of the bulls between the two world wars, but the DSC chose to skateboard from the bulls instead. Or when a volcano in one of the Caribbean islands erupted and as the population was being evacuated, a select group of DSC members flew in, walked to the top of the volcano and had luncheon out of a Fortnum and Mason hamper. The fumes were said to have rendered the food almost inedible. Or when they hired a boat to take them through two days of champagne drinking to the isolated island of Rockall in the Atlantic, which they climbed – with difficulty – consumed more champagne, and leaving two full bottles behind 'for the next people to come by', jumped into the water to be picked up and carted home again. Or when they gathered at the fashionable ski resort of St Moritz and went down the slopes with skis fitted to a huge blow-up elephant, a rowing eight, and a grand piano. Or when David Kirke floated across the English Channel at 10,000ft, suspended beneath three balloons, hoping the winds would blow him to France, and smack in the middle of the light aircraft corridor. I believe he came down by popping one of the balloons.

It was inevitable that David Kirke should be attracted to the New Aviation, even if elements of the New Aviation were always going to be uneasy about him. One of the 'rules' of the DSC is that no one should be a professional at doing anything. They espoused the cult of the gentleman amateur; training was for the 'hoi polloi'. A gentleman always knew how to do anything dangerous. What was important was not technique, but *style*. As Kirke put it, 'We insisted on beginner's luck and did our best to avoid the impositions of professionalism, expertise and all the other contemporary egocentricities that diminish one's sense of the unique by attempting to enhance it.'

In that spirit, with three hang glider flights behind him, barely enough to learn how to turn left or right, David Kirke took a hang glider to Greece and leapt off the 9,550ft-high Mount Olympus, home of the paramount God, Zeus. This led to an introduction to Bill and Steve Moyes, and when Kirke heard they planned to jump off Mount Kilimanjaro, at 19,430ft the highest mountain in Africa, he resolved the DSC should do it, too.

By this time Kirke had amassed the staggering total of twelve flights in a hang glider. Ian McCleod wrote a short account of what happened then:

> David Kirke marches to the sound of a different drum. With the help of a film-maker and money from a sponsoring company, permission for the Dangerous Sport Club to fly from 'Kili' was secured. Then came the climb. Sporting canes, and assisted by 70 porters, they contemplated being carried to the summit in sedan chairs, but settled in the end for a long walk. Because of pressure from the film crew, there was no waiting around to acclimatise to the drastic altitude changes. One DSC member began spitting blood at 12,000ft. By 15,000ft virtually everyone in the party was vomiting and had severe headaches. Afternoon cloud cover frequently reduced visibility to 50 yards.
>
> 'The theory,' said Kirke, 'was to snatch a few hours sleep and then start for the summit at midnight in order to take off at dawn before the cloud built up. At one stage we could only take a dozen paces before resting.'
>
> When the summit was reached, five pilots set up their gliders, David Kirke, Ashley Doubtfire, Alan Weston, Simon Keeling and Jonathan Hardy. Doubtfire was the most experienced of the flyers but went off on his own and launched first, calling on the others to follow him as he leapt into space. The others toasted each other in champagne and attempted to commit aviation. Kirke got away, 'after a moment's disbelief at finding oneself intact, all the pain vanished in the exultation of being the luckiest person in the world, dancing over the clouds with an aluminium wand to orchestrate the heavens. How many times since, when belaboured by the fools, demons, rattlepates and bureaucrats of everyday England, have I remembered that I was once up there.'
>
> Simon Keeling also got into the air in a flight nanoseconds from disaster, but Alan Weston was not so lucky. He was exhausted from the altitude and stalled his launch. Rising unhurt from the wreckage he smiled and said, 'Everything for a week on the mountain, and I only flew

30ft.' A fifth pilot, Jonathan Hardy, blacked out from oxygen starvation before he could launch. As for the landings, at the end of a 25-mile long sled run Kirke thought he had found an ideal spot in a field of cabbages. The 'cabbages' turned out to be coffee plants 8-feet high. Kirke wiped out a row of them. Doubtfire landed in the same patch, while Simon Keeling found an unsympathetic landowner who charged him a stiff fee before releasing him.

The New Aviation is not only hang gliding, paragliders and microlights. It is all the new forms of aerial adventure, mainly with soft sails, which have blossomed in the last twenty-five years, including BASE and bungee jumping. The word BASE covers the four structures that jumpers use: Buildings, Antenna, Spans (bridges) and Earth (cliffs). It has been attempted off the Empire State Building, and off 300ft cliffs. Going off a cliff thousands of feet up, BASE jumpers aim to free fall as long as they can before opening their chutes.

On 22 May 1992, a 25-year-old carpenter, Darren Newton, went up to the top of the Hilton Hotel on Park Lane in London, with a companion, David Claybyn. They had vague connections with the Dangerous Sports Club, and intended to BASE jump the hotel. Claybyn succeeded, but Newton, an experienced parachutist, launched himself wrongly and caught his feet in the lines. He swung into the building very heavily, which probably killed him, and then fell to the ground through a canopy, severing an arm and a foot. He was certainly dead when an ambulance arrived.

The *Daily Telegraph*, then edited by a normally brilliant journalist called Max Hastings who made his name in dangerous situations, including the 1982 Falklands War – he was accused of claiming to have led the British Army into the island's capital, Port Stanley – carried the following editorial on Newton's death:

> Spectacular acts of human folly often accompany heat waves. But, even by the standards of the genre, the death of a parachutist who jumped from the roof of the London Hilton hotel seems a depressingly futile sacrifice. Each year, society strives through legislation and technical advice to make daily life less hazardous. Ever more rigorous constraints

are imposed upon electrical appliances, smoking habits, road use, alcohol, industrial practices. A coroner's jury even reaches a finding that soldiers who died in a war were blame worthily killed, and seeks to apportion responsibility as if the dead men had been passengers in a civil airliner crash. It is a central thrust in contemporary life that risk and death should no longer be regarded as inevitable features of the human experience, but misfortunes which an enlightened democracy should strive to eliminate.

More than a few young men and women respond to this safety-first ethic by seeking progressively more hazardous challenges. Some of these are admirable, others – like the Hilton parachute jump – absurd. Flight seems to offer the last irresistible challenge for those bent on playing with death. Hang gliding, parachuting, gliding and piloting microlight aircraft grow in popularity. Most of those who practise them are content to do so by the rulebook. Others insist on tearing it up – and finish by wasting the time of coroners' juries.

It would, of course, be wrong to imagine that this is entirely a modern phenomenon. Past generations of Oxbridge undergraduates climbed medieval spires by night. Foxhunters have always cheerfully accepted an alarming casualty rate. The tradition of wantonly risking life and limb could be said to embrace medieval jousters, 18-century duellists and Victorian rural eccentrics. A passenger in a gig driven by the mad Squire Mytton in the last century was rash enough to remark that, in many years of rural travel, he had never had an accident. Whipping up the horse, the squire remarked contemptuously: 'Never been upturned in a gig? What a damn dull fellow you must be' and drove his hapless companion over a bank. Yet all these tales make better reading than the actual experience. It is a droll comment upon the response of some people to the humdrum appearance of modern life that they seek escapes which merely prove tragically silly.

This hypocritical and confused editorial illustrates a great deal of what is wrong in modern Britain. But it came in the *Daily Telegraph*, of all newspapers, which carried a wonderful article a few weeks previously about a middle-aged adventurer, John Ridgway – he once rowed the Atlantic with Chay Blyth – and his daughter Rebecca, then 22 – paddling canoes around Cape Horn. Both of them ran tremendous risks, with absolutely no scientific justification. In the whim that passed for editorial policy on the *Telegraph,* the Ridgway journey was a great adventure, while Darren Newton, possessed of exactly the same spirit, was 'tragically silly'. In the first time I have ever written to newspapers, I protested this view in a letter which I feel is a view from the New Aviation to the woke values of today. Only the paragraphs in italics were published:

> I am writing to protest, belatedly, at the tone and contents of your editorial – *Last Irresistible Challenge* – on the death of 25 year old Darren Newton, who failed to survive a parachute jump last month from the London Hilton Hotel in Park Lane.
>
> It is a late protest because, while I was deeply angered by the editorial when I read it, I fully expected it to be rubbished by your columnists like Auberon Waugh, Lord Deedes or Sir Peregrine Worsthorne. It was only when it was obvious that they, too, were going to ignore the issue that I decided I had, reluctantly, to write to you.
>
> *Darren Newton's death was not 'tragically silly'. People who take up the sports of hang gliding, parachuting, gliding and piloting microlight aircraft are not, as you put it, 'bent upon playing with death'.* They are, in fact, celebrating life at its highest and its best. But what is odd is that a newspaper with the history of the *Daily Telegraph* and your current editor Max Hastings, and championing the causes you do, should end up giving space to such a wrong-headed, trendy view.
>
> You carried, within the last few months, feature articles on the canoe voyage by John Ridgway and his daughter Rebecca around the islands of Cape Horn. What did they achieve that was, in any important way, different from what Darren Newton set out to achieve? There was no scientific excuse for the voyage the Ridgways made. It was more a rite

of passage between father and daughter. Rebecca described the challenge, in which their lives were at risk as surely as Darren's, in this way:

'You feel so alive that you think you will never feel it again. So you want to go back to see if you can find that aliveness again.'

The major part of the 'aliveness' of which Rebecca wrote is that the price of failure is sometimes death. If either of the Ridgways had died on that intrinsically useless voyage, would that mealy-mouthed leader writer have been hauled out of the hole you surely keep him in to write of their deaths as being 'silly'?

How can the *Daily Telegraph* commend the lunatic madness of fox-hunting, in which life and limb are so cheerfully put at risk in every chase of an inedible animal, and take the extraordinarily absurd view you took on Darren's death? Are not the qualities tested in the hunt the same as in Darren's flight, except that in the latter's case no animal's life was at risk? And how did you arrive at your mean-spirited view of the latest forms of aviation, to dismiss those who depart from the rulebook as 'wasting the time of coroners' juries'? How do you think the rulebooks are written in the first place?

In hang gliding, surely the purest form of flying, the best pilots are realising the real dreams of Leonardo da Vinci, of which the Boeing Jumbo is but a nightmare. When a man can spread his wings on a mountain, take off by foot leaving nothing behind him, and fly 300 miles, is it really a fair description to call him 'playing with death'? Surely he was reaching for something beyond the experience of the rest of us, which earlier generations of Englishmen would have had no trouble recognising. There is an element in hang gliding, when dinner is over, the third bottle of wine is broached and dreams are spun, when talk turns to launching and soaring Park Lane in a westerly wind. The people most qualified to speak on this subject are the same type of people as the man who first flew the 300 miles. Indeed, that man, Larry Tudor, wants to fly his hang glider *up* Mount Everest. Can your leader writer imagine anything more silly? Are we not all lucky that he can't find the money to do it?

In microlighting, an extraordinarily brave Frenchman called Guy Delage, in an aircraft with a dry weight roughly equal to a married couple, has just flown 2,350km <u>non-stop</u> across the South Atlantic, to emulate the 1933 pioneer Jean Mermoz, another Frenchman. Delage was in the air 26 hours, driven down to sea-level most of the way by storms, and twice hit flying fish. Aside from the joy of doing it – surely all that Darren Newton was setting out to achieve? – and the admiration of a small group of people (those of us 'bent upon playing with death'), what was served by Mr Delage's voyage? Can you imagine the meal your leader-writer would have made of Mr Delage's death, had it occurred, wringing his hands again over the 'wasting of time of coroners' juries?' Maybe not, though, because Mr Delage was a foreigner; perhaps foreigners are allowed to do that.

I know people in paragliding who fly with cameras on their legs, and in the air deliberately collapse the chute and free-fall, to see how they can open them again. They would say the experience is exciting, and they learn more about how to fly the canopies. The world champion is now an Englishman, but is that an excuse? Your leader writer could pick up much material for his whingeing from them.

There are two very English issues raised by your editorial that merit thought. Would the tone have changed if Mr Newton had been from the landed classes, instead of being a carpenter? Had he been, say, the son of a Cabinet Minister, dying not of an over-dose of drugs at Oxford, but because he wanted to achieve Rebecca Ridgway's 'rare form of aliveness' in something rather daring and physically difficult, would the *Daily Telegraph*, even Mr Waugh, Lord Deedes and Sir Peregrine, have treated his death differently?

Care to take a wager on it?

The second question is the different attitudes that seem to be emerging toward those who risk their lives professionally, and those who do it as amateurs. Your newspaper carries numerous articles on those paid to dice with death, not just the millionaires like Nigel Mansell and the whole motor-racing fraternity, but cameraman like Syd Perou and Leo Dickinson, and more traditional adventurers like Chay Blyth and John Ridgway. These are articles in which the word 'silly' is never mentioned. Should they die, there would be no disgusting cant about wasting the time of coroners' juries. Is it because money changes hands that they are excused this criticism, and we all understand that money excuses everything? Shouldn't we mark more clearly the death, in the 1990s, and in the pages of the *Daily Telegraph* no less, of the amateur ideal?

What is the intrinsic difference between Nigel Mansell risking his neck to go around a track faster, and Darren Newton parachuting off the Hilton? They are both brave men, at the edge of their experience, fully alive to the dangers. Both risked, but one lives, and one died. But Mr Mansell's speed is worth millions of pounds a year to cigarette manufacturers who sell us their products to make their profits; does that make the risk of his death the more noble? Would it be a different type of coroner's jury that listens to accounts of his death? And when Leo Dickinson risks his neck to take a picture, should he die merely to bring us a new angle on the world, will you wheel out the same 'damn dull fellow' you chose to write the obituary on Mr Newton?

Courage is a quality that, in another England, in another time, was considered supreme to all others. We were once more able to recognise it, across all classes, than we are today. Darren Newton had courage, and I admire him for it. I hope that Miss Sarah Walker, his girlfriend, who must bury him and put her life together afterwards, is able to see your miserable editorial in its true perspective. Miss Walker should take comfort that, in the days of preparation before the jump and the last few minutes before he leapt into space, her boyfriend was truly alive so that 'you think you'll never feel it again'. He was risking all he had, and must certainly have known it. When he and his companion slipped on to the roof of the Hilton that Wednesday evening, and unpacked their chutes to set up to fly, it would only take one look over the edge to know what could go wrong.

The fact that it did go wrong for Darren Newton was tragic, but his death was not a silly one. Miss Walker, when she puts her life together, may set out to find another man like him. She will, unfortunately, run across a great many men in the mould of the leader writer who dismissed her fiance's death as silly. But she should choose according to the values she found in Darren Newton, and eschew mediocrity.

Max Hastings wrote later and said we should agree to differ. I still cannot believe that he wrote the editorial, or even sanctioned it.

Chapter 2

Distances and Heights After 1981

The first ten years of hang gliding saw distance flown rise from 196ft at the First Lilienthal Meet, to Jim Lee's 168 miles. The next fifteen years saw a jump not quite as large as that, but pilots began chasing first, the Big 200, and then the Big 300; that is, 300 miles or 500km.

Like mainstream sailplane flying, and led by George Worthington, hang glider pilots had to be good at paperwork as well as flying. Height gains and distance flights must be corroborated by witnesses, and by carrying a sealed barograph that confirmed whether or not you had flown the whole distance. To actually attempt a record flight you needed an FAI Sporting Licence, not difficult to obtain but part of the taming and civilising of the New Aviation.

We all learned that record flights have to be approached professionally, but there was also a recognition that some pilots found themselves in a situation where a record was possible, and did it. Even though it could not be officially recognised, pilots knew the flight for what it was, and inside the community they were credited with the achievement. When John Pendry flew to his official world record of 187 miles on 13 July 1983, it was his name in the record books. On the same day, with poor paperwork, Larry Tudor flew 221 miles, 34 miles further, and first through the infamous '200-mile wall'. So Pendry was understandably chary about emphasising his record publicly.

The Pyrenees Challenge was framed in June, 1986, by a commercial company called Archiplumes. It was the oldest challenge of its type for flying in the Pyrenees. The prize was to be awarded to the first pilot to actually cross the Pyrenees, 150km, in one hang glider flight. XC flying over this range is outstandingly beautiful, but it requires a total commitment on the part of the pilot. The Pyrenees will never be like the highways of the Southern Alps, or certain parts of the Northern Alps.

DISTANCES AND HEIGHTS AFTER 1981

Since 1986, every time the weather was right the Souviron brothers, who lived not far away at Millau, travelled to the southern face or to Val Louron to attempt the Challenge. In 1987, Fabience Lemaire, Bernard Nonnon and Jean Souviron made 106, 107 and 108km, all three by different routes on the same day. Jean flew the north side, Bernard flew over the range and Fabienne along the south side. Days like this come once or twice a year.

In 1989, Jean and Gil Souviron pushed the Pyrenean distance record to a frustrating 144km, having been stopped by the Mediterranean sea breeze at Fort Romeu. Thereafter, a number of 100–120km distances were made via Val Louron, Blancas or Castejon de Sos.

In 1993, Eric Poulet and Jean Souviron made a joint flight of 145km, but, awed by the mountains, made a detour at the end and so missed the finish.

Then Gil Souviron decided to have the Challenge done, once and for all. As he himself recounts, it was not ideal conditions to do it. Another pilot at Castejon de Sos on the same day complained about 'infernal turbulence' in the middle of the day. That was at the exact time and place where Gil needed and got dynamic lift to complete the last 60km. At 3,000m in the Pyrenees, winds of 40kph pose a big risk.

Gil Souviron had already established a new European distance record of 430.6km, jointly shared with his brother Jean, on 19 July 1994, from Salamanca in Spain. Gil determined to crack the Pyrenees the following month, and carried his glider up to a site called Blanca. He left it there for a few days while too-strong winds made flying dangerous. Then ....

> Monday's sky is blue. At 12.30pm I am ready for takeoff. Conditions are fantastic. Sarogosse announces a 50kph SW wind over the Pyrenees, with a local stream of strato cumulus and a 3,000m ceiling. Like magic, a band of stratocumies makes its way over the site.
>
> I remain patient, waiting until 1pm to foot launch into a thin veil. La Sierra Tendenera, a great rocky mass, stands tall and erect, flirting with the clouds barely 150m above it. The few spots of sun reveal a spiky, tortured ridge. I have a strange sensation of plunging into a fairytale. The breeze, strengthened by the SW wind, allows me to circle above the magical scenery.

At the east ridge tip there are two options; either go for the magnificent well-exposed cliffs (Le Mandarruego) of Ordesa Park, or go south for the rather inhospitable Sierra. Regretfully, Ordesa is plastered with clouds 3,000m high, so I take the second option to the Sierras.

On the lee side of the Pueyo Ridge, I find myself all too quickly at 2,000m, just 100m above any landable fields and not even within a glide to Fanlo. Will I be obliged to do a fly-on-the-wall landing in the brush? I try clinging to the south slopes but continue to go down. At 1,900m a bubble at the edge of a canyon north of Fanlo takes me back up to 2,100m where, for 20 minutes, I scratch amidst the brush. Staring down at them for so long makes me think that some of them are not so un-landable after all.

'Keep on Gil!' I think, 'Don't give in.'

The next 10km are interminable. Finally my hang glider tunes into lift just past Nekin, which sends me vertically to 2,400m west of Aniselo Canyon. The place is a giant! What a trip! I fly over the 1.5km wide, 1,000m high canyon, hallucinating! The gorges of Tarn and Verdun look like miniatures compared to this. On the east side I am propelled to 2,900m and treated to a view of paradise; unending fields and a road lined with houses in the valley of Ainsa.

The high mountains are out of bounds because of the strengthening winds and lowering cloud base. I fly to Pena Montanesa where a 50km bonus awaits me. There is a fly-in for vultures going on, and I can practically go to sleep for a full 15kms at 2,300m, while the lift just carries me on. At the end I find a little bubble that pops me over to Campo Mountain. I was a bit distracted by the views of Castejon, but climb to 3,000m behind Turbon and let myself drift towards Vilaller where I keep heading towards San Marti and Lima Peak, a 10km long, well-exposed ridge at 2,700m.

The wind is no longer blocked by the high mountain and the clouds are swept into fractured cumuli, an indication of the acceleration of the winds. I am reduced to soaring over the ridge, which maintains me at 3,000m. In record time I reach the end of the Sierras where the remaining cumuli are

DISTANCES AND HEIGHTS AFTER 1981

purely decorative. After crossing the Sort Valley, I arrive on the western end of Lorry Peak, which is not recommended because of the lack of landing fields (and thermals). The wind picks up to 40kph. I drift too much and am obliged to go around to the lee-side of a 2,300m peak.

As the ridge recedes I inevitably sink, so I quickly change over to a little knob to the north to continue eastward. The south wind being perpendicular to the slopes allows me to get to the tip and keep going as far as Aravell, where I land at 6pm. Carine, my companion, drove over 300kms of mountain roads chasing me, and arrived 90 minutes later with the maps. We check the overall distance. It comes out at 150.6kms!

A last word on safety. Wings are becoming more and more aerodynamic with an impressive speed range. As a result, some pilots hesitate to use them for fear of overshooting a landing zone. But there is a solution; Patrick Bechean, for example, has an aerobrake parachute which makes smaller landing fields possible for faster wings. This new technique will undoubtedly offer a plus to hang gliding, and I am going to equip myself with one.

Extraordinary flights like Gil Souviron's are now possible in hang gliders, and virtually barred to sailplanes, because of the techniques we have evolved for landing in tight fields. Paragliders, of course, can land virtually anywhere. In the Pyrenees or the Alps, sailplane pilots must be constantly aware they could get trapped by poor conditions and be forced down in unsuitable places, with the risk of wrecking their aircraft and killing themselves. The fly-on-the-wall technique in hang gliding is just that; pilots dive and then zoom up the profile of the hill, losing speed, until pushing out and plonking safely on to the ground.

Another aid is the drogue parachutes, which have been some time in development. Early ones were carried on the back rigging by the control bar, and when released were supposed to slide up to the keel and slow gliders down. The major problem was that some caught on the rigging swages at the control bar, and tipped the gliders into vertical dives. Robert Close-Smith, a British League pilot, was paralysed in this way at Lachens, Mike de Glanville's home site in France. I saw a similar accident with a free-flyer in the 1985 World Championships at Kossen;

the pilot went in from 80ft and was killed instantly. The Americans have developed an umbrella-like parachute which is integral to the keel of the hang glider and does not have this problem.

The best hang glider pilots are capable of instant analysis in the air, and they are breaking into the big distances. Long flights were undertaken in Australia and in Europe, and South Africa and Namibia were just being 'discovered'. The US was where hungry pilots went, first to Owens, and later out into the prairies, where they are more likely to encounter killer 'dust devils'. The American pilot John Anderson had no qualms about taking his 'flimsy' hang glider into a dust devil, something a mainstream sailplane pilot might think twice about. It is a long way from the innocence of Graham Hobson, worrying about his glider 'getting an uppercut and hanging on for dear life' over Snowdon in 1976, just from a benign mountain thermal. Jim Lee, the American who, ten years after the First Lilienthal Meet, held the world distance record in 1981, opened the fearful can of worms that is 'dust devil soaring' in 1991. He asked:

Is dust devil soaring:

- A way to rise to a higher level through the use of a whirlwind common in dry regions?
- A desperation move by a half-crazed competition pilot?
- A common, though little-understood technique used by most hang glider pilots?

Which is the correct definition?

Sorry, this is not a multiple-choice question; all three are correct. It is a fact that pilots all over the world are using dust devils to make low saves, gain altitude and extend flights. Other pilots are making low saves by catching thermals that are really invisible dust devils.

You mean it's OK to fly dust devils? What about Dennis Pagen telling us in this book, 'Flying Conditions' to stay at least as far away from a dust devil as its visible height above the ground? The point I am making is to 'tell it like it is' and give food for thought, not to say, 'Go out and fly into any dust devil you see'.

Consider the Dirt: Not all dirt is created equal and neither are dust devils. Dirt varies from your basic sandy, rocky particles in the southwestern US desert, to the talcum powder-like dirt in the northwest, or even the 'clean' dirt found in the eastern US called 'grass'.

The Chelan, Washington State, area has some of the highest-quality dust found anywhere. Due in part to the fallow farming techniques which require tilling the bare soil over and over, the area grows some fine, knee-deep dust you have to land in to appreciate. It is so light that the merest disturbance of rising air produces a dust devil. Consequently, local pilots consider it common practice to fly from devil to devil.

How low can one fly into a dust devil?

On one particularly bad day for me during the 1986 Nationals, a landing was imminent in one of the dusty fields. I was ground-skimming on final when a dust devil sprang up about 60ft ahead. A couple of seconds of indecision afforded me the opportunity to centre-punch the thing. My wings rocked about 10 degrees as I passed through it, and returned to level as I flew out the other side to a stand-up landing. Behind me, drifting away downwind, it turned into the usual monster.

On the other side of the coin is the sandy soil of the southwest USA. Much denser than Chelan's, it requires a stronger thermal to pick it up. Only one of 50 Chelan thermals may be strong enough to form a southwestern devil. I would much rather fly into a Chelanese devil than a New Mexican one.

Now we come to the eastern US non-devils, or whirlwinds. About the only time you will see a dust devil here is when the whirlwind crosses a dirt road, flashes dust for a second and disappears again. However, it is common to see leaves, grass and various seeds floating up in a thermal. A whirlwind puts those particles in the air and would be a dust devil, if there were any dust. Invisible whirlwinds can be found anywhere where there is an absence of dust. It can be spotted shaking the trees, dancing across the grass or spinning across lakes.

Birth of a Thermal: The different convective theories concerning thermal development include the bubble, vortex ring and jet (or plume) theories. Thermals are usually a combination of all three. As a thermal mass gains enough buoyancy to break free from the earth, it can lift off as an isolated bubble or it may draw air from a continuous supply of heated air and form a column. During the ascent both types take on vortex ring characteristics. Either type may form a whirlwind, but the short-lived (at ground level) bubble has less chance of doing so.

A hang glider pilot flying into the top of a column thermal will usually get a smoother ride than one entering lower down, since the lower pilot must deal with more vertical wind sheers and turbulence. A pilot entering the thermal within a few hundred feet of its origin may also encounter a plume (or whirlwind) which, in addition to vertical wind sheers, contains a rotational factor as well. This pilot will get the roughest ride of all.

As for a thermal's size, a high lapse rate – the rate of change of temperature with height – and good solar heating will obviously make strong thermals. Also, light winds will allow for longer heating and more vigorous thermal action. Many other factors also apply. Strong thermals produce large whirlwinds and dust or other particles will make the whirlwind visible.

How big is big?

I was travelling to the 1979 Regionals in Crested Butte, Colorado, with Mike Robert when we spotted a very large dust devil ahead. It crossed the highway. We pulled over and got out of the truck, and watched it roll into the freshly bailed hay. The top of the 2,000 foot devil was dirt, and the bottom portion was hay. We watched as the 'hay devil' casually knocked hay bales aside, leaving a defined path in its wake. Coming upon a 10-foot wide stream, the devil centred upon the last bale in the field, sending it spinning in circles. It finally lifted the bale into the air and threw it across the stream, just as the devil became a water-spout. Watching the dust-hay-water devil drift away, we considered turning around and dragging our wimpy, single-surface rags back to Albuquerque.

DISTANCES AND HEIGHTS AFTER 1981

Many studies have shown that dust devils spin in both directions equally. You should always enter a suitable dust devil in the direction opposite the spin. Circling against the rotation decreases your groundspeed, leads to a reduction in centrifugal forces and yields a tighter circle. Also, climb rates and airspeeds remain more constant. Entering with the spin can cause you to stall suddenly! Be sure you have enough altitude to recover, no matter which direction you are going!

In many cases, you don't need to enter a devil to find lift. Dust devils can indicate the strongest part of an area of widespread lift, and often smoother more consistent lift can be found in the air surrounding the core. Sometimes multiple devils, or many strong devils dancing around a larger one, can be observed. This indicates multiple cores of the same thermal or perhaps separate columns of lift, some of which may be invisible.

OK, now fly with me on a real flight, the first day of the 1990 Hobbs Tow Meet. Due to an inadvertent release earlier, I am on my second tow of the day with John Forburger driving and my wife, Kathy riding as an observer. Climbing past 1,000ft AGL I notice a very large dust devil just off the end of the runway. Kathy asks me if I see it and I radio back that I do. It's a real snake with a jet-black core and rapidly swirling dust around the outside. It is only 50ft across at 1,000ft AGL, and extends another 1,000ft upwards. I continue to tow to 1,500ft AGL, release and turn downwind, away from the monster. I wanted nothing to do with it!

Lift is good on course to our goal at Portales, 100 miles away. Nevertheless, just past Tatum I am heading for the ground – fast. There are a couple of gliders on the ground, 400ft below. I start hitting patchy lift and begin to hunt for the thermal. Suddenly, a dust devil pops up about 400 yards downwind of me. I turn and head for it and it quickly rises to 200ft then 300ft as I approach. The diameter at my 150 foot level is 75ft across.

I note the counter-clockwise spin and so I enter the left edge, turning right against the spin with plenty of extra airspeed. I circle around the outside edge, banking tightly in surging lift, getting slapped around a bit, but it's acceptable (by my standards). The devil and I pass through an alfalfa field and it disappears but I can plainly see its footprint in the waving plants below. As I slowly climb in wildly varying lift, I notice the smell of alfalfa and manure. The climb rate improves to 300–400 fpm even though I'm flying fast and the dust re-appears as the devil leaves the alfalfa. My climb rate continues to improve as I get higher, and the ride smooths out, allowing me to slow down, relax and enjoy the low save while on my way to 5,000ft AGL. I leave the thermal in good shape to find another which gets me nearly to cloud base. I finish fourth for the day.

Upon landing at Portales I learned that Eric Aasletten had been killed on tow shortly after I departed the airport. Apparently the monster dust devil I had seen while on tow had hit the runway, become invisible, travelled the length of the runway and possibly hit Eric as he launched.

Like it or not, dust devil flight is common. Some pilots are even known for leaving good lift to head for a dust devil further away. As I said, we fly into invisible whirlwinds often. I have personally flown into about 50 dust devils in 14 years of hang gliding, while logging 17,000 XC miles. I have yet to kick the keel or have the bar ripped out of my hands. Am I lucky? You bet! But I also carry extra speed and hang on in tight turbulence, which definitely includes dust devils.

As one of my flying buddies says, 'If we could see the air, we'd probably quit flying.' When dust, smoke, and moisture make air visible, we can truly see that there are dragons in the woods. At least the dust in devils does us the service of showing the nature of the beast.

One of the most charming accounts of XC flight comes, as it should, from Ireland. Liavan Mallin ('Little Irish me' as she refers to herself) set a new Irish distance record in stark contrast to the macho whoops of Johan Anderson. I cannot understand why Liavan does not have the same sort of status in Ireland as the English-born football manager

DISTANCES AND HEIGHTS AFTER 1981

Jack Charlton had there, and she's home-grown stuff. She has courage, stamina, charm, an odd modesty so you only understand her ordeals 'sideways', in throwaway lines. It isn't as if Ireland or any other country has that many young heroines that it can afford to ignore someone of Miss Mallin's quality and style.

Her account of cracking the Irish distance record is genuinely witty; compare Larry Tudor's painstaking preparations and Liavan's blithe 'flutter over the back', because conditions are too rough on Ireland's highest mountain to land either at the top or bottom of it. And I would love to have been there when a farmer stumbled over her, lying comatose next to her wing, to find she was still alive!

> Oh no! It's blowing a gale and what's more it's southerly. Eddie said it was south-west at his house. I arrived at the top of Mount Leinster and Eddie and Jim had already rigged. Eddie was in the air in no time, and I helped Jim to take off. I rigged as fast as I could. While carrying my own glider to take off, my feet left the ground as I clung to the A-frame, and I wasn't even clipped in! Well, it looked OK in the air, top landing was definitely out and so was bottom landing, so I was all set for a flutter over the back.
>
> Eddie had already gone. It seemed like ages before a good cloud system came through which took me to cloud base 700ft above take-off. Things deteriorated rapidly over the back. I was below take-off and gliding to where Jim was circling under a nice cloud. I got a weak thermal which I worked for an eternity before it eventually took me to cloud base. Jim was racing crosswind. I decided to stay where I was as things were developing nicely downwind.
>
> My hands and feet were becoming numb with the cold, and ice was forming on my sleeves. My teeth were making very funny noises. Over Carlow, Jim seemed to be getting very low and struggling. Eddie must be at least ten miles downwind of us by now, as he's had half an hour head start. To the west things looked very over-developed, so I headed east to a developing cloud street. As I got lower the blood started rushing back into my hands and feet; the pain was excruciating. I caught a very broken thermal over

Stradbally and at about 500ft ATO went weightless a few times as I hung on for dear life. At about 1,000ft below cloud base, the thermal became smoother. This was the most spectacular part of the flight, climbing up past cloud base. I was surrounded by cloud in no time, but could still see the ground clearly, and cloud base, which was 500ft below me, was at about 4,500ft ASL.

I was enjoying the view, wondering what I was going to have for dinner, singing to myself, swinging out of the A-frame in budgie position, performing jogging exercises and was generally preoccupied at this stage. At about 3.30pm the situation was getting very serious downwind. The clouds were scraggy and I couldn't stay where I was because my cloud had died. Upwind the sky had totally over-developed. The next ten miles I flew 500–1,000ft ATO. As I came near to Lough Ennell I realised that I would not be able to cross it, so with 1,000ft I picked a deluxe landing field near a farmhouse and a main road.

Landing was quite turbulent. It took me a quarter of an hour to try and unclip myself, and unhook the nose catch. My fingers were not receiving my messages correctly. Lying down beside my glider, I slowly drifted into oblivion.

'Are you all right?'

I jumped up to see this massive farmer looking down at me. I mumbled some explanation, and asked him where I was. He looked at me as if I had a screw loose. When he said I was in County Westmeath I started dancing around my glider. He invited me in for a cup of tea and a sandwich. From his house, I phoned Bunclody, only to talk to Eddie who had landed in a ploughed field in Myshall, tête-à-tête with an earthworm. He severely reprimanded me for not carrying a radio, as he had been trying to follow my course after collecting Jim at Stradbally, but lost sight of me as I flew off into the sunset.

I had flown 61.5 miles, a new Irish record. Two regrets; not having bar mitts to keep my hands warm, and not being able to cross the Lake.

Chapter 3

Birds and the New Aviation

Because we are so exposed to the elements, hanging in the wind and flying comparatively slowly, we have a closer relationship to birds than other aircraft. An American scientist called Dr Pennicuick wrote an excellent article on the sink rates of vultures in East Africa after following them about the sky in a powered conventional glider in the 1960s, but he was only able to observe through his cockpit canopy, rather than experience what the birds were flying in. The BBC got much closer by sending British League pilot Jerome Fack, one of tall twin sons of the Dutch ambassador to Britain, into the middle of flocks of birds with a movie camera on a hang glider. It is quite common for us to mix it with birds, even big ones, virtually eyeball to eyeball in the same thermal. The easiest aircraft to commune with birds are the paragliders, then Rogallo wings, but even microlights, noisy though we are, can get quite close. On my way down the eastern Scottish coast, returning from my microlight flight around the world, I remember chasing a wild-eyed bird for twenty seconds, it being too stupid to fly left or right to get out of my way. Had I got too close, of course, I would have swerved, as it did in the end. In a more deliberate experience, dozens of geese in Canada were even persuaded by one curious pilot to see a microlight as their mother.

Some encounters with birds can be frightening, some fascinating, and some amusing. Britain's Judy Leden, for example, was competing against the top men in the Himalayas in 1983. She had beaten America's Larry Tudor, one to one, the hang gliding equivalent of racing Carl Lewis and winning, despite being so weak with one of India's tourist illnesses that another pilot carried her glider to take-off. As Judy dived for the finishing line:

> Suddenly I sensed something behind me. It couldn't possibly be! No, it wasn't Larry, but a 4-foot wingspan vulture

cruising about 6ft behind me. What an end to a wonderful flight! My own personal escort across the finishing line.

I was then drawn against the eventual competition winner, France's Gerard Thevenot, and looked forward to learning a lot from him during the task, a 50 km run to Daremsala. It was not to be. I found myself really low after takeoff, only to watch Gerard get into a good thermal, taking him to cloud base. Eventually I got back up and flew the rest of the race for practice. I met up with Josef Guggenmos on the way. We flew together for the rest of the course.

At one point I was heading across a wide gully with Josef slightly in front when a huge vulture appeared right behind him. It was obviously besotted with Josef, as it would start to overtake him and then stick down its legs to slow down and stay with him. Occasionally I would get in the way and the bird would indignantly weave around me to take up station again. I was in fits of giggles as it followed Josef for 15 minutes.

Judy went on to paragliding a few years later, and renewed her experience of flying with birds in South America, after which she wrote a lovely book on her experiences called *Flying with Condors*.

The 1988 World Hang Gliding Championships were held in Australia. Ricky Duncan won, still one of the Moyes Boys back then before setting up his own company, and the Aussies took the team prize too. One feature of the competition, according to Sherry Thevenot, Gerard's wife, was the irritated eagles stirred into action by men passing by on large silent wings and bleeping varios.

> Extraordinary, terrible, spectacular, frightening ... the frequent attacks by eagles defending their skies in Australia. Practically every pilot who went early for championship training had an experience of intimidation, if not a full-fledged attack by local eagles, who must have been in their nesting period. Many pilots had their wings ripped, usually about one metre from the wingtip, the rips a good 10 centimetres long.
>
> Analysing the various tales, three types of attack can be distinguished: intimidation with noisy screeching and

sweeps all too close in front, behind and just above the wing while positioning for attack; an actual attack on the wing tip, after a warning, with a good bit of damage to the sail (if the beak or claws did not slip on the trilam surface); or a direct attack on the kingpost with no warning at all from the aggressive bird who could only be spotted falling in front or behind the wing.

One pilot complained of having 10 centimetres of an upper cable unsheathed by a bird. Britain's Tony Hughes was attacked by two eagles, one with a three metre span who left a large hole in his right wing, a small one in the left wing, and a rip in the leading edge. Usually when two birds fly together the eagles would attack, one situated above the other. Although the threats continued throughout the championships, the attacks decreased during the finals, probably because pilots tended to fly in groups which was too much to handle for one bird.

Of course, now that it is over, it sounds amusing, but imagine yourself flying 6,000ft above the eucalyptus trees and spotting a great black mass shadowing your leading edge. It's a hell of a thing to be focussed on by an 'eagle eye', or catch a glimpse of the curved beak and readied claws that begin to drag with stiffened feathers.

Dr Jo Bathmann is the superb Austrian pilot who set the tasks for the 1985 World Championships in Kossen, involving fascinating races over 180km, including a final run to goal over Hitler's 'Eagle's Eyrie' in Berchtesgaden. Bathmann is one of the intellectuals of the air, always questioning what is happening in the mountains he flies. One year, he met an eagle to whom he gave the name Maximilian; the two would fly together. The following 'season' Bathmann bought a new glider, not in the same colours as the one Maximilian was familiar with. When they met again, Jo had reason to be thankful for man's polluting habits:

> I almost forgot him, the eagle, Maximilian. It was last year when the two of us became friends. But to feed Max from the air while I was flying my hang glider presented problems.

'You have to start to feed him, to make him accustomed to your person, and then you will have a real air show,' advised my friend Herwarth Voightmann, a scuba instructor. He has spent a lot of time and effort to train sharks to eat small bait fish out of his hands, even out of his mouth!

Last year I had to stop trying to tame Max because the weather was too poor for flying. I was feeding him small chunks of tender beef fillet, and we had become used to one another. We used to circle in the same thermal and fly side by side across the peaks of the Leogang Stone Mountain, admiring each other. There I met him again and again, when I was flying my long favourite cross-country route from Kossen to Zell am See.

Max has beautiful stone-grey wings with some very tasteful and harmoniously placed white feathers, and a majestic-looking head. His giant beak, which commands one's respect, shines in the sunlight, his claws hidden underneath his feathers. In those first meetings with Max, I was flying my hang glider with the rainbow-coloured double surface and a red leading edge, in a red cocoon harness which matched the glider's colours quite well. Maximilian must have liked that sail, and its colours. But he definitely did not like the new glider I am flying today!

There is no question that it is Maximilian. I recognise him easily. In the Alps, not many golden eagles of his giant size are left.

Instead of starting to circle as usual, both of us in the same thermal, Max rises to full size in front of me. He shows me his threatening beak. The feathers of his neck spread out into a waving collar, and the claws point fearsomely at me. He flies around me, turns back and aims first at me and then again at the sail above me.

Instinctively I draw in my neck because it is obvious it won't be possible to fly together in friendship anymore. But didn't he recognise me? Could it be that my new glider, with its different colours, looks different to him? Is he upset by the yellow double surface, or dazzled by the shiny mylar leading edge that catches glints from the brilliant sun?

BIRDS AND THE NEW AVIATION

I don't know and there isn't time to speculate. I fly a few wingovers, followed by steep and fast turns. Having lost 600ft of altitude, I escaped the attack. Had it been successful, my friend Max could have done serious damage to the sail.

Unfortunately, a field of cirrus clouds had dampened the sunlight during the past few minutes. The thermal activity becomes weaker, the up-winds sparse and not strong enough to gain altitude. Not far away I see pink smoke rising vertically from the chimney of the machinery works at Hochfilten. The words 'industrial thermal' spring to mind! I remember reports of sailplane pilots of the Ruhr area (the largest industrial area in Europe, in north-west Germany). These pilots have made five-hour flights, thermalling over power plants and big chimneys.

I speed up to get there. As I arrive in the vicinity, my vario indicates 200/400 fpm-up. But it stinks so caustically that I automatically stop breathing. My eyes begin to run with tears. After some coughing fits, I have to leave the smoke. I have gained almost 1,000ft and fly back to the slope, hoping to find enough clean lift to be able to hold on to the ridge. If I can hang on long enough perhaps the thermals will improve again. Then, I don't know where he came from, he is suddenly back again, Maximilian, the golden eagle!

He shows me his claws and that terrible beak again, then turns about to sit above me, ready to attack. I do not wish to have my new sail torn to pieces and dive away again in steep and fast turns, trying to escape. But this time the eagle follows me closely! He looks at me and then the sail above me, as if he is not sure which to attack first.

Let us see if the eagle likes industrial thermals.

He doesn't! You can almost see how he turns up his nose and flies away from the smoke. You already know what follows; coughing, swearing, tears in the eyes, and after an altitude gain of 1,000ft, back to the mountain.

This time I am on the look-out for my bad-tempered eagle. And right then, he breaks away from the big branch of a tall tree to circle beneath me, but in my thermal, which is now growing stronger.

He slowly comes closer from below. I centre the thermal more exactly to optimise my climb rate. We are both climbing, but who climbs faster? The 600 foot advantage that I gained in the industrial thermal is enough and I can disappear in the cloud forming above me.

Next time I will come back with small presents. But what would Max like? Should I try feeding him with a dead mouse? Perhaps I will meet Max with Mrs Max and baby Max? Then maybe all four of us will fly together.

I would not fancy my chances with Maximilian, but Jo Bathmann seems to have survived the experience. It is easy to see why birds, which have their own territorial claims, would get irritated with hang gliders, but in England a northern pilot with the unlikely pseudonym 'Dr Rook' took a series of photographs of the Mam Tor Crow. This crow liked hitching lifts on hang gliders:

We arrived at Hope in the Peak District at the end of May, 1991, and by the time we had located the sites it was getting around to 5.30pm. After talking to a local pilot we decided to fly Mam Tor. He also mentioned that a crow had been dive-bombing him when he flew. I took off on my Solar Wings Rumour 145, and flew for a couple of hours, but saw no sight of the crow.

Friday morning I was on site, ready to launch at 8.30am, complete with my trusty Halina 35mm camera. After flying for about half an hour, cloud base was over 500ft ATO, I heard a scratching noise on my port wing. I looked up and there was our infamous feathered friend hanging on to the trailing edge. It then let go and flew over to my starboard wing.

He continued this airborne ballet for the next couple of hours, taking off from his vantage point on the cliff, climbing above me and then diving with a squawk to land on the leading edge before sliding back to the trailing edge (hence the scratching noise). My passenger would then hang on to the batten elastic, at the same time pecking away, leaving – I found later – about three quarters of an inch at the end very frayed!

When I thought he had been there long enough I pulled on speed, forcing him to let go. He would then fly down to his perch on the rocks below for a rest before once again taking off and coming up for another free ride.

During this time I managed with great difficulty, to take a number of photographs.

Luckily I was the only one flying at the time, so I did not have to worry about avoiding other pilots while trying to look through the viewfinder of the camera, holding it with one hand and controlling the glider with another. It was a novel experience.

The best story to emerge about hang gliding and birds comes from Canada, where an environmentalist called Bill Lishman, living among the great forests of Ontario, became concerned that some birds were losing the skill to migrate. Putting an engine on his rigid wing hang glider, and then later using a soft-wing trike microlight, Lishman tried to teach a flock of birds how to migrate. The articles he wrote about his experiences later became the basis of a Hollywood film called *Fly Away Home*, about a young girl who uses a microlight to teach geese how to migrate. Lishman did the flying and the goose wrangling in the film:

> Essential to the survival of many species of birds is migration. Simply put, their healthy existence depends on the freedom to travel by air to better feeding grounds, according to the seasons. Most of these traditional migrations have evolved over millenniums and the routes have become a survival legacy passed on from one generation to the next. Many specific flocks of certain birds, through over-hunting or loss of habitat to man, have gone extinct in specific areas. Man has stepped in and tried to restore these flocks by bringing in breeding stock from distant flocks or birds that had been bred in captivity. However, since the migratory tradition was lost with the demise of the previous flock, there has been little success in getting the new birds on the block to

migrate. Self-sustaining migrating flocks have yet to be established!

It was not this noble cause that got me started flying with birds. Like many, I had been envious of bird flight since childhood. In the '70s I learned to fly by circuitous routes and retraced the steps of early flyers like Lilienthal and the Wright Brothers. By 1988, after several years of failed attempts, I had learned to fly with a flock of Canadian geese. Out of this success evolved the idea that what I had learned about flying with birds could possibly be used to develop new migration routes for several species of migratory waterfowl. What follows is the first part of a migration experiment.

In 1989 I met Professor William Sladen, a research scientist and swan expert who heads up the environmental studies department of the Airlie Centre near Warrenton, Virginia. Captivated by the idea, he invited us to try flying a flock of waterfowl from Ontario to his research centre. It was an adventurous project with the possibility of positive results that I could not pass up. There were a number of false starts. With the help of Dr Sladen, family and friends, we attempted an experiment in 1990 but were naive in our perception of the various governmental agencies involved in the management of wildfowl. They looked on the project as too risky. *It was truly interesting to note that their vision of microlight flying was that it was akin to Russian roulette.* Plus, somehow, we trod on some bureaucratic toes and the powers in the Canadian Wildlife Service saw fit to uncrecmoniously and illegally curtail our operations that year. It took until 1993 before we could get all the factors in place for a workable plan.

The experiment was to raise a flock of non-endangered Canada Geese, as I had in 1988–90, imprint them on a microlight aircraft, and fly them south 400 miles to the Airlie Centre in Virginia. Then to see if they would return to Ontario, on their own, the following Spring. Or, we might fly them back from Virginia, and see if they would return there the following Fall [autumn]. These geese would be guinea pigs, affording us insight on how we might introduce migration routes to the endangered species.

Covering all bases single-handedly would be impossible. I needed the help of another person who possessed that indefinable talent to relate to birds, and who could also fly a microlight. The right guy turned out to be Joe Duff, a professional photographer, long-time microlight pilot, and good guy.

In early April, Joe and I were out there collecting our future flying partners who came in little white spheroids located in well-concealed nests. For days we slogged through marshes and swamps, searching out those elusive treasures. Incidentally, Canada Geese have a highly workable back-up plan if they lose their eggs; they simply lay another clutch.

We bought a commercial incubator and studied up on the incubating process. Joe produced a wall chart to record temperatures, humidity and egg turning, which became a ritual. We candled the eggs at the appropriate times and eliminated a number of infertile eggs.

While I had used a rigid-wing biplane microlight in previous goose flights, my experience with the French-built Cosmos flex-wing trike looked like it might have better potential, fitting the specific requirements of a goose leader. The week prior to the incubated eggs hatching, Joe and I flew to Dijon in France, to meet Gerard Thevenot of La Mouette and test one of his new wing designs that he thought might meet our goose speed requirements. We spent a few days testing the speed range of the new 16 square-metre double surface wing called the Ghost. At that point we did not know of a trike that could be mated with that wing to give us the right speed envelope and range. Gerard concluded that he could modify the hang-glider flex-wing to permit the required slower speed, when mated to the Cosmos single-seater Echo trike.

We arrived home two days prior to the first eggs hatching. The goslings, wet and bedraggled at first, could hardly lift their heads, but within a day they were lively yellow fluffballs ready to take on the world. From then on it was a dawn-to-dusk labour, either playing parent to the quickly developing goslings, working on the next stage of permits, organising photos and videos, building pens, a mock-up aircraft and a second hangar.

We were in constant touch with Gerard [Thevenot] on the development of the wings. He test-flew them and his report was a little disheartening. It did not seem that the trike we had planned would fly slowly enough in its standard form with a 50 HP Rotax engine. However, my experience with Konig radial engines had been great; my Easy Riser biplane microlight had flown several hundred faultless hours. While putting out only 28 HP, it was just half the weight of the Rotax. We only wanted to fly 30 mph anyway, and the Konig sipped gasoline at only 7 litres an hour.

The goslings were turning from fluff to feathers, and starting to look like real geese. I ordered the trike from Cosmos, the engine from Konig, and the wing was en route from La Mouette. Nothing showed up on time and we were forced to use a hastily built ply-wood mock-up aircraft on the ground.

By 1 July the geese were fully feathered. They had developed their pecking order and their different personalities had started to emerge. It is important to spend time with growing birds, so to cover all the bases, either Joe or I would sit in the mock-up aircraft on the runway, surrounded by the geese, lap-top computer clicking away, and the portable phone to hand.

In early July we drove the route to Virginia to locate potential landings spots. At first we considered State parks or conservation areas, but thought again about another level of bureaucracy and opted for checking the possibility of private grass airstrips. With the help of the EAA (Experimental Aircraft Association) we identified a number of potential airfields. This took a week, but by the time we had returned from Virginia, we had found eight private airstrip owners more than willing to co-operate.

The Echo Trike arrived as a bare-bones box of parts, with no assembly instructions. Within days we designed, built and static-tested the engine mount, throttle-control system, goose/prop-guard, instrument panel, and also put the engine through its break-in procedure. Every hour or two we would take a break and spend some time with the geese, attempting to get them to follow us up and down the runway, pulling the dumb-looking mock-up.

We tried splitting them into several small flocks in an attempt to regain our position as flock leaders. This meant hurriedly building more pens.

On 13 July I test-flew the first aircraft from Willy Casteel's 3,000 foot strip on Scugog Island (my rough 900 foot strip is hardly suitable for test-flying). The Echo flew perfectly from the start. The moderate rate of climb of the Konig-powered version commanded enough respect; pitch-control was fine but like most double-surface high performance wings, it took some muscle to control the roll. The airspeed check seemed OK but hard to read as the wind-meter had to be repositioned according to the cruise altitude. We found that flying at goose-speed produced a great deal of strain.

The next move was to try it with the geese. The first flights were extremely disappointing. The geese, in several groups, flew in different patterns. Some would not fly more than a few feet above the trees; some would even fly down among the trees; some would just circle about and land immediately. None at first would come anywhere near the aircraft.

For three nerve-racking weeks we worked at getting those birds to follow us in the air. They were fine on the ground, but it took them the longest time to realise that we wanted them to fly with us. Besides that, they landed time and again in the strangest spots. We spent day after day, searching them out and walking them back to the pen. It was a real low in the whole project; we were on the verge of calling it quits.

The situation changed when we took another tack, made some modifications to the aircraft and it began to work. First two, then three birds would fly with us and we kept adding birds all the way up to eighteen.

It looked now as if the flight south might work and a new set of worries took over. Our first leg would incorporate crossing almost 40 miles of Lake Ontario. Would the geese follow us over that expanse of water? What if they get tuckered out and decide to land half-way across? How could we minimise the risks of an engine failure and possible ditching in the cold water? How to arrange customs and immigration clearance on the US side? How will we get accurate, up to date, weather? The last question was answered by Metech, a private weather-consulting firm which came to our aid and agreed to furnish us with detailed briefings throughout.

The flying now became more enjoyable and by early September we had the second Echo trike airworthy. We found that flying one fast wing and one slow wing was the right combination of goose leader and goose chaser.

Our first day of goose hunting season coincided with our first XC flight, to a strip about 35 miles north of home base. The route had to skirt Lake Scugog and the marsh area. The day looked great; only a few high cirrus clouds and virtually no wind. We had no difficulty getting the seventeen birds that we now had flying with us, off the ground and formed up on a steady 50 fpm climb to the northwest. At 700ft AGL the air was rock steady and everything was working like clockwork. I flew the slow wing; Joe cruised high behind and to my right. We passed over many hunters' blinds, looking down from a healthy altitude. One bird ('007') would often fly so close to the cockpit that I could reach out and let his wingtip brush my hand. It was a lovely feeling, the goose flying beside me looking up like a friendly dog on a walk. Once we arrived over the field it took almost an hour of difficult flying to get the geese to land at their first 'foreign' location. They were extremely cautious and made numerous low passes over the field prior to their final touchdown. We then discovered that we had one more goose than we had taken off with; a wild goose had joined the group en route!

The next week we did a second XC flight to Volk's field near Tottenham. It was below freezing on takeoff; we had to defrost the wings. The birds were distracted by every gravel pit we flew over.

BIRDS AND THE NEW AVIATION

For several months we lived and breathed gas fumes and goose droppings, grown hoarse with attempted goose calls, froze our fingers and never ever got enough sleep, but by mid-September we were almost convinced that the birds were following well enough for the project to become a reality. By mid-October we were ready to go.

Tuesday 19 Oct – After a one-day stand-down due to adverse winds, Metech inform us that conditions look good for a lake crossing. We are into almost military mode: the total scenario for crossing the lake has been worked out and carefully planned. Five aircraft, two rescue boats and five land vehicles were involved, plus 18 personnel, mostly volunteers.

At 0600 our kitchen seems to fill up with people and camera equipment. An ABC camera crew hustles about. The phone rings. It's the radio station and I do an interview after listening to a commercial for what seems forever, while I wait for the announcer.

It's time to go to the airstrip but it is still pitch black. There is an overcast day, no fog.

I walk over to the goose pen and say a few words to the geese, which are illuminated by the lights of the News van. Back in the hangar under the Pontiac headlights, I start suiting up. I turn on the GPS navigation system and watch it find the satellites. The camera crew is ready. Everything looks go.

Seated in the cockpit, I wave off Iain Mellows in 'Kodak One', a photo plane (Cosmos tandem) and wait while he disappears over the ridge. I give a sign to release the geese. Slowly at first the geese emerge from their haven and at once take wing. Full throttle, the goose leader trundles down the strip and is in the air. The birds are on my left; I veer towards them, just clearing the windsock. They keep veering left over the forest and then over the field to the north. Joe is airborne behind and to my left. He comes up on their flank and they loosely form up on him. He swings a wide arc to a southerly heading at about 300ft and passes over the spectators gathered with some cows on the ridge. I parallel him to the east. The geese are between us on a southerly heading. Joe crowds them further east and they gradually start to build up on his wingtip. We grind southeasterly toward our Newcastle turning point where my earphones start to crackle. The geese have broken away from Joe and are now flying midway between us in a ragged line. I call to them and gradually they move to form up on my wings. Several climb over the leading edge of the left wing forcing me to push hard to the right to maintain course. The wing pulses with their wing-beats. Eventually they settle out and string off the left tip.

After what seems an hour but is in truth only a few minutes, we cross the shoreline and the geese break formation; both Joe and I are silent. This was always a concern; will this huge body of water affect the birds? Will they decide to go down to land or turn back? Our fears are groundless. They move over and form again on my wing. We now have a new heading and our ground-speed picked up to 35 mph. Our fears of crossing the lake diminish in unison with the miles covered. The birds are like a string of beads off my right wing-tip.

We swing east now at about 700ft. There is a slight haze; about 100 people are waiting at the north end of the narrow grass strip, newspaper people, TV crews and neighbours. I fly straight in and land at a remote part of the airstrip, figuring the birds will follow. Not so. I ask the crowd to stay at the other end. Joe stays airborne and rounds up the birds. They are out of sight for a short period and we hear gunshots from the same direction. There is some trepidation but they all appear again and, after about ten near-landings, they fly right by me and land among the crowd in front of TV cameras. Everyone cheers.

Saturday 23 Oct – After delays due to ground fog and winds, we take off at 0730 and the birds form well. We set a southeast course and, aided by a brisk tailwind, make it to Jalamtra field near Bath, NY. We take off again at 1515 and cross into Pennsylvania with a slight tailwind. Now we are in the mountains and have to climb to 3,700ft ASL

BIRDS AND THE NEW AVIATION

to clear. The Apollo GPS is working well, and takes us to Jim Fink's field in Trout Run, north of Williamsport. The airfield, called Finkhaven, is in the bottom of a valley with 2,000 foot mountains steeply rising on either side. Joe likens it to landing in the bottom of a glass.

Sunday 24 Oct – The weather report is iffy but the geese have got the migration itch and are ready to fly. The winds are calm as we depart at 1045. The birds seem a little disorientated in the valley. We fly several circuits before they form up on us. We set course 180 degrees and fly for about an hour. Crossing the Susquehanna west of Williamsport, I note the groundspeed is down to 18 mph and the air is becoming turbulent. We carry on over the first ridge of mountains.

We spy a clearing in a valley with a track down the middle, and after several circuits I land. The geese land with little problem and Joe follows in. So we have an unscheduled camp-over, much to the surprise of the Miller family whose field we have dropped into.

Monday Oct 25 – We take off at frosty first light, climb eastwards for five miles before we have enough altitude to clear the first ridge of mountains. Our climb continues to 3,500ft ASL to clear subsequent east-west mountain ridges. Ground speed reading is 54 mph. There is fabulous visibility; smoke from many wood stoves rises straight up. We skirt the west of Harrisburg control zone and carry on in perfect air to land south of Gettysburg, Pa, at Brown's farm.

No one home at Brown's farm. The ground crew take two hours to catch up with us and miss the driveway. I jump up and wave frantically at them and inadvertently scare the geese into the air. I almost go into shock but my fears melt when in ten minutes they return and land at my feet.

Tuesday 26 Oct – In beautiful weather we get airborne at 1530 for the last leg into Airlie. It really is too warm for the geese but the forecast is for bad weather the next day. The geese pant the whole 2 hours and 30 minutes and will not climb. We have to maintain low altitude, 500ft over beautiful Virginia rolling countryside and fabulous homes.

Airborne spiders that ride the wind on long silk threads collect on our craft and their shining webs shimmer in the afternoon sun. The GPS brings us to Airlie at 1730. The afternoon light is perfect, and the air absolutely still. The whole scene is surrealistic and the geese need water badly.

I could fill a hundred pages on the trials and traumas that Joe, Bill Sladen and I went through in six months to hatch and raise a flock of Canada geese, simultaneously source, design and assemble the specialised flying hardware, and negotiate endlessly with multi-levels of a sceptical bureaucracy that required more paper than the weight of our aircraft. Not to mention the day-to-day dedication required to lovingly condition those birds to accompany us on a 400-mile flight from Ontario to Virginia.

There was a point in mid-summer when the birds simply refused to form up that we were ready to fold our wings. It seemed we were always on the uphill side of the curve. However, a change in wings and a new approach gave us enough hope to carry on, and gradually the project turned around. It certainly was a glorious day when we landed in that brightly-lit Virginia meadow with all eighteen geese.

Only then did the significance of it all begin to come through.

Bill Lishman and Joseph Duff are still conducting their experiment with so-called ultrageese (microlights are called ultralights in the US and Canada). There was a happy ending to their story. On the morning of 15 April 1994, ten Canada geese landed at Lishman's airstrip at Purple Hill, Ontario, near Toronto in Canada. They were ten of the original geese he and Duff had led to the Airlie Centre in Virginia in October 1993.

Over the winter the geese were allowed to fly freely at Airlie under the watchful eye of Dr William Sladen. The ultrageese were monitored on a daily basis by a team of biologists. The original plan was to equip several of the geese with radio transmitters and monitor their progress by satellite. This was found unworkable.

Lishman and Duff left their aircraft at Airlie and returned on three different occasions during the winter to fly with the birds. Two were lost over the winter, one to drowning under ice and one to an injury. When the geese had not departed from Airlie by the end of March, Lishman and Duff set out to Virginia by road to fly the remaining sixteen geese back to Ontario. The pilots arrived in Airlie on 5 April and discovered the ultrageese had not been seen since the evening of 1 April. They waited a few days before packing up their aircraft and heading north. They were almost home on 15 April when they received news that the ten geese had found their way back the 400 miles without the aid of their surrogate mechanical parents. There was no sign of the missing six geese. But the team of Lishman, Duff and Sladen were elated with the experiments to date. They expect the same geese to return to Airlie on their own.

Microlights have become sophisticated little aircraft, capable of long flights with geese, and yet still recognisably the children of John Dickenson, Francis Rogallo and Otto Lilienthal. They could lead geese, providing they can find fuel, over much bigger XCs.

But the New Aviators are contemplating something much more radical. Instead of living with the birds, confronting them or having them cadge lifts, we want to emulate them. There is no reason why, without an engine and with our wings and the power of the elements, we cannot migrate almost as well as the birds.

Chapter 4

Paragliding

The central thrust of the New Aviation until the end of the 1980s was the Rogallo wing. Then a new form of soft-wing flying began to appear on hills. It was called variously a parapente, paraglider, parasail, or in slang, Jellyfish, Blancmange, Mushroom, Wobbly. Some of the terms used by hang glider pilots for these new wings were as derogatory as those used about hang gliding by sailplane pilots in the 1970s.

In fact, they proved to be just as strong a New Aviation development as Rogallos, and in some countries have threatened to swamp the Rogallo community.

The FAI recognises the term 'paraglider' for these wings; they are technically Class 3 hang gliders. Their roots are the same as Rogallos, originally steerable descending parachutes, but they took a much different path than classical hang gliding before coming together in the early 1990s.

Back in the sixteenth century, the Italian Fausto Veranzio is said to have foot launched a single-surface square parachute, and survived the experience. In the nineteenth century people like the Australian Lawrence Hargrave and the British founder of the Boy Scouts, Robert Baden-Powell, flew in tethered kites. In the early part of the First World War, kites were used as observation platforms before being superseded by balloons and aeroplanes. Parachutes were developed as rescue devices and issued to British and German balloon observers, but not to RFC pilots because it was thought to encourage cowardice in the face of the enemy.

The world's military powers developed round canopies that were used on Crete by the Germans in 1941, and on D-Day and at Arnhem in 1944 by the Allies. In the late 1950s and early '60s, Pierre Lemoigne developed a gliding canopy, which, though round, had slots to enable it to manoeuvre. He used it for development and research. His work was picked up by Britain's Walter Neumark, who began to write training procedures for ascending parachutes in 1962 (ascending, in this case, was by towing, not by ridge lift or thermals).

Lemoigne went on to design the Paracommander, still used for towing today, and which Neumark encouraged to reach new heights under tow. Newmark's work ran in parallel with Bill Moyes' work on flat kites, but was unaffected by the Rogallo research John Dickenson was doing in Australia, and which led to Moyes 'seeding' hang gliding across the world.

In 1964, Domina Jalbert presented the ram-air inflated parafoils, and with other innovators like David Barrish used towing to develop the idea. The late 1960s saw the introduction of ram-air canopies in parascending, a term coined for the sport by Sir Godfrey Nicholson.

The early 1970s saw the pace of development hot up. Ascending round canopies, specifically designed and proofed (notably, in Britain, the Waterbird, designed by Brian Gaskin, an early hang glider pilot) were towed behind boats, starting the boom in this type of limited leisure flying. (Bill Moyes towed my 9-year-old daughter Jade up under one, over water, in 1988 in Australia, when my family joined me there after my three-axis CFM Shadow microlight flight from London to Sydney to celebrate Australia's bicentenary.)

In the US, Steve Snyder and Dick Morgan began to interest parachutists in the superior performance of the ram-air canopy, which, in flight, adopted an aerofoil shape more like a wing than an umbrella. Until 1973, parascending in Britain came under the control of the British Parachute Association. Then enthusiasts broke away and founded the British Association of Parascending Clubs (BAPC). Ram-air canopies, developed for parachutists who jumped out of aircraft, were now being towed into the air and released, and began to dominate competitions, still of the spot landing variety. Their speed gave more control approaching a target.

In 1977, when Rogallo wings were breaking away from ridge lift and going cross country, a company called Harley Chutes, formed by John Harbutt and Andy Cowley, began to manufacture British towing canopies. The 1970s ended with tandem launching and two-up flying. Walter Neumark was awarded a Tissander Diploma by the Royal Aero Club for his work establishing the sport.

I wrote a gossip column called 'Icarus Allsorts' in the hang gliding magazine *Wings!* in 1980, and wondered in print what had happened to

Brian Gaskin. He had been in the Welsh coastal site in Rhossili the week I made my first soaring hang glider flight in 1974, and been one of three pilots carted off to hospital for landing in rotor. A year later he was at the British Open in Mere, trying to sell his large Wasp CB240 hang glider, and I later heard he had gone off to work with parachutes. At the time I called this a backward step, 'going the other way to natural progress', but I was wrong; Gaskin had just set off to explore another rich aspect of the New Aviation, which exploded into our lives in the middle 1980s.

Consciously or unconsciously, the goal of the New Aviation is a search for the ability to foot launch and to fly, without anyone else being involved. Although records are being made from tow lines, and many sites nowadays require permission to take off or land, our underlying drive is for flight with no interference from anyone. This quest drove research strongly in the early 1980s, as those involved in parascending flight cast their eyes at Rogallos foot launching and said, 'that is where we want to be'. To rely on no one else, no winch operator, no pompous CFI, no aeroplane to get you up; just to turn up on a hill, pull the wing out, inflate it, lean into the wind ... and fly!

The obvious problem was glide angle. Parachutes can descend sweetly, but they were not renowned in the early days for actually going anywhere. It is no fun leaping off a mountain and then scraping your way down it because you do not have the performance to get away from the slope. A really brilliant parachute in those days would have a glide angle much less than a bog-rog, the very first Rogallos. Nevertheless, people began trying to fly them foot launched.

In 1985, Pierre Gevaux took off from the summit of K2 in the Himalayas, 28,280ft high and the second highest mountain in the world, and made a successful flight to a lower level. In the same year, Richard Trinquer soared Mieussy, in France, in a parachute, and achieved a duration record of five hours twenty minutes, which was to stand for two years. In hang gliding magazines, curious photographs started to appear of parachutes being flown from hills, top to bottom, in the same way as the early 1970s saw curious hang glider photographs in mainstream sailplane magazines.

In 1986, Paul Amiel conceived the Asterion, the first wing made from sailcloth, instead of rip-stop nylon, with a glide of 3.5:1. This model was adopted by sail-makers ITV in 1987, with its distinctive 'Amiel Tail', and copied by many manufacturers.

PARAGLIDING

In 1988 the shape of the paraglider began to change. The first elliptical wings appeared and the Genair, built and developed by Laurent de Kalbermatten, achieved a glide angle close to 5:1. But this was not a wing for amateurs, and led the French to develop a series of flight tests to put these parachutes through that rivalled the German Gutesiegal tests for hang gliders.

Cross-Country, the magazine-of-record of the New Aviation, superbly edited by Sherry Thevenot, the American-born wife of Gerard Thevenot, carried a discussion in its very first edition in 1988 on what to call these new 'wings'. There were three suggestions:

> Parapente (French, literally translated as paraslope). Use of a parachute, recognised by FAI and CIVL as a class 3 hang glider, in the same manner as a foot-launched hang glider. Translated into English as paraglider (the English term is recognised by the FAI).
>
> Parascender (British, coined by the president of BPA in 1968). Tow launching of parachutes, generally over land, as a sporting activity, which then cast off and descend and may hit spot landings.
>
> Parasailing (American). No formal training required. Flights rarely above 200ft, usually terminated without the release of the tow line.

Our concern is the paraglider, which the French call 'parapente', which has had such a deep effect on the New Aviation movement. Paragliders are made to three levels of skill; Level 1 for beginners or occasional pilots; Level 2 for intermediate; Level 3 experienced pilots capable of reacting calmly and quickly to deflations.

The development of wings was pressure-driven by their deceptive simplicity to fly. People saw them flown and said, 'I can do that, gissa wing!' Almost anyone could strap in, inflate, and run off a hill. To steer you pulled a right toggle to go right, left to go left, or both as you came in to land softly. But to get performance manufacturers had to trade off stability, and for those who moved over from hang gliding it was startling to look up sometimes and see half the wing flying and the other half flapping about. Funny things could happen above you, especially if you did not know what to do about them. We had to learn there are simple ways to make the wing fly again, so long as one has height and doesn't panic.

If a pilot is seeking records by jumping off places, there are a diminishing number of places he can use before he goes for the biggest of them all, Mount Everest, in the Himalayas. On 26 September 1988, Jean Marc Boivin made that jump, following a similar flight in a hang glider nine years earlier. But his description of the paraglider flight down takes only a few lines; most of his account is about getting up, of interest to mountaineers, not us.

A couple of years later, a photographer called Alain Desez also climbed to the top of Everest, intending to paraglide from the peak. His account of the flight down is much more immediate:

> On the summit of Everest the wind is too strong, making a take-off impossible. I descend towards the South Col in order to capture the sunset on film. There, too, a take-off is not possible, so I wait until the following day to fly and finally take the pictures I have in my heart.
>
> It is morning. The weather is beautiful. It is cold, the wind is blowing 25 mph. Only a few clouds hide the foot of the West Coomb, which leads to base camp. I unfold my wing in the snow. It has been packed for over a month, and I am happy to let it breathe again. Dennis Pivot helps me by holding the wing to prevent it sliding off the slope. He advises me not to hurry. Once in the harness, I take the controls and check that everything is in order. At this altitude, the smallest movements require great effort. It is more difficult to concentrate and therefore to respect the rules of safety.
>
> Dennis presents the leading edge to the wind. The wing is as impatient as I am to fly. A few steps, and I am flying. Indescribable!
>
> My feet are no longer touching the ground. For several weeks they have been sinking into the snow as they fought against its wretched gravity in the unrelenting climb to the summit. I notice Base Camp 3 below at 7,300m (23,950ft), which was so hard to achieve, and just after that I pass over Camp 2, pitched at 6,400m (20,997ft). It feels like I am

reliving a film of the ascent, but in reverse and at high speed. The camps seem so close to each other even though in reality they are separated by several hours of hard climbing.

I pull myself together again in the West Coomb and Camp 1 appears below my feet. The tents seem to be the size of pinheads. The Ice Fall, so dangerous to climb, now seems quite inoffensive. I no longer fear falling ice nor the enormous bottomless crevasses which we crossed at times on bizarrely patched up, wobbly ladders. I am still very high. I could land on the col at Lho La. I even ponder a while on prolonging my flight to Gorak Shep, an hour and half walk from base camp, where the terrain is less difficult. Nevertheless, I begin my approach toward the alluvial cone at Lho La, at 5,300m, and just a few minutes' walk from base camp. It is not easy to know how to make the approach; there are no points of reference, the density of the air is different up here, crevasses and boulders litter the area. Everything is going by very quickly! I feel myself hit the ground. Did I do a parachute landing roll to absorb the impact? Anyway, I find myself standing next to my wing without feeling the slightest shock.

Zebulon comes to meet me. He has also flown from the South Col in a dual flight with his father, Jean-Noel Roche. I pack up my wing and head back to Base Camp. The chef brings me a cup of tea while I tell my story to other members of the team. I will come back one day to fly from the summit.

Jean-Mark Boivin's flight off Everest in September 1988 seemed almost to act as a late starting gun. Why jump off things and fly down? Pilots want to go XC! In April 1988, Frenchman Pierre Bouilloux flew 42km around Lake Annecy. In February the following year, Uli Weismeier from Germany flew 49.3km after a winch launch, releasing at 250m and making 1,700m (5,577ft) height-gain in Forbes, Australia. In March 1989, Austrian Andre Bucher flew 60km. In September, Bucher went to Owens Valley (with a paraglider?!) and flew 78.4km. Then a Frenchman, Xavier Remond, covered 130km in Namibia with a height gain of 3,700m (12,139ft).

One of the prophets of the sport, France's Hubert Aupetit, had set up a Cap 111 to fly 111km in three days as a bird flies. It was seen as a worthy goal to aim for in the future; almost immediately a pilot does it in one flight!

All over the world there was an explosion of interest in paragliding. In Europe, the major countries are Germany, Austria and Switzerland, mountain regions. But it is in Japan that paragliding has really taken hold. There are now estimated to be more than 80,000 New Aviation flyers, hang gliders and paragliders, on that crowded island! Korea is another huge growth area.

This is logical, but alarming. It is logical because the East has a culture of kites and does not have to overcome the crippling 'poisonous butterfly' image that we have lived with in Britain since 1976. It is alarming because at the moment the best paragliding pilots come from Europe and Australia, but the real money is in Japan. The biggest paraglider manufacturer in the world is Edel of Korea. This financial muscle attracts top westerners to fly in Japan, where conditions are poor and often dangerous. It is on the cards that there will be a happy marriage of Western skills and Asian money, but an obvious effect is that indigenous European manufacturers cannot compete economically, and face going to the wall. Edel has set up in France, in partnership with a local manufacturer. I come from a country that once had a thriving motor-cycle manufacturing base, largely destroyed by Japanese manufacturers building better machines. I would not like to see the same happen to hang gliding and parasailing as happened to motorbikes.

Edel have taken a very aggressive financial view on winning market share in paragliding. In the 1995 season they offered the following incentives to those flying their wings in PWCs (Paragliding World Cup competitions) or national championships:

Each PWC – 1st, $3K; 2nd, $2K; 3rd, $1K. First woman: $1K.
Overall World Champion, $30K; 2nd, $10K, 3rd, $5K.
Women's World Champion, $10K; 2nd, $5K; 3rd. $3K.

For National Championships or League Finals (overall ranking)
1st: $5K; 2nd: $3K; 3rd: $2K; 4th: $1K; 5th: $500
First woman: $2K

These were peanuts prizes compared to snooker or darts players, and hardly worth blinking about in golf, but they were serious money in paragliding and an indication of a large potential income.

PARAGLIDING

Meanwhile, in the UK in October 1992, the BAPC merged with the BHGA to become the British Hang Gliding and Paragliding Association (BHPA). The old *Wings!* had become the new *Skywings* sometime earlier. Rapid lessons were learned about how hang gliding progressed, to use as a model for paragliding. The first Paragliding (PG) World Championships were held in Kossen in 1989. There were not enough tasks for the FAI to make it valid, but Carlo Dalla Rosa from Italy won individual gold ahead of Austria's Andre Bucher. Germany won team gold. Britain's team came sixth, although Lucy McSwinney took the individual women's gold. The British team included three League hang glider pilots.

Paragliding is particularly attractive to those in Britain who want to fly. The wing squeezes into a rucksack, so you do not have to carry a socking great glider up the hill. It is not physically difficult to fly a paraglider, so the sport attracts more women (an estimated 20 per cent of paraglider pilots are women). What is striking, too, is that most people going into paragliding are young, in their early 20s, while the best hang glider pilots are at least ten years older. As sailplane gliding became, by and large, a haven for older flyers in the 1970s and the young went into hang gliding, so a similar pattern developed in the 1990s, with the young in paragliding. But there is a two-way traffic, pilots with one discipline learning the other, much more than there was in gliding and hang gliding.

Women also feel in paragliding that they can compete, one to one, with men, and the gulf that opened in hang gliding has not opened in paragliding. So although women are judged against other women, they fly with the men in the same air in the same competition.

Inevitably, there has been a backlash, most famously in the Southern Hang Gliding Club, which has a sensitive and overcrowded site called Devil's Dyke. Some traditional hang glider pilots wanted to ban paragliders from the site (how they were physically going to do this never came up). Paragliders, they said, were too slow, got in the way, and made things dangerous for the faster, more sophisticated hang glider pilots. When a thermal came through, dozens of slow-moving paragliders mushroomed off the hill, and when it died they sank back on top. There was, hang glider pilots felt, no room left.

In contrast to the behaviour of sailplane clubs in the 1970s, there was debate on the issue. The two sides met and talked. We were determined not to ape the behaviour of BGA clubs like the Long Mynd or Sutton Bank or Dunstable, either to say, in effect, 'sod off' to the paragliders, or appeal to lawyers for legal tricks to force fellow flyers to go away. But it was a painful debate in which Johnny Carr, SHGC chairman and the most distinguished pilot in the club, suffered lots of abuse for fighting to integrate with the paragliders, although he never flew one himself. The vote went overwhelmingly against any ban, and instead the two close disciplines worked out rules to live with each other.

It is not possible to describe in detail the records that have been set in paragliding, because what I write this year will be totally out of date in the next. All the creative, liberating energy that has characterised the New Aviation since 23 May 1971 was now being poured into making better soft paraglider wings. Though they are not Rogallo wings, they fulfil the original dream of Francis Rogallo for a completely non-rigid wing, without even the solid leading edges of modern hang gliders. By the middle of 1994, these were the records established in paragliding.

Record Pilot	Km	Yr	Take-off
World (FAI) Alex Loew (S. Africa)	281.5	92	Kuruman, SA
Women (FAI) Judy Leden (GB)	128	92	Vryburg, SA
Tandem (FAI A Haincourt (F)/P Collot (F)	136	93	Tocopilla, Chile
Triangle (FAI) Pierre Bouilloux (F)	153.3	94	Chamonix, France
Out & Return Xavier Remond (F)	134.8	92	Billing, India
Altitude (FAI) Urs Haari (CH) (This is a height gain of 18,537ft!)	5,650m	92	Vryburg, SA
Duration Jean Yves Fauste (F)	11h23	88	Makapu, Hawaii
Tandem alt gain Urs Haari (CH)	4,230m	93	Kuruman, SA
Dec Dist (FAI)Masihiro Minegishi (J)	183.2	92	Kuruman, SA
Europe John Silvester (GB)	202.4	94	S. Estrala, Port

PARAGLIDING

The height gains compared very favourably with those in classical Rogallo hang gliding, while the distances were just over half what have been made by Rogallo wings. Notice that South Africa has become a popular place to set records, all of them off a winch. The last claim for a world distance record was 283.5km, so records are tumbling all the time.

Paragliders are so easy to fly that people become over-confident, and there has been the same pattern of accidents as occurred in early hang gliding. In Japan, for example, schools popped up all over the place, there was little formal pattern to the training, and by 1994 more than forty pilots had been killed.

A study of paraglider accidents covering the period 1987–90 was conducted in Switzerland, and later published for discussion. The statistics confirmed that the major cause of accidents was pilot error. While their frequency is relatively low (per year/per pilot), they were usually of a serious nature. Nearly 85 per cent were very dangerous or fatal. Less experienced pilots were warned by the authors that training, judgement and flying in the company of responsible peers was imperative.

The Swiss study was based on 118 paraglider accident patients cared for at Sion Hospital.

Its first conclusion was that in Switzerland the number of accidents was stabilising, although more and more people were taking up the sport. The frequency of accidents was relatively low, and the number of fatalities was decreasing.

The second conclusion covered pilot experience, and revealed that two thirds of all accidents occurred during the first 100 flights. The authors felt this indicated a lack of training or peer responsibility among the less-experienced pilots. Another incidence of accidents occurred at about 200 flights, due possibly to the increasing risks taken by a confident pilot. With experienced pilots (500 flights) accidents occurred while aspiring to ever higher performance levels (going for it!).

Dealing with licences and permits, the study concluded that a licence is no guarantee against accidents, while admitting that unlicensed pilots had more frequent and more serious injuries.

On causes, the authors found that 30 per cent of accidents occurred at take-off: falls during the running start, stalls right after take-off, turns into the slope, and take-offs in stormy or gusty conditions.

The study found that 25 per cent of accidents occurred during the flight; turbulence close to ridges, collisions with obstacles (in competition, 90 per cent of accidents happened in flight!).

Landings accounted for 40 per cent of accidents: landing during squalls, gusts or crosswind landings outside the landing area, and also collisions and stalls.

The remaining 5 per cent of accidents happened in other circumstances, such as winch-towed flights.

There was a section on injuries, describing the number of sprains, wounds, bruises and fractures. More than 59 per cent of the accidents at Sion Hospital showed injury to a pilot's legs, his landing gear.

The second incidence of injuries was the spinal column, with close to 40 per cent of vertebral fractures, occurring in 44 cases out of 115 (the other 3 of the 118 were killed).

The consequences of a paraglider pilot's injuries were usually major. Sometimes, physical integrity was irreversibly impaired (paralysis or serious after-effects). Accidents were fatal in 3 per cent of all cases.

After evaluating all the accidents the authors issued the following warnings: never fly without a licence, always wear the correct footwear, check the weather report before each flight, never fly with a wing that is inappropriate or of too high a performance for one's capacities.

They underlined one golden rule: know when to say NO, because therein lies true courage. They advised all those who wanted to become pilots to start classes during the winter, when the snow cushions falls, and the cold air (being heavier) creates less dangerous turbulence. Also, snow-covered take-off and landing areas were more regular and sure-footed. One should also remind occasional practitioners who haven't flown for some time to take a few more lessons to get back into the swing of things.

The study ended by saying the worst accidents were usually caused by the most stupid blunders. The authors called for better pilot training and a parallel system of experienced guides, as in mountain climbing.

Spinal fractures	44 (38.2%)
Concussions	15 (13.0%)
Dorsal contusions	13 (11.3%)
Broken ankles	13 (11.3%)
Sprained ankles	12 (10.4%)

Tibia or fibula fractures	10 (8.6%)
Wrist fractures	9 (7.8%)
Pelvic fractures	8 (6.9%)
Femur fractures	7 (6.0%)
Face and head wounds	4 (3.4%)
Rib/breast bone fractures	4 (3.4%)

Since then, a series of imaginative safety devices have come on the market. Most paraglider pilots fly with a back-up parachute. There are spine protectors sold to absorb the energy of a heavy landing, and even instant blow-up airbags around the seated harness so a pilot virtually bounces on his landing.

As in classical hang gliding, the big competitions forced changes in performance, and as paragliders flew better, top hang glider pilots were attracted over. Part of it was commercial; there were many more paraglider pilots, so it made sense to go into the big markets. Also, outside commercial sponsors seemed more attracted to paragliding than hang gliding, and wanted to associate their products with it.

In the 1991 World PG Championships, the three top British pilots were famous names from hang gliding. Robbie Whittall won the gold medal position, with Bruce Goldsmith seventh and John Pendry fourteenth. The Swiss won team gold, just ahead of the British. Goldsmith and Pendry both went on to become World Champions.

But paragliding soon evolved into a world series system of competitions, deciding champions not by one contest but by four, the way hang gliding tried in 1990–91 with the Superleague, but failed. The idea, I suggest, was modelled on the original British League back in 1977. Tasks jumped very quickly to follow those in classical hang gliding, out with spot landings, in with speed flights across country, but so far they have all been foot launched off hills and mountains.

The 1995 men's World Champion was Stephen Steigler of Austria, with Hans Bollinger of Switzerland in silver medal position; Jocky Sanderson of Britain won bronze. The top woman paraglider pilot was a familiar name, Judy Leden of Britain, who, like Robbie Whittall, has now been World Champion in both hang gliding and paragliding. Judy was the only woman in the top thirty in the competition, held in Japan. (Oddly, in this decade when there is so much emphasis on women's achievements, Judy has only ever been awarded one silver medal by the Royal Aero Club, compared to Robbie's unprecedented pair of gold medals, although she was awarded an MBE). Again, the Swiss won team gold, with Britain second, followed by Austria, France, Japan, Germany, Italy, South Africa, Australia and Korea.

You may notice that the US does not appear in these rankings. American hang glider pilots did not embrace paragliding with the same enthusiasm as Europe and Asia. There was no American pilot in the top thirty rankings at the World Championships. One factor has to be the image of the fashionable American hang glider pilot, based in California, and described in 1980 by W.A. Roecker ('Pork') as 'goforit boys, sky-surfin', bet-I-can-do-a-loop, pot-partying, flat-spinning, hard-drinkin', womanising, home-growed, philosophising, self-taught artist musicians'. Did they feel paragliding wasn't manly enough for them?

Cameron Young, Australian hang gliding champion in 1993, was asked if paragliding really fitted in to the Australian macho scene, an atmosphere similar to that in the US …

'In the beginning that was certainly the case; the "Woossie paragliders" to quote every HG pilot at Stanwell Park. But now we're making very good distance and keeping up with them, we're actually getting quite a number of the good pilots coming over to have a go on a "jellyfish".'

A promotional film was made by Airwave on the Isle of Wight, then one of the biggest paraglider manufacturers in Europe, featuring Bruce Goldsmith, who designed their wings. He wears a video camera on his knee, is linked up for sound, and then towed to 2,000ft to see if he can destroy his wings. As he tumbles out of the sky, first one way and then another, demonstrating everything that can go wrong, you see the fluttering paraglider wing above him. He calmly explains what has gone wrong and then demonstrates how to get out of it. He once took his father, John Goldsmith, to the French Alps to video him tumbling out of the sky to discover, from another angle, what was going wrong with the wings. Woossie paragliders indeed!

Foot-launched flight off a hill remained the favourite, indeed, more pure way to get airborne, and that was the launch method for the first 100-mile paraglider flight in England in 1994, thirteen years after Bob Calvert first broke the 100-mile barrier on a hang glider. In England, pilots have no problems finding roads but generally do not fly with chase vehicles, and in the ensuing record flight it was delightful to note that at least one of the pilots suffered from the problems the rest of us

PARAGLIDING

non-supermen go through. Also, English skies seem, on this flight, to have become a vast playground for Mainstream and New Aviators alike. Three pilots were involved, Matthew Cook (MC), Richard Carter (RC) and Mark Grimshaw (MG), and despite the hill launch, much of their flight was over the eastern English flatlands:

MC: Saturday, 13 August 1994, proved to be as cool and clear as forecast. I made rather a late start and arrived at Bradwell shortly after 11am to find only a handful of others on the hill. The wind was blowing steadily as we laid out our canopies and folded maps. We said we would try for Skegness (a seaside resort) and arranged a rendezvous in whichever pub was closest to the clock tower. Richard coaxed us into flying as a group to maximise our chances. Who was I to argue? I decided to launch first – too often I have been on the ground as Richard headed off into the distance.

RC: I let Matthew launch first. I was in no hurry to get off as the sailplanes launching from Camphill were telling me all I needed to know about the day. Although cumuli were forming, the thermals did not appear to be strong enough to get to cloud-base yet. I also noticed the sailplanes were finding the most regular lift near the bowl to the south. Matthew and others were on the north end of the ridge, but as nothing was going on at their end, I turned south and began to climb away, but decided to wait for the others as it was still early. It would be more fun flying as a gaggle and faster too because of our improved search capacity. We all got up on the next thermal, along with John Avill, the only airborne hang glider.

MG: Once we had left the hill I adopted what I called a 'farming' mode of flying ie working the lift to stay as high as possible, using other pilots, clouds and sunny patches to aid my decisions. Over Curbar, making the best of the poor lift under the scraps of cloud, I spotted the beginnings of a new cumulus just upwind. Gliding over to investigate, I soon centre a 5-up core, and then told Richard, who glided over to join me.

MC: We all made cloud-base with this one and drifted off towards Chesterfield. The glide from there was looking like it might be terminal, but it showed that despite the comparative small size (23 square metres) of my standard B3 paraglider, I could still glide competitively with the two UPs. We were saved at the coke works with a slow climb which became stronger and better organised as we gained height. Richard and Mark set off on a glide just as I centred into a good strong core. I opted to stay in it to get back to cloud-base but watched the others all the while for signs of a good climb.

RC: I have flown with Mark a lot, using the radio, and we work well together. Unfortunately, Matthew wasn't in on the radio conversation. Just beyond Chesterfield we were averaging 400 fpm, and watching a sailplane climb better than us east of Junction 29 on the Motorway. Feeling confident, the two of us went off to join him. We flew through several strong cores on the way which greatly improved our glide. On reaching the lift my vario gave an 800 fpm average climb to cloud-base at 6,800ft. The time was 2pm and I was thinking, 'at this rate we are on for 8 grand in height somewhere out in Lincolnshire this afternoon!'

MC: With the others clearly climbing well, I set off to join them, arriving level with them. We climbed together and once more spread out slightly to increase our chances of finding lift. North of Mansfield the smoke from the factory chimneys was showing a good deal of northerly component, so all thoughts of the coast were abandoned and we headed off south towards the slim gap between the ATZs (Air Traffic Zones) of Syerston and Newton RAF bases. This glide saw Mark getting lower than Richard and me. It felt like a long time before we found some weak lift. Richard soon found a core and climbed away. Mark worked for a while before setting off and I was left struggling to climb in the middle.

RC: I now had a choice of two sources for the next climb: cornfields in the sun with good clouds above, or the Calverton coal tip in a semi-shaded area. Hang glider pilot

PARAGLIDING

Mark Clarkson, having caught us up from Bradwell, came screaming into the coal tip on his Solar Wings Rumour like a man possessed and started to go ballistic in an average 1,000 fpm climb. No contest! Matthew and I joined forces again over the tip and hoofed it up. The Rumour was gone by the time we topped out, off down the edge of the now very spread out 6/8 cloud cover. This is where we lost Mark Grimshaw.

MG: My demise was due to several small problems, which combined to make me feel rather uncomfortable in the air. I list them here so as to be a lesson to you all: (1) a hangover, (2) I hadn't sorted out the adjustment of my harness properly and I couldn't sit comfortably (get your equipment properly sorted before a big day arrives!); (3) a call of nature meant I wasn't just crossing my legs to aid the turning of my glider (make sure you go before take-off!); (4) I was cold (I should have worn much warmer clothing). Two hours plus at high altitude and you soon realise it is cold up at cloud-base. All this meant my concentration was elsewhere instead of on the flying.

MC: This is the point when I wished I had brought my radio to ask Richard how the hell we were going to get through the tiny gap in the ATZs. The problem was solved by the good climb from the mine, and we flew over Newton ATZ up in space somewhere, even getting extra height under cloud for part of the way across. We were now passed by Danny Clerkson, also flying fast on his Rumour and on his way to Crowland. We then flew under a dream cloud, 15 km long and with loads of good lift.

RC: Gliding along under the edge of the cloud, I realised I had overdone the previous climb and should have started gliding 1,000ft lower. I spent much of the next 10 to 15 kms flying with big ears (pulling both canopy edges down to lose height; the wing looks like it has ear muffs on – BM), trying to avoid being sucked into cloud. I passed straight over the town of Bingham where I had lived as a kid, and could easily recognise my old schools.

MC: I was able to make up some of the distance I had lost to Richard by using full speed bar to limit my climb. With 2–4 up on my vario, and racing along until my legs were shaking with the effort, I made a major error; one minute I was congratulating myself that we were 80km out, 5,000ft high and doing 8-up in a straight line (and it's only 3pm so I won't bother circling in this lift). Five minutes later I was down to 2,500ft and watching Richard pull out a 5km lead. I flew south into a thermal just as a sailplane below me flew north into it, and we both climbed for about 5 minutes in it before he raced off again. I still needed more height, but the thermal slowly increased in strength and I started to relax again. Near cloud-base I pulled big ears to stay out of cloud, but this proved to be insufficient and I was drawn up until I lost sight of the ground and decided I would have to B-line. I hate B-lining! I don't know why but it scares me to death. At least I was going down. I popped back out of cloud rather cold and nervous, then flew the next 5km in a straight line, shaking like a leaf!

RC: I had lost sight of Matthew now and was a bit concerned that he had flown too far under the large cloud and into the shade. I was just off Saltby Gliding Club, and went over to join a circling K13. No sooner had I centred in the thermal about 100ft lower than him that he left, apparently frightened off by the arrival of a parachute! I spotted Matthew again, gliding towards me, and hung around for a while so we could fly together again. The next 20km didn't look too inspiring as the slim strip of sunshine we were following, caused by two of the large cloud sheets almost meeting, nearly faded out. By accepting slower climb rates, together we were able to tip-toe through.

MC: Having flown within sight of each other so far, from here to Peterborough we really flew quite properly as a pair. We climbed quite slowly but still made it to about 5,500ft before gliding off in parallel and centring on whichever one of us was climbing the best when we reached the next thermal, by which time we had generally dropped to about

3,000ft. Peterborough now looked to be only a glide away and I started harbouring thoughts of landing there. Plenty of potential witnesses was one reason; another was that 5 hours of flying, drinking water on the glides and getting cold at cloud-base was starting to take effect. I was not confident about trying to take a pee in the air with the prospect of some serious hitch-hiking ahead of me! (and smelling strongly of pee was hardly the way a hitch-hiking pilot could endear himself to a pick-up driver – BM). As we drew near to Peterborough we hit the by-now inevitable thermal and it was a question of crossing my legs and going up again.

RC: I had had various conversations on the radio, including one with hang glider pilot Gordon Rigg who was decked short of Chesterfield. For the last hour or two the radio had been silent, but then, waking me up, over the airwaves came Mark Clarkson again. He was down at Whittlesea, south-east of Peterborough, having flown too far east into the sea breeze, though the clouds to the east showed no sign of it being there. The smoke from chimneys in that direction had an awful lot of easterly component, yet to the west smoke from another chimney was blowing from the north-west. We talked about a retrieve as he went back to the phone. I hung back now behind Matthew, gaining as much height as possible. It was 5.30 and it was not going to be long before the lift died.

MC: The dark cloud over the town centre and beyond was working well and I was tempted to fly in a straight line to make as much ground as possible in the time available. I also had to refold my map as we were heading for a group of ATZs and it would have been foolish to fly through airspace after all this distance. I was getting tired by now and spending too long map reading. I opted just to glide as far as I could and not to bother seeking a final thermal.

RC: Mark came back on the radio. The Bricklayers Arms, Whittlesea. Phil Higgins is coming to pick us up.

Yippee! I like days like this when retrieve is organised before you hit the ground!

MC: Richard was a little way behind and above me. With touching naivety I imagined us landing in the same field to claim a shared record. However, as soon as it became apparent that I was on final glide, Richard set off further east chasing the last of the sun.

RC: I was now in 100 per cent competition mode. We had passed the old record mark; now all we had to do was sort out which of us could go the furthest. I could not work out why Matthew was gliding into the gloom when there was sunshine to the east, but I needed to know he was on the ground so I marked him until I was confident he would go down, and then went off to the sunshine. I had lost a lot of height on this glide, and although I found lift it was too weak and incoherent at this low altitude to get up.

MC: I touched down a little before 6pm in the village of Bluntisham. For a whole 10 minutes I was the British paragliding distance record holder, which must be a record for the briefest held record! Still, it 'counts'!

RC: 6.05pm. I turned to land in front of two farmers who had just finished cutting the corn from my landing field a couple of km SE of Sutton, near Ely in Cambridgeshire. I am sure many of you have been there already. You spend the next 15 minutes explaining the sport of paragliding or hang gliding to a complete layman, hoping they will offer you a lift. These two, with only a tractor and a combine harvester between them, were not much use. It was quicker to walk.

MC: Even the retrieve was a dream. A phone call to arrange to meet Ajay at Leicester services, 4 very quick hitches, and I was back home in Manchester by 11pm, tired out, grinning like a lunatic, and completely unable to get to sleep.

RC: I hitched to my prearranged pub, getting a good lift from a bunch of lads who were smoking more than just their tyres on the road.

PARAGLIDING

MC: Fame at last? Not quite! The following week Merthyr Radio blurted: 'Have you heard? Richard Carter has broken the record again. 160 odd kms. Amazing. Oh, and some guy on a B3 went with him too.'

RC: 163.9 kms (101.8 miles), and 6h in the air. Max average climb was 860 fpm, max altitude 6,800ft (2,072m), and average ground speed of 27.3 kph. Cloud-base, surprisingly, went down to the south of the River Trent. I have been saying for a while now that 160km would be a realistic figure for a good day in Britain. Now I am revising that figure! On a day with less cloud cover, and eliminating all the mistakes we made, something like 190/200km should be on the cards.

Very few mainstream pilots talk about the problems of going to the toilet on their journeys, yet Matthew Cook and Mark Grimshaw could have flown further had they not been cracking for a pee. This utterly brilliant joint account of what turned out to be a master class in dealing with a playground in the sky just emphasises how much progress has been made in the New Aviation. First, contrast the easy skills at which this intrepid trio was able to cope with weather changes, and second weigh up the conflict between hang glider pilots and traditional sailplanes that was down to the mean-minded way some pilots in traditional aviation could not see how bigoted they were to us newcomers.

As for the toilet issue, on my microlight flight to Australia I wouldn't take off until I had walked around and convinced my body to have its morning constitutional. Once I even leapt out just before lining up to take-off for that last pee, nervous that six hours later, struggling through monsoon clouds over Indonesia, my attention would be distracted from trying to stay alive by desperately trying not to pee. This must have happened to pioneers Amy Johnson and Ross Smith. Eve Jackson spent eight hours on her microlight flight from Rangoon and had to land at a military airfield short of Bangkok and speak rather curtly to anyone near her while she tore off to the toilet.

Before I set off for Australia, a salesman came to see me, convinced I would be a good marketing tool (as it were) for his product. His company sold an apparatus to the military to enable a jet fighter pilot to stay in the air for eighteen hours, with constant refuelling. It was all straps and tubes and rubber, and so horrific looking that I just thought of the impression that would be created if I was pulled out of the wreckage of my aircraft wearing it, that I resolved never to do so. Instead, I carried a bottle, and hoped to get the urge passing over Genoa in Italy, which had given me such a hard time on a practice flight. There was a hole in the cockpit where the front wheel was located, and I could have tipped the contents of my loo bottle through it as a comment on Genoa's bureaucrats. Alas, it never came.

I still have the apparatus in a dark part of our cellar. As I saw the salesman out of the door I wondered two things: what he told his children he did for a living, and what would happen if his briefcase burst open on a train and the pink plastic thingey that he used to demonstrate how his product worked popped on to the floor. That salesman could do worse, though, than approach some of the New Aviation pilots intent on long flights.

We are in the era, in paragliding and hang gliding, of chasing records that are still possible for ordinary human beings. You have to have the Right Stuff, but you don't need the money of Howard Hughes or Richard Branson or the resources behind Chuck Yeager. Yet records are just records. They are here today, and gone when someone else takes them away. The soul of the New Aviation is not about getting records, though they are necessary to learn about long flight. Paragliding, like hang gliding, is taking a path 180 degrees in the opposite direction to Mainstream Aviation.

One of the most poetic accounts of the sort of flying we are heading towards comes from Hubert Aupetit, a French pilot of great experience on hang gliders and paragliders. Aupetit is one of the founders of the 444, the seminal competition of the New Aviation, because it is against the elements and oneself. The rules existed thousands of years ago, are still adhered to by birds, and are the ultimate goal of the New Aviators. In his account, 'Scotland is for Me', Aupetit touches on the real differences between the New Aviation and the Mainstream, which could never do this type of flying:

> I definitely know what I like to do with a paraglider. Although I am tired of those 50 aggressive pilots jammed into the same gaggle, giving each other hell, and chilled by a few hair-raising close calls in a tormented aerology, I am

still keen on performance. But only with the appropriate apparatus; a hang glider, sailplane or a rigid wing, all of which are designed for difficult conditions. But there are certain journeys which none can adapt to. When you are in a mood to idle about for a few days between earth and heaven, only our slow, light flexible wings will do.

To me, a paraglider is an absolute aircraft, an alternative to explore the aerial world, a spur for my two legs to pace the landscape and keep me mobile. It hoists me away from the stiffness of social life which has so cut me off from nature.

Still half asleep on the bus that goes from Glasgow to Inverness, I catch a glimpse of Scotland awakening. A sober landscape of bare mountains, covered only with grass and heather, with sheep as inhabitants, large valleys shaped by the ever-abundant streams fed by frequent rain, and majestic dark lakes, those famous lochs of unfathomable depths that shelter strange creatures. Each of these noble reliefs makes you want to stop and climb with a twig between your teeth and a bouquet fixed to your backpack (the Scots believe they bring luck).

Facing me, a girl with liquid violet eyes, opens them at the Aviemore shop, the only vulgar spot in the otherwise untouched beauty. With Claire, time will pass slowly. She is returning to her hometown, only a few miles from the battlefield at Culloden, where the last Stuart pretender to the throne was implacably defeated in 1746, and along with him all the chiefs of the highland clans. Sad memory for Claire.

I leave her at Inverness station and prepare to head for the end of the world. Aultbea is the last western village before the Isles of Hebrides. I drop in to see a friend and ready myself to confront the 'Meal Ham Meallan', a beautiful 450 foot slope stretching towards the sea, 6 miles away. A car offers me a lift, but I refuse. My desire is to renew myself with Scotland again, and with no intermediaries apart from my hands and my feet. I have been visiting Scotland faithfully for 15 years, and now I am discovering its stunning autumn colours. Burned are the grass tufts, withered the ferns, decadent the bells of heather. Before me is a palette of reds, rust-colour, ochres, greens and violets, as you find them faithfully reproduced on the tweed clothes or lambswool sweaters the locals fancy.

I reach the summit easily, but in a state of visual drunkenness. My feet are resigned to getting wet. After ten useless minutes trying to avoid pools of water, I gather my journey is destined to be placed under the sign of the soaked sock. I unfold my paraglider, an Arbison, painlessly in a light northeast wind, and off I go.

The high mountains around are caught in what I would call a 'traine molle', a sort of wet and sticky perturbation (I gather that France and England are covered with storms). Dozens of islands surge from the silver sea and create a black and white landscape. The lift is not vigorous, though enough to have fun. The site reminds me of those in Yorkshire, the Dales, where you always wonder how you ever managed to take off and actually hold lift on the slope, so even and wet is the landscape.

Half an hour later I land on a tiny patch of smoked green grass near the water. I pack up and resume my walk around the little peninsula of Rubha Mor. The coast under the wind is fresh and sandy. A triumphant sunshine watches me undress. I dive into the water, do two or three invigorating strokes, and put my itchy clothes back on again. Evening at the pub. To me, this is a perfect day.

Two days later I leave for Aultbea. Cars rumble down the roads, eating up mileage, with synthetic music vomiting from the windows. It is a world I do not wish to know. I pick up my things and head south. A few cars give me a lift. In between rides I eat berries along the roadside, and read Joseph Kessel's *Mermoz*. [What a great aeronautical spirit – non-stop across the south Atlantic in 1933 – BM.] After an endless walk in a deep, open, ever-the-same-and-ever-changing valley, as mesmerising as Celtic music, I arrive in Torridon, a true paradise for the parapentist interested in something other than the beep-beep of his vario. A vast fjord surrounded by summits over 3,000ft high, and frequented, I am told, by the finest of British mountaineers.

Bewildered as I am before the magnificent landscape, I do not hear a car that stops nearby. An old, white-haired, kilt-dressed man steps out. He speaks with the slow, harsh local diction, and apologises for not speaking French. 'Any well-educated person spoke French fluently before English rulership.' He takes me to a cousin of his wife's who will be my host tonight. We speak Gaelic over a cup of tea. I am grateful to my guide, Iain Macgregor, who hates Margaret Thatcher, John Major, and today's outrageous power of money. He is a separatist. I suddenly feel the weight of my wing, built by Pyrenean idealists. 'Friendship is the only thing that counts in this world,' he concludes.

Five o'clock, two hours of daylight left. I immediately attack Ben Damph ('Ben' means summit in Gaelic), 1,200ft agl, the edge over an abyss, and no wind. It is somewhat difficult to inflate my wing amid the pools of water. It droops to the left. Eventually, I run crab-like and manage to take off. Oh, the infinite pleasures of being able to pull oneself away from the turf and heather; what joy to simply be in the air and brush against the pine tree-tops, to say nothing of landing quietly on a grey sand beach between cows and sheep, which ignites the hilarity of the seagulls.

Night is drawing in, and the local pub welcomes me into its warm atmosphere. Before a turf-flavoured malt whisky, distilled on the Isle of Islay, a couple from Aberdeen recount their day tour. Ben Alligin, 'the summit of the jewel', 3,000ft above sea level. 'What is it like up there?' (typical parapentist's question). 'A huge curved plateau followed by a line of hairy crests.' The plateau is enough for me. I drift to sleep after a last whisky, recalling that solemn sentence of my friend Iain Macgregor, 'We are light and we will return to light …'

It is a 3-mile walk along the river's edge before I arrive at the Alligin track. Then I find myself in a multi-coloured wood full of silver birches, camellias, rhododendrons, swarming with luxuriant birds, red berries and Caledonian pine trees. There used to be more of the trees, especially in the highland forests, but many of them were destroyed or burned for the needs of the Realm (the 'Clearances'). The same fate was dealt to the small, strong, Gaelic bulls. In fact, whole families of the valleys were simply chased away to make woollen clothes for the armies. Very few of those impressive trees are left now, and they proudly resist wind and tide.

I leave the woods and follow a small brook – a 'burn', the Scots call it – where a herd of deer disappear behind a dorsal. Climbing is easy and ends up along a streamlet in a stony gully. Once up there you are on a different planet. Clouds above and below, stretches of water gleaming between patches of mist, endless dark crest lines all around. You cannot tell whether they belong to the continent, or to the dozens of islands around. The boundaries between sky, earth and water seem to have vanished. This is Scotland, a land always haunted by the sea. I leave my backpack behind and start walking along the crest of a summit with peaks up to 3,000ft. But the turn of the weather makes me go back. There is scarcely any wind, humidity and sun, nothing that will help me predict whether visibility will improve. The wide plateau is now completely covered in mists. Fortunately, I left some marks (thanks to a certain Pyrenean experience). I climb down 300ft to the base of the clouds. A nice moss-covered slope, some wind behind me, the ground appears to be just slightly curved and comfortable to go for a launch.

The unmistakable feeling of being alone on a mountain with the rest of the world totally unaware of your presence makes me prepare each step even more carefully. I take off at first attempt, find myself pushed around a bit in a scarf of clouds that has come hovering up the slope. For a few seconds I do not belong to the sphere of man anymore, not quite sure whether I am flying, swimming or walking in the air in that landscape where all the elements seem as one. But the laws of aerodynamics slowly bring me back to my natural state. The isles disappear one after the other behind

PARAGLIDING

the loch. The mountains resume their dimensions. I land near the river, following the direction graciously given to me by a heron.

It took me a long time to know exactly what I was looking for in a flight. I believe it is having a hold over the places you go to instead of passing through them like a tourist. I will never buy my freedom wrapped up in a catalogue, or over a counter. I will always invent it and try to be worthy of it.

After that flight, I still had resources. I went back up Ben Damph as fast as a cable car for the ultimate bliss of heather and mud, for splashing about in pools, or mingling with nature with my feet, my hands and my wing. The next day at dawn I took a coach back to France. Scotland was probably the only place in Europe, while I was there, where it had been good to fly.

Chapter 5

Women and the New Aviation

There is no physical reason why a woman should not be as good a hang glider pilot as a man. She does not need the shoulder development of an orang-utan or Sylvester Stallone to be a flyer. She has to be fit, but providing a woman pilot, generally smaller and lighter than a man, chooses a wing suitable for her weight, she should be able to compete just as well, get higher even, certainly fly XC as far. For a long time it did not happen like that.

In the early days of the 1970s, women pilots were outnumbered at least 20-1 by men. At the first US Nationals sponsored by Annie Green Springs in 1973, of the thirty-six competitors, one – Donita Holland (Mrs Dave Kilbourne) – was a woman. I only remember one woman pilot in the freezing cold of the Long Mynd (Paul Bridge's wife, Lesley), and none hacking up Rhossili in the 1970s, though if we looked down at a training slope, some of those undergoing instruction were women.

Part of the problem was the way we taught students to fly. I was taught by being hurled off a 500ft hill, the Devil's Dyke near Brighton, but I think I was one of the last to 'learn' like that. Schools evolved a teaching method called 'low and slow', which involved flying down gentle slopes ... and walking back up the hill carrying the hang glider. This is back-breaking work and puts a lot of students off, male and female. In Bruce Goldsmith's original Imperial College class of eighty who signed on to learn hang gliding in 1981, just two went through to soaring. Only the toughest stick at it because, in those days, there was no other way to learn. A girl could hardly fly to the bottom and flutter her eyelashes at a husky male pilot to persuade him to carry the wing back up again ... at least not more than once.

Glancing through early *Wings!* magazines, men flew and women watched, made sandwiches or tried to make friends with other pilot's girls on the hill. We used to line up at the hotel phone in Rhossili, southwest Wales, after a day's flying and call home, ostensibly to say how good the flying had been but really to tell our wives we were still alive and uninjured. Many of them did not fancy huddling for hours in a gale-force wind, waiting for the right conditions to fly, when they themselves did not fly.

An article entitled 'Sexist Battles' by Rex Grogan from the Mercian Club, then the wittiest club in Britain, appeared in *Wings!* in 1980. It summed up the prevailing male culture of hang gliding, and was reprinted in hang gliding magazines around the world. Grogan's piece was very amusing, but it also had a lot of truth in it. The article purported to be a guide to a red-blooded male hang glider pilot, keen on flying but in a constant battle with his reluctant partner:

> It must be reckoned at the outset that women and hang gliding are mutually incompatible. Women, with their in-built instinct for combating anything which conflicts with their interests, have evolved a series of anti-hang gliding tactics which are divulged for the first time here. Obviously this can only be a brief résumé; it would require a second Pavlov to cover the entire subject. Remember though, an enemy even half-recognised is close to being defeated.
>
> It is important to be aware that the Hang Glider Pilot's Wife (HGPW) – 'wife' here being used to include girlfriends – will move to meet the threat of the conflicting hobby or interest in a series of conditioned reflexes. Counter-attack comes in two stages:
>
> 1. Prior Perception and Awareness (PP&A). Only by the earliest possible recognition of the impending danger can the correct counter be applied.
> 2. The selection of the proper Controlled Nullifying Response (CNR) is of paramount importance and early application will achieve the desirable end of peaceful coexistence.
>
> Although basic opposition tactics are itemised below, you should be aware that sub-categories or multi-category attacks are possible.

WILD ADVENTURES OF THE NEW AVIATORS

PP&A (1) Hang Gliding is Dangerous. 1. HGPW is seen reading *Wings!* and tut-tutting over accident reports. Insurance policies are scrutinised, especially the small print. Grumbles about inflation eroding value of insurance cover.

CNR (1a) Offer to take up more stimulating hobby eg Lion taming, high-wire juggling, pot-holing. (1b) Get *Wings!* sent to another address. (1c) Point out that only idiots get hurt and I'm no idiot – proof – look who I married. NB Very effective but not to be used more than twice a year.

PP&A (2) Hang Gliding is silly and childish. 2. Derogatory terms used for important items of equipment – kite becomes 'your 747' or 'flying tent frame'. Harness = 'truss'. Boots = 'undercarriage'. Preparations for that day's flying greeted with 'going to play aeroplanes again?'

CNR (2) Enter into spirit of joke – laugh uproariously, hold sides, fall about. Repeat phrases to friends, point out good fortune to have wife with sense of humour. Make disparaging remarks about other po-faced HGPWs.

PP&A (3) Hang gliding is just an excuse for swilling beer at the pub. 3a. Keen interest shown in site and local geography of day's flying ie 'Anywhere near the Red Lion, dear?' 3b. Rigid check on money being taken. 3c. Casual requests for packets of crisps on return. 3d. References to psychological effects of drink e.g. 'You needn't come back smelling like a brewery/behaving all soppy/covered in lipstick again/with your flies open like last time.'

CNR 3a. Make serious remarks about other pilots drinking and dangers resulting therefrom. 3b. Agree about after-effects but indicate 'All that is in the past – turned over a new leaf, etc, etc'. 3c Promise crisps but never, never bring them '… all the shops (heavy emphasis on "shops") were closed'.

PP&A (4). You are always going off and leaving me. Sulks, tears, remarks about togetherness of other couples, threats of going home to mother, headaches at inconvenient times.

CNR 4. Enthuse about sturdiness of other HGPWs and ability to carry heavy loads of equipment up hills. Use word

WOMEN AND THE NEW AVIATION

'we' frequently but with oblique references to privations – 'you don't mind a few spiders, do you?' – 'what a shame we shall have to walk through all that mud' – 'the ladies' loo is only 35 minutes walk away' – 'I think we shall have some snow today'.

PP&A (5) How can you spend all that money when ... (a) We need a ... (b) I haven't had a stitch of clothing since ...

5a (i) Items of domestic equipment develop alarmingly high accident rate. (ii) Advertisements for expensive and desired items left in conspicuous places e.g. pasted to loo door. (iii) Coveted articles pointed out when seen in other people's houses, on TV, in shops, accompanied by heavy sighs.

5b (i) Appearance of items of outmoded clothing e.g. navy blue knickers, gym slips. (ii) References to nice appearance greeted with scornful laughter. (iii) Claims that we 'will need to visit Scout Jumble Sale soon.'

CNR 5a & b. (i) Counter-attack with catalogues implying heavy expenditure under consideration – Porsche Turbo, power boat, etc. (ii) Bribe friends to say 'New kite a good investment, bound to be worth double soon.' (iii) Look thoughtful when discussing rich friends, e.g. 'He's got his own plane and a Range Rover.'

PP&A (6) Hang gliding is just an excuse for mixing with vulgar loud-mouthed males. 6. Observations about lowering of moral tone, increasing vulgarity, coarseness of behaviour. Gushing praise about dutiful hen-pecked, polite, smarmy acquaintances (non H-Ging, of course).

CNR – 6a. Invite home smooth, polished, courteous but very boring H-G friend (every club has one). Appear to hang on his every word. Afterwards, comment effusively about his wit, erudition, stimulating conversation. 6b. Refrain from even traces of a grin when hearing slightly blue jokes, express ignorance of meaning, ask HGPW to explain. 6c. Rush to offer help in house, peeling potatoes, washing up and similar menial jobs. With skill, offer can be timed to be just too late. If offer is accepted, make a hopeless mess of job until ordered out.

PP&A (7) Hang Gliding is bad for you. 7. Recurring use of phrase, 'But you're always too tired after you've been H-Ging', 'You poor thing, you look tired out', 'You'll catch your death of cold H-Ging this weather', 'Of course H-Ging is really a sport for a much younger man'. There are many variations of these, but anything cooed in a solicitous tone is a firm indication of a type-7 attack.

CNR 7. Fiddle bathroom scales to show reduced weight. Buy sunray lamp and use when HGPW has gone to mother's. Leap out of bed on H-Ging days 'accidentally' dragging bedclothes off HGPW in process. Throw away sexy aftershave and buy 5-gallon drum of strong-smelling embrocation. Borrow Bull-Worker, exercise bicycle and barbells. Retire to bedroom, lock door and make strenuous exercise noises while reading *Mayfair* or *Playboy* (warning: complaints of tiredness likely to be replaced by complaints of excessive enthusiasm – you can never win).

When British teams went to the American Cups in Chattanooga we came upon women hang glider pilots. We heard that Cyndee Moore, whose trademarks were high-heeled boots, tight jeans and curly hair, was a good pilot, and also Liz Sharp, who later organised international hang gliding teams. The magazine *Glider Rider* carried a feature on women pilots in 1979, triggered off by the first American Cup, where one of the wind dummies (sent up to check conditions, a skilled job) was a woman, Patty Bentz. Other names mentioned included Jan Case, owner of a hang glider shop called Chandelle in San Francisco and a hang gliding teacher, and Sondi Baker. The article, written by a woman, was uneasy about its terms, whether to emphasise a pilot's flying ability, or her beauty. ('When I first saw Cyndee launch at Torrey, she was wearing leather knee boots and a beautiful suede jacket. She looked very feminine … if it's OK to say that these days …')

Pilots like Robert Bailey who went to the Grouse Mountain Competition in Vancouver in Canada used to hope loudly that their one-on-one competitions, by which they advanced a round, would give them a girl opponent. The girls were tough and serious, but not in the same flying class as the men were.

WOMEN AND THE NEW AVIATION

It was not a question of attitude. They could be just as aggressive as the men. Rich Pfieffer tells this story about coming up against his own wife, Paige, in the Southern California Regionals in 1980 ...

> It's a duration contest between me and Paige Pfieffer (my wife at the time). She's above me and I'm just about resolved to the idea of losing when she starts yelling: 'Hey, what are you doing down there? I thought you were supposed to be such a hotshot competition pilot!' and so on. This is more than enough to jar me out of giving up. I head out on a glide, hoping she'll follow me since I know I can out-glide her. There's a chance I won't be able to make it back to the landing area, but I decide I'd rather land out than go into the landing area with her announcing to everyone that I'm losing. She doesn't follow me and I manage to catch a lucky thermal and make it back to the landing area as well, to beat her by a few seconds.

Paige Pfieffer was probably the best of the early woman pilots, whatever her relationship was with Rich. George Worthington wrote admiringly about her in his regular column in *Wings!*

> Paige Pfieffer, a 22-year-old blonde San Diego pilot, has been flying hang gliders for about two years. She is married to Rich, a very ambitious pilot who in the summer of 1978 flew flights of 70, 75 and 81 miles at Cerro Gordo (Scareyergordoff). It looks to me like Rich is the driving force which got Paige into the sport. When they are both at the Pacific coastal site at Torrey Pines, Rich is always in the air and often the only pilot who will fly the cliff on certain days when the lift is very, very marginal. Paige, on the other hand, flies far less, and less aggressively. There may be a reason for this. Paige has twice made hard landings which have thrown her arm painfully out of socket. Each time, it has taken her a month to recover. Yet on July 30, 1978, Paige took off from Cerro Gordo at about 2.40pm in a UP Firefly. By the time she had landed, about 2½ hours later, she had covered a straight-line distance of 51 miles. I took

off only 30 minutes earlier than Paige and the very best I could do that day was 25 miles.

Coming from George Worthington, who would move over for nobody, this is high praise (though some modern women would think it patronising). Paige herself said that being in the air for three hours absolutely exhausted her, and she could not cope with the six-hour flights Rich often made. Paige was one of four women who, in the late 1970s, formed themselves into the United States Women's Hang Gliding Team, but they were famous more because of their glamorous looks than for their flying skills. None of them featured highly in skill or competitions ratings against men.

For a long time the world tandem distance record was jointly held by a woman, Eri Fujita. Larry Tudor, one of the Owens Valley princes, spent a lot of time teaching the Japanese to fly, so that they are now the biggest national hang gliding and paragliding community in the world (nearly 100,000, and 20 per cent are women!). In 1985, Larry took Eri Fujita, a young Japanese girl, on a flight of 165km along Owens Valley, and from the interview she did three years later with Gerard Thevenot, one wonders if she enjoyed the experience:

GT: Eri Fujita, you have held several tandem world records with Larry Tudor that are well known in the hang gliding world, yet few people know anything about you. Can you tell us about your hang gliding career?

EF: I am 28 years old and have been flying 5 years. I weigh 41 kgs (90 lbs) and I am married to Naomi Fukita, one of the pioneers of hang gliding in Japan who has remained at the top of the competition list all these years. My longest solo flight XC is 45 kms.

GT: Owens is reputed for extreme aeronautical conditions, and frequent landings in the desert where there is neither civilisation nor water ... were you afraid during the flight?

EF: (hesitation) No, but I was very cold and my eyes hurt because I did not have sunglasses, and after one hour in flight I felt sick in my stomach. Because of that, Larry decided to land but after a long slide down to a landing area he asked me how I felt. 'Better', I said, so he started up again and my sickness came back. In order to distract me, Larry sang songs and described the landscape and to keep me from getting really sick he thermalled as little as possible, We were both afraid in fact because at landing we realised that our hang straps had broken.

GT: Did you help Larry during the flight?

EF: No, very little. I held the control bar while he put on his gloves and took photos, that's all.

GT: Have you made any solo flights in the Owens?

EJ: Yes, twice after the record, but I only did about 30 kms. In any case, the flights with Larry taught me a lot about technique in XC flying.

GT: How would you describe Larry?

EF: He is very nice and kind, but in the air he has an incredible sense of combativity.

GT: Have you ever flown with your husband?

EF: Yes. Even though tandem flying is barely done in Japan, I have made two tandem flights with my husband ... but I prefer flying with Larry.

GT: Would you do it all over again if someone broke your record?

EF: (long hesitation) Yes!

I first became aware of women as serious pilots while trying to pick up British team members on XC during the Blériot Competition in France in August 1980. We drove all over the place to find our pilots, and often picked up a free-flying French girl called Odile, small, delicate, extremely feminine, and obviously a superb pilot in that she was matching scores with some of my pilots. None of the French pilots commented on her, but that could have been a wind-up.

By the end of that year there was a small group of women pilots in England with ambitions to get off XC and start taking on the men. Jenny Ganderton, an English girl who later became the top woman pilot in Australia, sat me down on a hill that winter and said she and some other women wanted a Women's League, like the men's but scoring against women. We worked out that women's competition, because of the way the League worked, could be grafted on to the men's competition, particularly in XC tasks, but they could be split into heats against themselves at no real extra cost.

(I didn't, as becomes evident, make it all happen but Derek Evans took my promise on and made it work. Years later I donated the Harriet Quimby Trophy to encourage women's flying; Miss Quimby, a beautiful American known in San Francisco clubs in 1906 as the 'Dresden Doll', was the first US woman to earn a pilot's licence. She was also the first woman to fly the English Channel, in 1912. Unfortunately, she did it the day the *Titanic* sank, so few people have heard of her. She was killed later that year, falling 500ft into Boston Harbour. The US postal authorities used Miss Quimby's face on 25 cent air mail stamps.)

One of the girls who became a British Women's Champion through the League system was Kay Simpson, the girl, if you remember, proposed to by Dave Simpson while tandem flying 500ft over Dunstable. Her account of how she became a pilot highlights the difficult obstacles she had to overcome. She called it 'Persistence Pays!'

> 'I can't do it.'
> 'Yes you can.'
> 'The wings won't stay level.' (he doesn't understand!)
> 'Stop behaving like a woman!'
> 'But I AM a woman. I'm COLD.'
> I was standing at the top of a 50-foot man-made ridge in Milton Keynes, wrestling with a borrowed Vega II weighing about 45 lbs. It was the first time I had clipped into a hang glider and I wasn't having fun. My instructor (and friend) made encouraging noises, and amid the words of comfort I heard, 'Don't be disappointed if you don't get to the soaring stage.'
> CLANG! It was like being hit by John Duncker's lunch box. Then what was the point to all this?

WOMEN AND THE NEW AVIATION

That was ten years ago, a decade, and around 500 flying hours spent looking at the world from a completely different perspective. Ten years of obsession, ten years of new goals appearing at every goal achieved. It has influenced my choice of friends, where I live, how I earn a living and where I go on holiday. It has probably had an influence on my personality and has certainly influenced my values and what I consider to be important in my life.

I find it hard to call it a hobby. It has become a way of life.

Go to any hang gliding site in the world and you will meet people who understand you. There is no need to explain why you are there or what you are waiting for. You can have an elating or demoralising experience, and other pilots will know how you are feeling. It's not even necessary to speak the same language. At the first Women's International Competition in Sederon, France, I seemed to land almost every day in the same field as a Swiss lady pilot. We hardly spoke each other's language, but we made a lot of hand signals and did a lot of smiling and nodding. We haven't met since but we pass greetings to and fro through other pilots.

I suspect that the girls in the sport share a form of camaraderie not experienced by our male counterparts. That isn't intended to sound smug, but tends to be the natural order of things where there are minority groups in any walks of life. In Britain, lady hang glider pilots are probably the most rare of minorities.

The British Ladies Championships held over the last 4 years has always had an atmosphere unlike other competitions I have attended. Of course, individuals still want to win, but experience is more freely shared and advice and support more forthcoming than is the norm.

The standard of flying and interest in the competition has increased noticeably each year, and it is clear we must encourage and build on these skills if we are to have a hope of retaining the gold medal in next year's Women's International competition. Yes, we have Judy Leden who is improving her performance every season, but we will not get a team gold on the strength of one person's performance, or even 3, or 5 girls. We need to build a pool of girls from whom selection can be made.

If you ask, why are there so few lady hang glider pilots, the answer is that they have to want to learn to fly more than anything else. They need to be sufficiently inspired by the thought of flight to initiate contacting schools. Perhaps there are fewer women than men in this group?

I first saw hang gliders on Dunstable Downs in 1977 from a bus window. I was inspired, but my medical student boyfriend gave me a knowledgeable summary of the various parts of one's anatomy that could be modified by hang gliding. The sun shone out of his stethoscope, so I put it in a pigeon hole in the back of my mind for investigation in the future.

Once you have enrolled on a course, and you experience your first few days of wind, rain, mud, cow pats, stinging nettles, bruises, exhaustion, and lack of 'appropriate amenities', the inspiration for flight may become a little jaded. This appears to be directly proportional to how long it takes you to get your EPC (Elementary Pilot Certificate). It doesn't apply just to the girls but, if you have a strength disadvantage you may take a little longer to get through the course than your macho friends. It's easy to become disillusioned when everyone is patting themselves on the back after their first soaring flight and you haven't had one yet.

I was very fortunate. I had a friend who was an instructor and he helped me through the doubts I sowed in my own mind. He believed I could do it when I was not so sure. Richard Bach says in *Illusions* ... 'Argue for your limitations and sure enough, they're yours'. Easy to do when you are cold, tired and hungry.

At last you get your EPC, you leave the school and join a club. This is the stage where any new pilot feels vulnerable. You hear people confidently talking about aspect ratios, lapse rates and ground effect, expressing disappointment at having 'blown it' after just 20 miles. You see them rig their shiny gliders and put their kit on whilst joking and holding a conversation at the same time. They clip in, hang check, and take off.

They don't make 3 trips to the bushes beforehand, it doesn't take them 5 attempts to get the wings level, they even sing while they are flying! What is hard to appreciate is that they were standing in your shoes a few years ago, and that one day you will be standing in theirs.

I managed to amass 1 hour 36 minutes in my first year of flying, but must have spent at least 300 hours standing on hillsides. I used to ask everybody what conditions were like.

'Oh, it's great, some nice thermals coming through.'

My heart would sink. Thermals were anathema to me; thermals meant bumps, and bumps meant out of control with my heart in my mouth.

The protracted apprenticeship continued throughout the following year until at last I managed to soar Dunstable Downs. That was entered triumphantly in my log book on 25.3.81 followed by a line which reads, 'broke my collarbone the next day'. Textbook accident statistic, 5 hours air-time, downwind stall ... ouch. I didn't enjoy my flying for some time but I kept telling myself it was only a passing phase. Eventually I started to relax again but it meant progress was fairly slow.

Now I get 100 hours airtime a year, and less experienced lady pilots tell me how despondent they are at only getting 5 or 10 hours in their first year. They ask how on earth I ever manage to carry my glider, and sometimes think I don't understand their suffering at carrying a glider up from the bottom for the umpteenth time, when they see me land back on top.

If only they could have seen me with my biceps trembling, trying to get my 45lb Vega on to my roof-rack, and breaking my aerial for the 6th time ... or at the bottom of Dunstable Downs, trying to carry my rigged glider up the path in a crosswind, and weeping with frustration ... or landing in a bog miles from any other living soul, and deciding that I'd much rather die in that hole than try walking out ...

My instructor was right. He did understand. I can do it, and so can you, but only if you keep the inspiration alive.

The 1980s was the decade in which women really burst upon the hang gliding scene. Five years after Paige Pfieffer's flight of 51 miles, the women's world record climbed to 146 miles. By 1988, a woman had made a height gain of 13,000ft, while another had been towed to 15,000ft over Mont Blanc, and one of three hang gliders towed in to the air by a trike had a woman pilot. Women had flown hang gliders off Kilimanjaro. Eve Jackson had flown a microlight to Australia, the first person – not just the first woman – to do so, and won a gold medal from the Royal Aero Club and that year's prestigious Segrave Trophy. Three women pilots had entered the German League, on merit. Four women graduated to the British League on the same terms, having been nursed through specialist women's competitions.

At the last count, two of the top one hundred pilots in the world, Kari Castle of the US and Judy Leden of Britain, are women. It is the toughest hang gliding list you can get on. Some of the flights they describe would have been difficult for angels, never mind men. Take this second story by the modest and witty Irish girl Liavan Mallin, who went to Owens Valley for the experience, and despite her protests ('I think Australia is the place for little Irish me, but haven't you read tons of articles describing Owens as the ultimate hang gliding site?') had an extraordinary experience trying for a new world record:

> We (Mark, Ken, Rab and I) finally made it to Owens late June of 1989, and for the first two weeks the flying conditions were disastrous. When we did get some flying in, the weather was so stable that even a 50-mile flight was a real struggle. Depression set in, and the only thing to counter it was our briefing in the jacuzzi every evening. At least we had time to get to know the Owens Valley characters. One, Geoff Loyns, an English ex-patriot, acted as our mentor. Conditions can only get better, he said. It was the worst year he had ever known at Owens. It was Geoff who suggested Basalt, in Nevada, as my first objective.

All the women were setting goals at take-off so there was a real spirit of competition.

On July 10th, Mark, Rab and I took off at 1015. Ken was retrieve driver. Mark went down in Onion Valley, 35 miles from take-off. Rab and I were able to continue along the Sierra, but took 3 hours 30 minutes to reach the crossing point, a difficult 20-mile gap from the Sierras to the White Mountains. After struggling for a time on Black Mountain, I managed to stay with a broken thermal which eventually took me to 15,000ft. At Gunther I got low again but was so convinced that I would get up that I ventured into a canyon from which I could not have made the road.

The two gliders that had been flying beside me left and glided out to the road. After circling very close to the hill in a smooth 1/2-up for half an hour, continuously losing 50ft and gaining again, thermals started to develop and brought me up to 14,000ft. I was safe and had no problem staying high for the rest of the flight. In fact I arrived over goal with 12,000ft, seven and a half hours after take-off.

Three days later the flight along the Sierras was a dream. I never went below 10,000ft but the last mountain, Tinamaha, from which one crosses the valley, was really rough. I had just completed the first 60 miles when I heard Rab's voice over the radio: 'Geoff Loyns tucked and had to deploy his chute over Gunther!'

I arrived over Mina, my goal, with 14,000ft and had to decide whether to land or continue to try and beat Judy Leden's open distance record of 146 miles. There were no other gliders in sight. The temptation was aggravating. Rab was waiting to witness my landing at Mina. Should I save the record for the next time? I would not know until the next day how far the other women had flown. I stopped with 132 miles. As it turns out, it was a new Women's Distance-to-Goal World Record!

The following week brought days that overdeveloped by 2pm. Once I scared the life out of myself by flying around a large-looking rain shower with thunder and lightning, trying desperately to get down into the valley that was lifting. Just after landing I nearly lost my glider as a violent gust front ploughed through taking bushes and sand ...

Finally on our last day, blue skies returned. It was my day to drive. I was trying to be cheerful, helping the others unload but I was bitterly disappointed. Then Rab offered to drive and minutes later I was setting my goal at Gabbs, 170 miles away.

After take-off at 10.45 I was racing down the Sierras making the best time ever. At the end of the Sierras, thermals were getting rough, as always. At Mt Tinamaha, I was higher than usual, at about 12,500ft and expecting to go up to 16,000ft before crossing the valley. Entering a 6-up broken thermal, I turned and fell out of it, then pulled on speed to enter again and find the core. Suddenly I was no longer in control. The glider had been tossed upside down in the thermal and I was looking at the sky and plummeting towards a rock face in a flat spin with one wing at right angles to the other.

With one hand on the bottom bar I tried to pull the parachute out with the other, but it wouldn't come. I started to panic, tearing desperately at the parachute handle with both hands. This time I pulled the container out, threw it into the open space below and waited. There was a little tug but I was still sinking fast. All I could feel now was the G-force, all I could see was the glider that was now in front of me. I clung to an upright. The bottom bar was way above my head. I couldn't see the chute so assumed that it had got caught in the rigging and had not deployed.

My plan was to roll myself into a ball to try and avoid spinal injury. I opened my harness and attempted to bring my legs up to my chin but this only increased the spinning. I was being thrown around so much that I couldn't keep my legs up anyway. There was nothing to do but cling to the upright above me and wait. I hit the rock face but as the glider went in first it took all of the impact. I came in on top of it, just hitting my knees as I landed. Then the keel fell on my back and trapped me under the glider. Miraculously I was OK and could move all my limbs.

WOMEN AND THE NEW AVIATION

But I had another problem! I was perched about 500ft from the top of the mountain on a 65 degree scree slope, and every time I moved the glider would slip a few inches down the slope. From my position I could not reach up and unclip the carabiner, which meant that if any wind or thermal caught my glider, we would end up tumbling down 4,000ft of sheer rock together.

Usually I carry a seat-belt cutter in my harness, but I had replaced it with my camera. The only solution was to try and wedge out of my harness. Slowly rotating my legs towards my hands, I undid my laces and kicked off my boots. With my shoulder unclipped, I freed myself from the oxygen tube. With radio cable draped around my neck I managed to crawl away from the glider.

The parachute had deployed. It was lying above the glider.

I found a ledge, lay down in shock and wondered whether a world record could ever be worth such a narrow escape!

It was then that I witnessed the most terrifying sight. Another glider was approaching the mountain! The pilot, having spotted me, shouted, 'Are you OK?'

I screamed at him to fly away because of the turbulence.

Seconds later I watched in terror as his wing broke. He threw his parachute but it got caught in the tumbling glider and flapped uselessly. When I lost sight of him I felt incredibly helpless. I tried crawling down the face but I couldn't put any pressure on my legs.

Then the faint sound of a helicopter brought tremendous relief. I waved madly and they signalled me to stay put. I crawled back to my perch and tried to sleep but couldn't, worrying both about the poor pilot who tried to assist me, and sliding off the mountain.

If I had only known earlier that he had, in fact, landed safely in some bushes and managed to walk out, it would have made my long wait almost enjoyable.

Eight hours (!) later a rescue crew strapped me into a climbing harness and carried me to the summit, where we spent a cold night in the open air.

> The long safe way down was on the lee side of the mountain. Another rescue group climbed up the next morning to help carry my stretcher. Twenty-six volunteers were involved in my rescue operation! There was no possible way I could show them my appreciation. The next day I hobbled out of hospital on crutches with nothing more than bruised knees and faced the press about my 'World Record'. But believe me, that was incidental.

After such an extraordinary flight, which she describes in such an understated way, you could have forgiven Liavan Mallin for retiring to a nunnery. Instead, she tacked on the bottom of her article the following credit: 'I wish to thank John Pendry, Chris Johnson and Sarah Fenwick at Airwave who pulled out all the stops to get my glider repaired in time for the National Airshow in August which allowed me more media coverage for my sponsors. Xtra-Vision got their money's worth.'

One of the great difficulties about writing of women and the New Aviation is that, for the last twelve years one Englishwoman has been a virtual giant in the sport, against whom everyone else takes measurements. Her name, as is obvious from every account of women's flying, is Judy Leden. If I start writing about her when she started, in 1979, then it appears to diminish the achievements of other women, and I think it better to let other women speak first before turning to Judy.

She wasn't the first woman in the world to fly more than 100 miles; that was Jenny Ganderton, the girl who asked me when I had the power for a women's League competition, who did 115 miles in Owens on 12 July 1983.

But Jenny's record lasted less than twenty-four hours, and the record Judy set the following day, 146 miles, was unbeaten for six years, in a period when records elsewhere were tumbling every year. The girl who took it from Judy was an American, Katherine Yardley, and her account is a chronicle of amazing physical courage as well as a tribute to Judy:

> July 13, 1989, and I felt my face starting to get red. The sun was so low that it had been shining in under my sail for the last hour. This flying off into the sunset stuff can give you a mean sunburn. Now I flew north along some dirt road, running out my altitude from 12,000 ASL, on a glide. A lazy

360 brought Boundary Peak into view about 70 miles back to the south. Low on water, no food, radio dead, nine and a half hours in the air, looking at a good long walk out, and I was grinning from ear to ear. I did not know exactly where I was, but I knew I had just flown my hang glider about 170 miles, further than any woman in the world.

With barely any pull-in left, I flared off the back wires for a sweet landing in the still desert air, my smoke bomb (indicating wind direction) billowing up gently from the dry lake bed. Sitting down seemed like a good idea for starters, because my knees kept buckling when I tried to walk. But I quickly dragged myself upright on the down-tubes to get at my barograph and confirm a useable trace. The old Repogle ticked away, showing a forest of lines all over the chart between 5,000ft and 17,000ft; the seal was intact so I could make a claim on the world record. And I was a happy pilot. I turned toward the setting sun and hoisted my near-empty water bottle in a toast to the day and to Judy Leden.

July, 1983. Judy was the first pilot I ever saw fly with a barograph. I was reacquainting myself with the Owens Valley after knee reconstruction, and Judy, a member of the British National Team, had come with a group to fly there for a month. World records were her goal. She hooked up with our crew for a few days, and I got to see how the big girls do it [Judy is tiny – BM]. In the same time it took me to set up my ProStar glider, she would already have camera clamped on, sponsor's logo in place, pre-launch photos taken, and be standing on launch ready to go. Every day she had a goal. On typical days, it was ambitious. On disappointing days, it was amazingly optimistic. She had to fly every day because she only had a month in the Owens and she was determined to be in the air on that magic day when, as the late Jeff Scott used to say, it would be 'semi-soarable'. That is, the boomer OV day when even a semi is soarable and the flight of your dreams is laid out like a highway before you.

My new and improved knee worked great, but all too soon our crew had to blast off for Los Angeles. Judy stayed on and she was at the new OV (Owens Valley) launch,

Horseshoe Meadows, on that semi-soarable day, July 13, 1983, when the magic happened and she flew past Luning, Nevada, to set a new women's world record for distance in a straight line of 145.35 miles. I was not surprised at her accomplishment. I had already witnessed her determination and energy for the project when we flew together. What really dazzled me were her photographs. From a point well along on her flight to the north, she turned at 17,000ft ASL and snapped a view back towards her launch point in the south. Yet the Horseshoe Meadows launch was not visible in the picture. It was so far away that it had been obscured by the curve of the earth.

What a photo! What a concept! From the day I saw those pictures of hers I wanted to share Judy's experience. I wanted to see my launch point recede and disappear under the horizon as I soared off into the wild blue yonder – with heroic soundtrack.

So I figured I had better learn to land. I had been flying five years by 1983 and, using many different and imaginative techniques on landing, I had managed to tear a cruciate knee ligament and break three arms. If you are counting, that's the same arm in two different places – California and Utah. Taking tumbling at the gym, and swapping my ProStar for a Comet helped my landings, then a windfall of cash courtesy of the California Lottery stepped me up to a shiny new Wills Wing HP and I learned to fly ridge-rocket style, low and fast.

My XC distances grew while I zoomed around learning to appreciate new scenery and deal with the challenges of landing out. Blasting through the big 100-mile barrier in 1986, I stalled at that distance for three years, unable to find the combination of altitude, energy and ideas that would extend my personal best out towards Judy's world record distance. But when I figured out that a handful of my previous personal bests could have been world records on their own, if documented, I knew that world records could be a reality for me too. The more I thought about it, the more the idea appealed to me. I had toyed with contest flying and found I didn't much enjoy sharing the skies with a snarling, contentious bunch of competition jocks. But world record attempts were different. Competition with oneself to maximize the conditions and best an established standard fitted my temperament much more comfortably, while obviously demanding a big stretch of my piloting abilities.

More techno-toys were required to be a real contender in the world records race. I had been screaming into and cursing at my CB for years. Now I became a licensed ham radio technician (KC6EAE) and my CB was replaced with a two-metre FM radio with crystal-clear reception and myriad tiny buttons. My 10-year old Litek vario worked like a charm, but it needed to be accompanied by a barograph that would record all my derring-do. My old cocoon harness caused something like paralysis of the lower extremities in flights over four hours, and replacing it with the super-comfy CG1000 pod made possible record-length flights, after which you could actually use your legs to land instead of your face. Trading up to my Moyes GTR from an HP proved a beneficial change by allowing me to relax a bit in the air, so I could comfortably fly for longer periods. Colour me fully-prepared and ready to go.

July, 1989. We had been planning this OV trip since last summer. My Sylmar flying buddy, Julia Chandler, and I felt that two weeks of hard flying in prime time ought to get each of us a world record or two for the den wall. Julia went up early and reported disappointing conditions, early blow-outs and no one having great flights. When I arrived, we hooked up with a new pal, Mike Barber from Florida, a self-proclaimed adrenaline-junkie and hard-core XC enthusiast. Our team was completed by Paul Yardley, hang driver extraordinaire. Conditions were still not fabulous. Suffice it to say that we had our afternoons free since we had already crept in and crapped-out by noon each day after sled-rides.

But on July 13, exactly six years to the day from Judy Leden's record flight, the cumies began to pop on the Sierras and, having both declared Mina, Nevada for

Distance-to-a-Goal, Julia and I were looking good at 15,000ft ASL after travelling 50 miles down range to the traditional point for crossing from the Sierras to the Whites. Julia hung on tenaciously but couldn't get back up after her crossing, and finally landed at the Bishop training hill, having flown about 65 miles. Mike and I hung really tough and were finally sucked up off the valley floor, losing radio contact as we ran under the cloud streets at over 14,000ft ASL into Nevada, with hardly a circle for 50 miles.

When you get to Nevada things look a lot more confusing. Instead of a nice straight mountain range to fly along, you get to pick your way through small mountains here and there, mixed with dry lakes and dirt roads. An important flying aid here would be a map, which I had failed to bring. I would love to say I was at my mental and physical best at this point, but prolonged flying at over 14,000ft without oxygen had its classic effect, and I got just a little bit stupid, resulting in a total overfly of my goal at Mina. Thank heavens for that, because a lovely Irish lass (Liavan Mallin) had already declared and achieved Mina for her Distance-to-a-Goal world record that same day. If I had landed at Mina it would not have been a record for me. By being lost, I inadvertently took the same course the big boys use to fly 200 miles +, and when I lost radio contact with the chase car, I decided to forget all about Mina and head north, following what looked like a major road. The cloud streets were still lifting at 7pm when I thermalled up for the last time and began my glide into mystery valley.

A full moon was already high in the sky when I stowed my gear and began the long march to whatever passed for civilisation in that part of the desert. There were no lights except the moon in any direction from my position. Figuring it would take about four hours to get back to the last major highway intersection, I made a deal with myself: march until the moon goes down, then sit and have a good cry if you still feel like it.

About an hour and a half into the walk I had a feeling I would be taking advantage of that deal, but I was saved

Above: Robert Bailey.

Below: Swans.

Above: 3 Johnny Carr UK Bronze Joseph Guggenmoss Germany Gold Gerard Thevenot France Silver.

Below: British League Competition Take Off 1981.

Above: Landing in high winds.

Right: American Cup Take Off.

Above: The Dalgety Flyer above the Persian Gulf – England to Australia 1987-88.

Below: The Dalgety Flyer Christmas 1987 in the Persian Gulf.

Right: Judy Leden.

Below: Liavin Mallin.

Left: Liavin Mallin.

Below: Ridge Racing.

Author meeting Prince Charles 1979.

Above: Tangled Landing.

Left: Author, Glider Rider Cover 1978.

Author, Disaster Flight Article.

Above: Author receives The National Trophy from Queen Elizabeth II 1985.

Below: Heathrow.

Above left: Judy Leden.

Above right: Keith Cockroft.

Below: American Cup Take Off.

Author and Keith Reynolds flying around the world 1998.

Spiraling to target.

Didier Favre.

Didier Favre Take Off.

Above: Didier Favre.

Below: Author World record solo flight around the world 1998.

from despair by a load of bailing wire. Chet Smith was bringing home a truckload of wire when I flagged him down on the dirt road at 10pm. It turned out that Chet is a pilot himself, flying his private plane from a landing strip there in the desert, and Chet got a big kick out of the whole situation. He gave me a lift to his alfafa farm and explained that, because they were so remote, they had no telephone. Lela, his wife, jumped up to make me a country breakfast that could not be beat, then drove me another 20 miles into Gabbs, Nevada, so I could contact my chase crew. If there is a heaven, Chet and Lela already have reserved seats.

At midnight I made my call to the prearranged telephone contact, rented a motel room, took the most wonderful hot shower of my life, hung streamers on my motel door and sank into a fitful slumber, only to be awakened at 4.30am by Paul, Julia and Mike. Mike had gotten lost too, confusing east with north, and had flown doggedly along in a headwind to Tonopah, Nevada, for 120+ miles. Of course, the guy with the most miles that day was Paul, having driven all over tarnation trying to find his misplaced pilots.

The official claim forms are completed and submitted. I am currently the unofficial world record holder for distance in a straight line (feminine category), at 164 miles. Was I lucky? You bet. Was I skilful? I like to think so. Was I prepared? A definite maybe. Significant additions to equipment and mental preparations are already planned for next time, including an on-board map and oxygen to prevent brain lock.

What's next? The 200-mile flight, of course. And I'll have a lot of company. There is a gaggle of talented female pilots out there with the capability and desire to blow right through 200 miles. We are all just waiting for that next semi-soarable day.

Katherine Yardley's record lasted two years, for among the gaggle of talented female pilots 'out there' was a tall, tough blonde called Kari Castle. Judy Leden was first woman to make the Top 100 World list; Kari was second, and when she went to Austria in 1991 in the US national women's team, her friends in America were tipping her for the World Championship title. Things did not quite work out like that, but what did happen neatly illustrates that Kay Simpson was right in saying the atmosphere in women's hang gliding is much different to men's. Kari, the US champion, found herself ranked in the 40s after four days:

> I wasn't flying the way I knew I could. Up until that time, I did the physical practice of flying and never thought much about the mental side of it. But at that Meet I had to go inside my head and say, 'Kari, what are you doing to yourself?' When I left home for the competition I had a lot of pressure from everyone I knew. 'You're the best,' they said, 'You're going to win.' Deep down, I believed I could win.
>
> At the Meet, Judy Leden (who did win to become 1991 World Champion) noticed that I was having a hard time and came over and talked to me. 'I know where you're at right now,' she said. 'I've had hard competitions where everything's going bad. But you've got to forget about winning. Concentrate on what you're doing at the moment instead of thinking about your standing. You can't win at this point anyway.'
>
> It hurt to realise it, but she was right. I had gone there to win and I was in panic-mode. I had to do well.
>
> 'Forget about it,' Judy said. 'Just go out there and fly. Concentrate on each and every thermal you're in. Don't think ahead. If you make a bad move, don't worry about it. Just go on and think about the here and now.'
>
> That is what was happening on the earlier days. My head was just spinning. I was thinking way too far ahead. When I was at the first turn-point, I was already thinking what I was going to do at goal. I followed Judy's advice for the last two days of the competition and flew much better.

There cannot be many pilots who, halfway through a World Championships, would go up to one of their principal rivals and help her to fly better. Mind you, Judy ensured that, when she talked to Kari Castle, Kari had no chance of coming back to overtake her. But Kari

Castle seemed to have put her mind back together quickly, and worked out the best therapy for losing; which was breaking the 200-mile wall. Her account of the flight is very American:

> Chicago International Airport. I can only think of escaping, but the airline has cancelled my flight home. After a month in Austria for the Women's Worlds, this airport feels like a jailhouse. I've gotta make just one phone call to my boyfriend Mark 'Gibbo' Gibson in the Sierra Nevadas. He is the best person to psyche me up for flying. 'The weather in the Owens is shaping up for a big day,' he says, 'a two hundred miler at least off the Horseshoe launch above Lone Pine.' Dreaming of cloud streets and bottled oxygen, I hardly take notice of my dismal surroundings.
>
> Home again, it's July 20th, up at 5.30am, rush out to the Horseshoe launch area, spread the wings, throw out the lawn chairs, absorb the morning sun and sip coffee.
>
> Good Morning!
>
> Mark and I are both off the hill before 9.30am and up to cloud-base in no time. The day looks like it will over-develop so we race along the Sierra Nevadas all the way to Bishop, then, for fun, head back as far as we can, almost reaching Big Pine.
>
> After flying the big Wills Wings HPAT 158 in Austria, it sure felt good to be on my little ol' 145 HPAT again.
>
> The following day I made my first record attempt, declaring an Open Distance. The cu's are poppin' and the day looks great, especially when the paragliders take off at 9am and fly straight out going up the whole time. We're off the hill at 9.30, steaming down the awesome Sierra Nevadas. Mark is the perfect thermal snooper, radioing in, 'Gotta hurry, baby, before it over-develops.'
>
> At Birch Mountain near Big Pine, we're low, but in no time a ripper comes through. It's time to make my first crossing. Mark goes first, after leaving light stuff a quarter of the way out. I stay back and eventually take a light one up to 13,000ft. By then Mark is in serious sink. He reaches Black Mountain and scratches his buns off. Meanwhile

I pass over his head, get to the next spine and away I go. Next thing I catch on the radio, 'Hit the deck!' Oh Nooo!

I knew he'd be spewing.

'Kari, are you gonna keep going?'

'I can't see any reason why not. I just crossed the valley for the first time and I'm up at 14,000ft. Yeah, I'll keep going.'

Silence, then, 'If I drive for you, that means you drive for me tomorrow, right?'

'Ha, ha ... no, comrade.'

'It's gonna be a long walk home!'

I turned off the radio. This was a trick I learned from Gibbo, when someone is ground-sucking you. Before long he mellowed out, got in the car and encouraged me on my way.

I landed 142 miles away behind Pilot's Peak, with a serious desire to pee!

Next day, July 22nd, I announce an Open Distance and Declared Goal at Austin Airport. This time I am prepared (adult diapers – nappies!). Nothing will stop me! The sky looks awesome, cu's poppin' at 7am!

We mess around on launch until 10.30, filling oxygen bottles, arranging a driver and drawing a map for him to Austin Airport. When we finally do get off the hill, boy, it's good! This time I lead Mark all the way down the range to Onion Valley. We get high just before crossing. I chose the back route. But all of a sudden the Onion Valley Grunnion decides otherwise. Luckily I like to hang on to the bar real tight, because I go on a real Yah Hoo ride past 90 degrees. I am not going to argue. I just take the front route. Mark gets ahead of me on this one. Without talking to each other we simultaneously decide it is time to cross.

At Mazerka Peak, we climb to cloud-base, blaze Westguard Pass and glide until we hit Gunther launch. We fly over the windsock that is blowing across and down. Ya Hoo! Mark dives to the white spot on the hill across Coldwater Canyon and I am getting drilled, so we head out towards Raydeans. The clouds look so good I'm certain something is going up somewhere. Sure enough, out over the mine just before Piute, I hook a light one and drift with it straight down the Valley. Cool, I think, I'll just cruise down the valley to the end, but it peters out around 11,000ft, so I dive back into the hills and proceed to get my butt kicked. I leave, thinking the next one has to be better or I'll just go land.

Before long, I am low in front of Boundary Peak, thinking if I don't get up now, forget it. The clouds look so awesome in Nevada, I have to do it.

Boom! Hang on, this is it, 1,500ft/min up! I hang on to cloud-base, then I am outa there! There's 100 miles down, 100+ to go.

And now the best part of the flight; nothing but beautiful cloud streets and small hills everywhere. Mark is at cloud-base 10 miles ahead. We keep radio communication to a minimum because our radios weren't charged the night before. Just before Mina I turn my radio on to discover that Mark is heading towards Luning for a cloud street heading north. Sounds good to me.

And boy, is it! The rest of the flight is a piece of cake. Flatland flying is so enjoyable after wrestling with big mountains. Drift with the thermals and stay high. I can handle that!

Soon I see the 200-mile mark while my ground crew, right below, cheers me on. Around 6.30pm I drift past the 200 mark with a grin on my face that doesn't quit! It really does not seem real. At 6.50 I touch down in the middle of Nevada, 210 miles from launch and I am greeted with three more grins and cold beer. Here's one Happy Girl!

Katherine Yardley marked the end of the period in women's hang gliding, and Kari Castle's brilliant flight confirmed it, when Judy Leden was British, European and World Women's Hang Gliding Champion. At the same time Judy held, with three separate flights, the British, European and World open distance records, which is the record everyone wants. The only way Judy could go in women's hang gliding was down, unless she took on the men.

She had difficulty at first, because she was in the same air as men who taught her, and it took a few sturdy sessions with a sports psychologist to break through the mind barrier that men seemed to pose. But Judy was the pathfinder, the Amy Johnson of her age. She began beating men regularly in the air, starting in the Himalayas in 1983 when she took out the legendary Larry Tudor one-on-one, and placed third in a competition where Steve Moyes was behind her. Judy also began doing things in hang gliding that no one had done before.

She was the first person to jump off the highest active volcano in the world, Cotopaxi in Ecuador, 20,500ft. A television film was made of that event, and the way it was played it looked easy. But Cotopaxi had been a target for the Dangerous Sports Club, which made two very determined attempts that failed, and DSC founder David Kirke stayed in Ecuador for a month afterwards and made repeated attempts. Judy made it look too easy to make a decent film of it.

She was the first woman to hang glide across the English Channel. One man had beaten her to that goal, Ken Messenger, back in 1977, while I had failed on the same day. Again, Judy made it look easy.

Judy flew a trike from London to Amman in Jordan, a journey dedicated to the memory of a young Jordanian girl called Yasmin who died of cancer, to raise more than £100,000 for cancer victims (Judy named her first child, a girl, Yasmin).

Judy Leden has, on merit, captained British hang gliding teams in which she has been a flying member, and all the other competitors have been men. As British teams were, consistently, among the best in the world through the 1980s, it follows that there are few national teams from other countries that would not include Judy as a member (even Bill Moyes would possibly think about it).

She went to South America in 1988, the only woman to fly in the Venezuelan Open against dozens of pilots who wore their machismo on their sleeves, and she won. It was not a fluke because she went back another year, and won again. She did the same in Bulgaria a year later. She has twice won the Curryong Cup in Australia. Judy has an MBE, which entitled her, among other perks, to get married in St Paul's Cathedral in London, where Princess Diana was married.

When I first met Judy in 1980, she was a student nurse, small, bouncing with excitement, and cuddly. Fifteen years later she was still small and cuddly, but she turned that bouncing excitement into a rare determination to get to the top in hang gliding, and she had. In the New Aviation we have an elective royalty. You don't have to win the most competitions, or always fly further than anyone else. Bill Moyes hasn't, for example, and nor has Bettina Gray. But in our world, they are royalty. Among all the princes and princesses, dukes and duchesses and so on, Judy is queen. Perhaps she does not have the open distance record in hang gliding right at this moment, but that may be because she will have a baby instead. Afterwards, if she wants the open distance record back, the woman who has it will have to fight a lot harder than George Worthington did to stop Judy getting it.

Judy is a beautiful writer as well as being a natural television performer, and there are numerous accounts to choose from to show her skill and courage. Among the best is the account (extracted from her book *Flying with Condors*) of the Jordanian balloon drop, a world record – men and women – that still stands. For fifteen minutes after she fell away from her balloon, her eyes were frozen shut and she had to fly, literally, blind.

In reading Judy's brilliant and insightful account of her world record balloon drop, you should know that at that time I still held the world two-man hang glider drop record with a man called Graham Driscoll, at 13,770ft. The contrast between Judy's careful measures that she took to stay alive and the amateur way Graham and I went about our mission in November 1976, that is eighteen years earlier, shows how far the New Aviation has progressed. The individual steps Judy took in her flight over Wadi Rum in Jordan in October 1993, and the casual way Graham and I approached our own drop, makes me realise how lucky I was in actually being alive afterwards. So although this is a chapter about women flyers, please forgive the short account of my own balloon drop to provide a contrast with hers. Mine, with Graham, was a record that lasted twenty-one years until it was taken from us, inevitably, by Judy herself in a televised 'wheeze'.

I had come second in the National Championships in 1976, undeservedly, and was in the process of founding the National Hang Gliding League to raise competition standards, but I had never done a balloon drop. Then Graham, a fellow member of Alvin Russell's Long Mynd Hang Gliding Club, phoned me one night at my home in St Albans.

'How would you like to drop off a balloon for a new world record for a two-man flight?' he asked. 'We want to go above 10,000ft.'

At the time the world record was 3,500ft, so it would be a big jump. Of course, I said yes.

Graham had linked up with the pilot of a balloon sponsored by J&B Whisky, Phillip Hutchins, who was game to go above 10,000ft, an unusual height for a balloon, in which the risk was he could be too high when fuel reserves got low and run out of fuel on the way down, with fatal consequences. Graham found us two parachutes, but we had no instruction, beyond being told that if we had to cut free, we should ensure we were not close to each other when we pulled the release. Two other balloons were found with experienced pilots, Don Cameron and Dick Wirth, one to carry a TV cameraman from ATV, which then covered the Midland region of England, the other to carry a stills cameraman, a friend called John Cookson.

My wife Fiona and I drove up to Shropshire with our 16-month-old son James on a Friday night, and at the crack of dawn on a Saturday we turned up in a frosty field to watch the three balloons being inflated. I helped Graham rig the big American-built hang glider, a Will's Wing Swallowtail. Our simple harness had been cobbled together, with a 'spreader bar' hooked on to a carabiner, from which two plastic seats were hung on pieces of rope, across which we each had a lap-strap. The drop mechanism – I was in the left seat, Graham in the right – was on the right side of the control bar, and looked like an old-fashioned lavatory chain; pull strongly and we were released. We had thought of training, but didn't do any, and we had no oxygen, though we were intending to climb thousands of feet higher than the 10,000ft level above which oxygen is usually required. This may have accounted, according to the BHGA's Dr Dunstan Hadley later, for the bizarre 'fighter pilot' tactics we adopted after 'the Drop', in which we whistled past the descending balloons rather more closely than we should have.

At the time I was a twenty-a-day cigarette smoker. Graham also smoked, but I had thought to bring a packet of cigarettes and he had not. So when the ground fell away from between our feet and we went through the dangerous moments getting to 300ft – any separation lower than that could easily have been fatal – Graham began cadging cigarettes as we climbed into the cold November air. Having parachutes was a comfort, but I have a vivid memory of how much I felt we needed them after tossing away a cigarette as we passed through 8,000ft and watching it fall into the void. Every now and again, Phillip shouted down at us, asking if we were OK, to which we shouted back that we were. We could see the other two balloons climbing with us, and we were supposed to wave enthusiastically when we were ready to drop off.

Eventually, after another cigarette, we reached 15,000ft where the air was quite thin. Phillip stopped using his burner, and he told us we were going to descend. Graham had told me he wanted to wait until the sails of the hang glider filled in the descent, and then he would pull the chain. Our back-up was Phillip up above with a carving knife, to just cut the rope. I had been told that, in this process, we would feel every single molecule of the knife blade before the rope parted.

I have seen John Cookson's photograph of the drop, taken just after we waved at the cameramen and Graham pulled the chain. We were both seated, but Graham had his feet well back, as if flying prone, while I was just hanging on. The whole wing rotated, but not beyond vertical, and with both our arms stretched out we went into a zooming dive and turn. It was terrifically exciting and we had a long sled ride down, zooming into 360-degree turns and laughing with sheer *joie de vivre*. Coming into land in a field with a slope on it, I was conscious of how fast we were going, but we co-ordinated to push our arms out and landed safely. I spent the next ninety minutes walking constantly the length and breadth of the field, almost unable to cope with the huge build-up of adrenaline that had coursed through me. We had a pie and beer for lunch, while we checked the barograph and had our height confirmed.

We were amateurs. It was done for thrills and bragging rights. By contrast, Judy Leden was the consummate professional. No one has since bettered her, and it is not difficult to see why:

> I shiver in the early morning chill as I dress with immense care, aware that everything has to be right today. Chris Dawes and Simon rig the hang glider as Anders connects my pre-breathing system to my mask. I put on my helmet and push the mask's bayonet-attachments into their slots, securing it to my mouth and nose. For the next five hours I will be inhaling 100 per cent pure oxygen. I can hear nothing except the rhythm of my own breathing through the snug earphones that cut off all sound. Completely isolated, there is nothing to do but reflect on how I came to be sitting

in the middle of a desert in Jordan at 3am, about to be lifted to the edge of the stratosphere.

I had wanted to break the balloon-drop record since 1988. The catalyst that finally made the project possible was meeting Per Lindstrand, the pioneer balloonist, who was keen to be involved. Royal Jordanian Airlines agreed to sponsor the project, and National Geographic was to film the expedition.

Per had the inspired idea of doing the flight from Wadi Rum in Jordan. It is the most spectacular place I have ever been to, and a perfect backdrop for the film. I asked His Majesty King Hussein for permission and he not only agreed, but, in his generous style, immediately offered assistance in the form of transport, accommodation and helicopters!

Our three biggest dangers would be hypoxia, the 'bends', and very low temperatures. We needed sophisticated oxygen equipment as pressure breathing would be essential above 38,000ft. At this height the 100 per cent oxygen coming through the mask would no longer have sufficient pressure to be absorbed through the lung walls, thus leading to hypoxia. This would be overcome by increasing the pressure of the oxygen fed into the mask. The effect of this feels strange. Instead of inhalation being an active manoeuvre requiring muscular expansion, it becomes passive, and exhalation requires effort. In practice, it feels like someone is holding a hand over your mouth as you try to breath out, and you have to force the air out against the pressure of this hand.

The Swedish Air Force was unreservedly helpful in providing us with training and equipment. We flew to Linkoping Air Base to be fitted with fighter pilot's partial pressure suits, helmets and masks. The helmets and masks were made to measure, moulded to our heads and faces for a snug fit. The function of the partial pressure suit is to brace the torso against the pressure of the incoming oxygen and to help restore atmospheric pressure to the body. Visually they are not attractive garments, unless you are into bondage. Made from green canvas, they are small bladders covering the chest, abdomen and legs, tightened to ensure a close fit to the body by means of a complex network of straps and laces around the back. During the fitting of the gear, it became glaringly apparent that I was not in for a comfortable flight.

My hang glider had to be built quickly. With the oxygen system weighing over 20kg and a lot of extra clothing, I had to move up a size to a medium glider. I chose an Airwave Klassic 14m. I sent them Royal Jordanian's artwork and gave them free rein to do any modifications they thought necessary to strengthen the glider. The problems were twofold. I was almost certain, having watched Rory Carter drop from 34,780ft in 1984, that if a glider were taken any higher the rotation on release would be so severe that it would probably tumble. The other problem was, assuming the tumble could be prevented, the chance of a structural failure would be increased due to the tremendous speed that it would reach in the dive and the subsequent pull-out. Airwave made the necessary calculations, shortened the luff-lines a little and sleeved the keel.

Having done many balloon drops in the past, I was convinced the way to reduce the glider's rotation was to hang it in a nose-down attitude. What I needed was a way of altering the angle just prior to release, as taking off with the glider's nose already down was both impractical and very uncomfortable. Having established a basic model using a potato peeler and string, I recruited the help of Simon Lawrence to make the life-size version. His engineering skills and initiative produced a multitude of pulleys, extra rigging wires, straps and varying diameter rope. I consulted all the aerodynamic 'gurus' I could think of and the consensus was that a 45 degree nose-down attitude would probably keep the glider from tumbling.

The proof of the pudding was to be at the Bristol Balloon Fiesta. Dangling underneath the British Gas balloon, I was surrounded by dozens of other balloons of every shape and colour and was being orbited by a helicopter containing the film crew. Per gave his unique count-down – 1, 5, 3, 2, 1 – and it worked! The glider dipped its nose and started to fly without the usual violent rotation. I landed to find that some concerned Bristolian had called the police to report that 'a microlight is stuck under a balloon and a helicopter was trying to rescue it!'

I was confident in the system and ready to go for the record. The expedition was set for mid-October and the organisation began in earnest. I had to have all my old fillings replaced in my teeth, as any air trapped in them could have caused, at best, extreme pain, and at worst, the tooth could have shattered. After seven appointments, each an hour long, I emerged with new fillings, a sore jaw, and a firm resolve never to eat chocolate again!

Airwave built me the strangest-shaped Race harness ever made. Once dressed in my pressure suit (3 thick thermal layers, down jacket and trousers) I was almost spherical! They added a front-mounted parachute, side bags for the camera recorders and batteries, and numerous attachment points for the oxygen cylinder, emergency bottle and regulator.

I had to plan what to wear as the temperature above 33,000ft would be -55C and would drop with the wind-chill factor once I had released from the balloon. Never had I fretted so long about an outfit! I consulted everyone I could think of – cavers, mountaineers, trans-Everest balloonists and extreme parachutists. Two days before we left I had spent a small fortune but was finally happy. Working from the inside, I had thermal underwear, the pressure suit, 2 Buffalo jackets, Buffalo trousers, a huge down duvet jacket, 2 pairs of gloves, bar-mitts, 2 balaclavas, 2 pairs of ski socks and moon boots. We arrived at Heathrow with enough equipment to sink a battleship.

All 16 of us including 6 film crew, 2 balloon crew, a stills photographer, Anders (a Swedish oxygen expert), Simon, Chris and microlight pilot Ben Ashman whisked through customs into a waiting vehicle which took us to the luxurious Intercontinental Hotel as their guests.

The following day we loaded the trucks and headed for Wadi Rum. As we entered the valley, the cathedral rocks towered 3,000ft above us in the haze of the midday sun. We drove up to the rest-house at Wadi Rum as camels ambled by with their lazy, long eyelashes. Bedouin looked on, forever amused by the antics of the Westerners. The army had erected a tent village for us and a huge Bedouin tent with the floor strewn with mats and cushions. There was always tea on the fire and a host of army personnel had been drafted in to help us.

The oxygen cylinder I had to carry was huge. It had to provide me with 100 per cent oxygen for up to 6 hours and also to pressurize the suit. It was attached to the back of the harness and stretched from my shoulders to my knees. The implications of landing with this contraption worried me. It weighed over 20kgs and any mis-timed landing, tripping in soft sand or an early flare and resulting hard thump on the cylinder could spell disaster. The best solution would be to land on wheels. Steve Hudson from the Sheffield HGC lent me a pair of day-one trainer wheels, having convinced me that 'big is beautiful'. My first test was aero-towing behind Ben's microlight, taking off from the road in Wadi Rum. We climbed easily in the gentle morning breeze. Wadi Rum had never looked so beautiful. The colours of the angular cliffs glowed as we climbed through the inversion into the crystal air above. Ben towed me 10kms to the hard flats of Disi, where the huge circular fields of the agricultural project stand out incongruously green among the mixed browns of the desert. I released and lined up for my first desert wheel landing. It felt strange to have my face so close to the ground.

Simon worked on the angle of 'dangle' during the day and in the evening Ben towed me to Disi once more. We returned to Wadi Rum just after sunset. As we climbed away from Disi, the sun reappeared again above the silhouetted cliffs. Simultaneously, the full moon appeared behind us. Ben and I are lost for words, marvelling at the sight.

The following morning we made the first practice balloon-drop. The purpose was to test my new 3-ring release system to allow me to control the cut-away from the balloon. In the past I have always favoured the 'Stanley Knife' technique where the balloon pilot cuts the umbilical cord connecting us. The reasons for wanting to release myself are two-fold: first, if something happened to Per and he could not release me, and second, in case of radio failure. The 45 degree nose-down attitude was uncomfortable to hold for any length of time so when I was ready to go I wanted to be able to.

We rose at 5am and set up the glider. It seemed to take forever to rig the cameras, but we were finally ready to go at 7.15, long after the sun had risen and the penetrating heat had started. The lift-off was clean as the balloon was released from its tethers. The initial ascent was slow, giving me a long look at the shear rock face as we meandered upwards. As we reached 5,000ft I pulled my 'angle of dangle' rope. From the resulting 45 per cent nose-down angle, I was looking straight down the cliff below me. Per confirmed our descent rate and told me to release when ready. The idea behind having the balloon descend before releasing is to decrease the glider's rotation slightly, and also to reduce the distortion of the balloon when it suddenly loses the weight of the wing. I counted down for the cameras and pulled my release handle. It required quite a tug but the effect was perfect. The glider dived, gathering speed, and converted, climbing out above the balloon. Trailing coloured smoke, I circled around Per, drinking in the scenery. One more problem solved, leaving only one more to go: whether I could fly wearing all the kit and gear necessary to keep me alive at 40,000ft. The next and final test would be a full dress rehearsal at 10,000ft.

I spent the morning with Miranda making a face-mask. A friend from the 'Flight for Life' expedition, London to Amman in Jordan, Miranda thought I would need some help, bought herself a ticket to Jordan and turned up in Wadi Rum. Her creative needlework skills and unfailing good humour were invaluable. My face was the only part of my body that was as yet unprotected from the cold. We had lots of Neoprene and fleece material, so it was just a question of fitting it to my goggles and oxygen mask. With endless patience, Miranda produced a masterpiece, designed to cover all exposed areas.

The following morning I climbed groggily from bed at 4.30am and started dressing. Per had been to high altitudes before in a balloon and so didn't need to put on all his gear for the rehearsal. I had to wear everything that I would have on the actual attempt and it was stifling. The down jacket sealed in all the heat, so I felt like a roasting turkey.

We were delayed again, this time by the valley wind that wafts down the Wadi for a short time each morning. With such a big balloon (140,000 cu ft), conditions need to be calm, so we waited for half an hour. By the time we took off I felt weak through over-heating and claustrophobia. I put on my goggles just before launch and they fogged up immediately. As we took off, I just hung my arms over the bar, desperately needing to cool down. By the time we passed 2,000ft drops of sweat were gathering in the goggles and I couldn't see anything. I took a glove off to wipe them and was rewarded with a magnificent view of the Sea of Galilee, the Dead Sea and the Red Sea. We climbed to 15,000ft and I released at 10,000ft. I was still unbearably hot and had taken my goggles off completely before cutting away. The drop was problem-free and I followed the balloon down. As Per landed in the middle of the desert, vehicles appeared from every direction. The helicopter landed alongside, Ben arrived on his trike, our lorries and film crew Land Rovers descended on the site like the cavalry! My landing was smooth, but I was exhausted by the heat. Chris and Simon raced over and pulled off my harness and thick outer layers of insulation. The relief was immense to feel cool air reaching me at last. I was soaked through with sweat and suffering from heat exhaustion.

All the tests were completed and we were ready to go for the record. My husband Chris spent the day checking the oxygen system with Anders, Simon made a sealed temperature-proof cover for my Davron 800 instrument pack, with a Perspex window so I could see the altitude and climb rate. Miranda modified the face mask after the morning's test. Jules disappeared to confirm our intentions to the air force, the air traffic controllers and the met office. The weather throughout our stay was consistently good with clear skies and light winds. The forecast for the following morning was perfect, predicting 50kt SW at altitude. The temperature at 40,000ft had dropped to around -62C. It was as good a forecast as we were ever going to get. The crew was ready, and the record attempt set for the morning. I was nervous but excited as I attended to the final details. The whole team had worked hard and each person was focussed on his individual role for the morning.

October 25, 1994: It's now 4.30am and I have been pre-breathing pure oxygen for 1h30m to avoid getting the bends during our rapid ascent. My mind returns to the job in hand as Miranda, mistress of the wardrobe, brings me clothes, piece by piece, and helps me into them. She tightens the laces of the pressure-suit so that it fits closely. Two hoses protrude from the left side of the suit. These will connect to the regulator – the 'brains' – of the oxygen system which will control the onset of the pressure breathing. The regulator is attached to the side of the harness, on top of the emergency oxygen cylinder. There is a hole in front of the harness for the hoses to go through, and they have to pass unobstructed through each layer of clothing in turn. I dress slowly and calmly, allowing Miranda to check each layer. I feel surprisingly calm, concentrating on the job ahead. In my mind I go through the emergency drill that I have arranged with Per in the event of radio failure. We are to give each other a different series of 'jolts' to indicate that either 'descent has started', 'release speed attained', or 'I have an emergency, descend immediately'.

The minutes move slowly, interminably. Chris and Simon have finished rigging and checking the glider, conscious that my life depends on their thorough inspection of the equipment. The balloon is being inflated and cameras are being attached to both balloon and glider.

Miranda helps me put on two balaclavas, I remove the helmet, holding the mask to my face. I hold my breath, remove the mask and pull them over my face, replacing the mask to breathe again. Just one breath of normal air at this point would introduce nitrogen back into my body and joints, risking the bends, and we would have to delay the flight.

Chris brings my E.W. Avionics barograph for me to set. Janet, our FAI Observer, witnesses it. Chris sets the Davron 800 and Janet seals both of Per's barographs. We have four between us in true 'belt and braces' style! Miranda finishes dressing me with the final layer of down jacket, trousers and moon boots. I move into the pick-up truck which has its air-conditioning on full blast. I am desperate to avoid the debilitating over-heating which I experienced on the practice drop. Finally, Per Lindstrand joins me and we are driven to the balloon. It stands turgid and ready, the gold Hashemite crown, emblem of Royal Jordanian Airlines, shines in the early light. Per gets out and I watch as he wades over to the basket. It is smothered with people, checking and double-checking tethers, cameras, instruments, propane and hydrogen. Finally, we drive to the hang glider. Dwarfed by the enormous balloon and dripping with ropes and pulleys, it sits patiently in the sand, unaware of the long, cold flight ahead.

Slowly, I walk to the glider, turn and reverse into the harness. I am so bulky in all my clothing that my arms have to be guided into position. Simon supports the weight of the oxygen cylinder as Chris does up the zip and buckles. Anders comes close to shout instructions to me as he changes my oxygen from the pre-breathing tank to my personal cylinder attached to my back. Under his guidance, I hold my breath while he disconnects one and reconnects the other. I am now a self-sufficient unit with my own life-support system.

Miranda checks my neoprene mask, ensuring that all the exposed flesh is covered. My goggles are around my neck, waiting until I am high and cold to put them on so that they don't fog up again. I have wiped them with alcohol and stuck silica sachets to them in the hope of keeping them clear. I lie down in the harness for a hang-check. Chris puts on my gloves, liners first, then huge gauntlets. I am cooking already and want to go. I feel restricted with umbilical cords attaching me to oxygen, camera recorders, sound wiring and push-to-talk buttons. We do radio checks – the sound is crystal clear through the headphones. It is time to attach the glider to the balloon. As I cannot get up with the weight of the cylinder on my back, Chris and Simon wheel me backwards towards the basket. I am blind, deaf and mute. I can only look straight ahead and have to rely entirely on my helpers. I can only hear the intermittent, dull roar of the burners as the balloon is ready for take-off. Chris comes on the radio 'OK Per, let's go'. I know he is aware of my over-heating and I silently thank him for speeding things up. I sense an increased urgency amongst the people around me. Simon disappears behind me to connect me to the basket. His face reappears in front of me. He gives me the thumbs up and shouts that the connection is good and all ropes are tangle free. Chris connects my emergency oxygen handle as the last thing. The balloon takes my weight and we start to climb. The tethers are released and we are on our own. The quiet consumes me. We rise into the clear skies above and I feel a fatalistic peace wash over me. We are fully committed and within four hours it will all be over, for better or worse.

Down below, the crowd cheers, then falls silent. Chris, a non-smoker, draws heavily on a cigarette. We climb fast, drifting NE to start with, then passing back over Wadi Rum as we contact the south-westerlies at 10,000ft. I am lost in the spectacular landscape below. For a moment the record is forgotten as the reds and golds of the desert glow, the long shadows of the crags retreat, scurrying away from the heat.

The green circles of the Disi fields are clearly visible, providing an excellent landmark. Ahead lies Iraq, miles away but directly on track if the jet-stream is stronger than forecast. Simon has done a great job on the Davron. Snug in its neoprene jacket, I can see through the Perspex that our climb rate is a healthy 800 fpm. The Red Sea comes into view, and with it Egypt and Israel. There are some altocumulus clouds to the west but we are above them now.

The silence is eerie. There are six people on the ground with radios, but no one speaks. Per Lindstrand is busy coaxing every ounce of performance out of the balloon. The noise of the burners is constant and I know that he must be heating the envelope to its limit. We pass through 34,000ft and a spangling shower of ice crystals comes streaming past me as we leave a vapour trail.

At 36,000ft the oxygen feels strange. I am aware that if something goes wrong with it at this altitude I have only 45 seconds to act before lapsing into unconsciousness. I massage the exhaust valve on the mask in case it is iced up. The system we are using is tested to -30C and we are already down to -55C. I monitor my breathing closely. I feel a slight pressure on my body and realise with surprise that pressure breathing has kicked in – not the extreme uncomfortable suffocating experience I remember from Sweden, but a gently increasing pressure, allowing me to function normally despite the rarefied atmosphere.

Fifty minutes after take-off we are above the cirrus clouds. The sky beyond is dark and the curvature of the earth is clearly visible as we reach 8 miles high. The bitter cold begins to penetrate my gloves and I ease them into the bar mitts. I feel surprisingly comfortable – the thick layers are working well. Only my face feels uncomfortably cold. I try once again to put on the goggles. They fog immediately and I despair of them, leaving them dangling and just use the visor, which is warm enough – just. Per comes over the radio to say that we have reached maximum altitude and that we will start descent. He sounds clear but a little breathless due to the difficulty of talking against the pressure of oxygen. Two minutes to the drop. I focus concentration on the release. My body is as far over the bar as possible and I have no option but to look straight down. The air is clear and the desert so featureless that the perspective is hard to judge. The only guide is the tiny line of pimples which are the huge cliffs of Wadi Rum. My heart is racing and a surge of fear courses through me. I wish I had taken up knitting instead! Too late for second thoughts.

Per speaks again. 'We are at descent speed, release when you are ready'. There is no time to wait. Descending now at 1,500 fpm, a short delay now would lose us the record. I grab my release handle, hold my breath, and pull. Nothing happens. I pull harder. Still nothing. The 3-ring release has frozen solid. I call Per, 'Cut me now!' I know he is ready as we arranged, with his knife poised. Instantly I feel the glider fall and rotate around me. It is at least vertical, maybe past vertical. I am in free-fall, harness straps slack. My feet hit the keel. I feel the oxygen cylinder catch on the back wires. Still the glider falls. 'Fly, please fly!' The air doesn't catch me but at least the glider has stopped rotating and I probably won't tumble. At last the glider bites. With a smooth surge, it pitches up, my cylinder pings clear of the wires and I am flying. The rush of relief is immediately replaced by pain. The wind whips under my visor and freezes my eyelids shut. I can feel the skin on my face burn with cold. I shove my padded arm against my face to try to block the gap under the visor. I can't see anything and I don't care. The cold is all-consuming. The wind-chill factor has brought the temperature plummeting to around -85C. Everything freezes – bar mitts, harness zip, compass, feet, hands – but it's my face that hurts. After a few minutes I start to think more clearly. I don't know exactly where I am, but with a stiff breeze and a super-fast ground speed due to the thin air, I may well be heading towards Iraqi airspace. I turn the glider and find the brightness of the sun through my still-closed eyes. I continue until I sense the darkest part of the circle and straighten up. At least now I am heading west, back to the friendly reception of Jordan.

Fifteen minutes later my eyes unfreeze. I squint in the bright sunshine, still unbearably cold but I know it will get warmer as I sink towards the desert 7 miles below. I hear no one, but I feel as if I can see the ends of the world. God, I'm cold! I need to find out where I am. I can still see the agricultural plant. We are only 15 miles past it. We are expecting to drift at least 50 miles further. I can hear the helicopters trying to locate us. Suddenly I catch sight of

Per Lindstrand, a tiny orb miles below me. An even smaller white dot is circling him and I know Ben has found him in his microlight. I try again to ease my hands into the bar mitts but they are still frozen and I can't get my huge gloves inside. I try the zip again, wanting to close the harness to try and unfreeze my feet, but it is locked with ice. I try and distract myself from the cold. The road from Jordan to Saudi Arabia is clearly visible, the desert stretching as far as I can see to the east. I can see Per's shadow close to the balloon; he must be about to land. He touches down lightly. The balloon stands proud for a moment and then deflates, sprawling across the sand, lifeless, its mission accomplished.

At 10,000ft my hands unfreeze. With the returning feeling comes the 'hot aches'. They have been numb for 1h30 and I bang them against the base bar to ease the pain. I check my altimeter and detach one side of the mask, letting it hang, releasing the oxygen into the air. The feeling of freedom is wonderful as I inhale deep breaths of the fresh desert air. Finally I manage to zip up my harness, though it makes no difference to my still-frozen feet. I begin to see detail below. Per has landed in a rough area with uneven ground and scattered rocks. The collapsed balloon makes a good windsock, but I elect to land cross-wind along the rough channels on the ground. I can't see a smooth area and it's going to be a case of making the best of it. The second helicopter lands and spews out the film crew who hurry to their positions. The ground rushes up. I focus what concentration I can muster and touch down right on a lump, bouncing me back into the air momentarily, and then the glider settles. It's over, we're OK and we have the record. I don't care about it now.

I slump with fatigue and relief. I can't move – the harness weighs a ton and I am connected to everything via pipes and ropes. I am aware of people around me pulling, disconnecting and freeing me from the equipment. I feel the weight disappear and Chris is there helping me to my feet. I lean against him as he takes off the down jacket. Per comes over and gives me a Swedish bear-hug. He is bubbling with it and we jabber together. At the highest point, the propane was so cold that it was coming out of the cylinder as 'snow', igniting and falling on him in flaming lumps! When he cut me free, he was on the floor of the basket, peering through the camera viewing hole. He saw me plummet but he didn't see the glider recover. For a moment he was worried, and then he saw me at the same level as him, circling, and he happily descended. He didn't realise that I was flying blind. It would have been somewhat embarrassing if the only two aircraft flying at 40,000ft had collided!

The Davron displayed a maximum altitude of 41,370ft. We still had to work out the exact drop height, but we knew we had the record. Simon de-rigged the glider, but he had to leave it in the sun for half an hour to defrost, as he couldn't fold the wings in! I had mild frostbite on my face which disappeared in a few days. We threw a party that night. The whole team had worked so hard to make it happen. The moon rose over the ridge into the star-studded night, as the beer flowed. I lasted until 10pm before the day's excitement combined with an early start caught up with me. I sloped off, climbed into my sleeping bag and was asleep before my head touched the pillow.

Chapter 6

Events After 1980

Beginning in 1981, the British moved into a dominant position in world competition hang gliding. They did not win everything and often locked, head to head, with the Australians and Americans, but the British became the team everyone wanted to beat, the standard other teams measured themselves by, a situation that lasted for ten years and only ended in the 1990s.

The engine that drove the then British dominance was the National League I had created in 1977. It involved up to fifty competitors a year, men and women, who flew against each other, often in dreadful weather conditions off hills that in other countries would not even be considered worth driving up to look at. It was a feature of the National League, from its 1977 origins, that if it was possible to fly during the competition dates, we all did so. Crucially, this included me, because most of the flyers came to the correct conclusion they were better flyers than I was. If I was willing to fly, so were they. There were very few accidents, and none fatal, despite this go-for-it spirit.

A second factor that underlined the depth and power of British hang gliding was the formation in 1980 of the Cross-Country League, founded by Dave Harrison, brother of BHGA Flying and Training Officer, Bob Harrison. For the first four years of the National League, we had run special competitions to bring in new blood; Dave Harrison's XC League gave us a ready-to-wear option to pick the best XC pilots in the country. A lot of National League pilots competed in the XC League and many of them were leading flyers in it, but the system encouraged XC flying all over Britain, and pilots would 'go over the back' at the slightest excuse, because they knew it was meaningful. Harrison's monthly table of distances flown enabled pilots to measure their skills against each other, and the best were offered a place in the National League and a chance to fly for their country. In passing, the XC League also offered those who sneered at competition pilots as cultivating 'artificial' skills, a chance to see if they could fly further.

In 1981, the year after the Americans pounded us in the third American Cup in Tennessee and let loose the UP Comet upon the world, the biggest competition was the FAI Worlds in Japan. The FAI, *Federation Aeronautique Internationale*, is the official body that regulates all civilian flying, Mainstream as well as the New Aviation. Within the FAI our international governing body is CIVL, the *Confederation Internationale de Vol Libre* (broadly translated as 'free flight'). These organisations have a strong French flavour, reflecting the earliest French passion for flying since the last few years of the nineteenth century. The FAI only authorises a certain number of competitions; World Championships, for example, in odd years (1981, '83, etc), and the European Championships in even years. In 1981, Japan secured the World Championships, and ran their competition from the northern city of Beppu.

The FAI, being official, often lags behind thinking in competition hang gliding. Everyone was raging to do XC tasks, distance and speed; the Japanese were restricted by both terrain and thinking from actually running such a competition. There were five tasks on the books, including XC, which was not called, and a goal distance task up to 20km, called once. So the great names of hang gliding were in Beppu – Rich Pfieffer, Steve Moyes, Gerard Thevenot – but they were not fully tested. Duration/spots, as in Kossen five years earlier, was the main test, along with speed runs. Micky Mouse stuff.

Rich Pfieffer calculated that he would win more points if he got to the ground quicker than anyone else, even if he crashed. And that is just what he did, time after time, wiping out the uprights of his wing so that in the end the US team ran out of spares. Pfieffer placed second after the Brazilian who had showed so much promise in Tennessee a year earlier, Pepe Lopez. Graham Slater of Britain placed third, ahead of 1979 World Champion Josef Guggenmos, with Gerard Thevenot fifth and Johnny Carr sixth. The British, for the first time, won the team event, well ahead of Switzerland, with Germany third and Canada fourth. The US team was eighth!

The 1982 Europeans at Millau in France was a massacre. It was essentially a cross-country competition, mostly involving Europeans, though US pilot Jeff Scott and World Champion Pepe Lopez also flew (placing seventh and thirteenth). There was an extraordinary argument about Michael Carnet, a Frenchman resident in England, flying for the British, and lots of the usual politics that often work behind the scenes at all sporting events. But when the competition was over, British pilots were placed first, second, third and fifth (Tony Hughes, Graham Hobson, Robert Bailey and Bob Calvert), with only the previous two-time European Champion, France's Gerard Thevenot, splitting them up. Britain also easily took the team prize, with Switzerland second, Norway third and the hosts, France, fourth.

We were supposed to stage the 1983 Worlds in Britain, but this fell through, and it went to Tegelberg in the south of what was then West Germany. The German organisers let in a South African team, which meant the British lost any Sports Council backing and did the competition on a shoestring. There were a lot of XC tasks, but little speed testing, so a pilot completing the 90km course in an hour would get almost the same score as a pilot taking twice as long. The eight-man heats also meant that class didn't show against a large enough number of pilots. Teams were of six pilots, with the top four scores counting. Despite these shortcomings, in the end there were worthy winners.

Australia ended with the individual champion, Steve Moyes, and also the team prize. Stew Smith, from the US, placed second, ahead of Britain's Graham Hobson, with Australia's Ricky Duncan fourth, Pfieffer fifth, and Robert Bailey sixth. It is an indication of how much hang gliding was becoming a sport, a real and consistent measurement of excellence, that acknowledged great names like Guggenmos, Thevenot, Carr, Slater, Jarman, were among the top sixteen pilots, year after year. It must have been brilliant for Bill Moyes, having done so much to create hang gliding, to see his own son as champion of the world. Team placings went to Australia, Britain, USA, Canada, West Germany, France, Brazil. All the British pilots flew Airwave wings, and that company's Magic 3 began selling all over the world. Some Germans even tried to buy the gliders from British team members before the competition was over.

So far, the best British competition pilots came out of the League. But then a Englishman began winning international competition who had never flown in the League, and who was, all on his own, making his name in the big meets. John Pendry was destined to become the single most successful competition pilot of his time, displacing the legendary Australian Steve Moyes.

Pendry began flying in February 1974, at the age of 16, only five months after Ken Messenger jumped off Snowdon. This was the beginning of the year that saw hang gliding explode in Britain, when Johnny Carr first emerged as a champion. But the young Pendry stuck with his bog-rog for nearly four years when everyone else was moving into the Phoenix 6B, the Wills Wing SST and then into fourth-generation British wings. Pendry bought an American SST in 1977 and flew that until graduating from college in 1981. During all this time, despite our search in Britain for any flying talent to promote, his name never came up as a serious prospect for League flying.

Pendry spent the summer of 1981 flying with Mike and Caroline de Glanville in the Alpes Maritime, and the fabulous Lachens site. He wind-dummied the French Nationals that September, and did his first 50-mile XC. His first British competition was the 1982 Fosters Open on the Isle of Wight, won by Johnny Carr, but which Pendry didn't enjoy. Its flying values were very poor. Gerard Thevenot suggested Pendry try the Lariano Triangle competition in Italy. It was his first really serious competition, and he came second to Gerard, 'as much a surprise to me,' Pendry said later, 'as it was to anyone else'.

In 1982 Planters Peanuts, through a family connection, sponsored Pendry, earning him the nickname of 'Peanut Pendry'. He now had the money to travel, and went to Australia to compete, to take on the Moyes Boys in their own territory. Pendry spent the summer of 1983 at Owens Valley, and on 13 July flew 187 miles, an official FAI World Distance Record (but only because his paperwork was better than Larry Tudor's, who flew 221 miles on the same day). Planters were delighted, and felt they were getting a good return for their money. Pendry won his first competition that year, the Wyoming XC Open, then finished second in the US Nationals and third in the US Masters. These were serious competitions.

That winter, Pendry won the 1984 Australian Nationals for the first time, and finally joined the British League. As a virtual celebration, he took the UK distance record up to 130 miles in a technically superb flight along the south coast of England, from Ditchling Beacon to Colyton in Devon. It was unusual because of the various different types of lift he found – thermal, ridge and convergence (when a sea breeze meets an inland wind) – any one of which could have dumped him. At one time he was 300ft AGL and preparing to land, when he found something to stay up on and continued. In Europe's summer Pendry went to Kossen, in Austria and won the pre-world meeting there, making him one of the favourites to win the 1985 worlds.

Pendry was in the British team sent to Norway for the 1984 Europeans, which proved to be the last with target landings, those leftovers from our steerable parachute days. There was one task, speed around a four-pylon course of nearly 36km and then a target landing, with an open window every day so competitors chose when they wanted to go. But the weather was poor, and the full course was only possible in two of seven rounds. Only nine competitors actually did it. Overall winner was Tony Hughes of Britain, the reigning European Champion, but the Germans won team gold, followed by the French and then the British.

That year, the British had beaten the French in the Anglo-French Blériot competition, Len Hull had won the Hungarian Eger Cup (Judy Leden was third!), and Johnny Carr had won the Spanish Cup. Tony Hughes, meanwhile, had won the European championships twice, and in 1983 had gone to Owens Valley and beaten all the Americans to win the great OV Classic, the first foreigner to do so. Hughes had come a long way from the raw 'Yosser' I first met in the League; he almost single-handedly saved Britain's team reputation in the 1982 American Cup in Yorkshire, in which I was then coaching the Americans.

John Pendry went back to Australia that winter and continued his fierce duel with Steve Moyes, then World Champion. On the first day of the Blue Stratos Classic at Mount Buffalo, Pendry was flung upside down by a vicious thermal, breaking his bottom bar and safety luff-lines at the same time. He threw his parachute, landed in the bush close to the road (his girlfriend then, Hilary Smith, got more scratched in a frantic search for him than he did from his fall). His driver picked Pendry up, rushed to the hotel, collected a spare bottom bar and more luff-lines, repaired the glider and road-rallied to the top for another go. Pendry finished fifth that day, and went on to beat Steve Moyes on the final day.

Moyes and Pendry met again in the 1985 World Championships in Kossen; the story is complicated – and epic – and I will deal with it later.

Pendry, by now recognised as a giant in the sport (aside from being 6ft 5in tall) won five competitions in a row in 1986 – the Australian Nationals, the Lawrence Hargrave, the Venezuelan XC, the first British League and Bassano. He went on that year to win Como, and later that summer became British champion for the first time (it was then he said the British League was the toughest of all competitions to win). Pendry's reputation in Australia was so high that Bill Moyes tried to claim, only half as a joke, that he looked on Pendry as an honorary Australian, an unheard of remark from that source about a Pom!

The 1986 European Championships were in Hungary. Again, Britain won the team event, while Pendry was individual champion.

The 1987 World Championships took place in 1988 in Australia, at Mt Buffalo. Conditions were close to those in California and Owens, and the Americans fielded a particularly strong team. The Australians, on home ground, would have been difficult to beat anywhere, but only really beat the Americans at the last round. It was all XC flying, with strong thermals, some of which could be picked up less than 100ft from the ground. Being attacked by eagles was one of the extra risks run by competitors. Only four British pilots made the cut-off point, compared to six Americans and seven Australians. Ricky Duncan, whom we first met as a 16-year-old at the 1976 British Open at Mere, became World Champion, with Steve Moyes third. They were split by Bruce Case, of the US, and another American, Ted Boyse, placed fourth. The top British pilot was Bruce Goldsmith, at fifth, and Larry Tudor was sixth. Australia won team gold, USA silver, Britain bronze, and Japan made an excellent showing, coming fifth after Brazil.

Bruce Goldsmith was my particular protégé, for I had taught him to soar hang gliders when he was an engineering student back in 1981. He lived next door to the house my family moved into in Bristol. Bruce was keen to get beyond the top-to-bottom flights he had done up to then at Imperial College, London, whose club he had joined. I went out to a coastal site called Bossington to guide Bruce through his first soaring and top-landing flight. It was obvious within two minutes he had exceptional ability. That day, for example, he was in the air for two and a half hours, his first soaring day! Within a month he had borrowed my high-performance wing and, without instruments and in the same air as British team captain Robert Bailey, flew his first XC, 17 miles compared to Bailey's 10. I wrote to Johnny Carr on the BHGA competitions committee asking him to look after Bruce, whom I saw as a League pilot soon. Johnny wrote back later to say it quickly became a question of Bruce looking after him.

In 1987, when I had a promise of £100,000 sponsorship from the billionaire Kerry Packer to fly a microlight to Australia, I offered Bruce the job of organising the flight. We agreed to wait until I actually had a cheque in my hand before Bruce left his job. On Friday, 1 April, Bruce said he had been posted to Paris, and had to make a decision that day to either go or resign the job.

'Have you any reason to think Kerry Packer won't come through?' he asked.

Nope, I said, so at 3pm Bruce resigned his job. At 6.30pm that same day, Linton Taylor, Kerry Packer's right-hand man, telephoned me in the East End of London to say the sponsorship was off; the flight to Australia was too risky and too expensive. I faxed an imploring letter asking for a change of mind, without success. So I faxed another imploring letter, explaining Bruce's situation, and saying that Mr Packer should consider sponsoring Goldsmith, as a potential World Champion. Back came the question, how much? Bruce tore around to produce, at twenty-four hours' notice, a full year's competition programme costing about £16,000. Mr Packer said, OK! A year later, Bruce placed fifth in the Worlds. I *was* pleased. Aside from being a brilliant pilot, if hang gliding has intellectuals, Bruce Goldsmith is one, a thinking man's pilot.

The 1988 European Championship in Italy was another massacre, Britain taking gold, Germany silver and Italy bronze. Individually, we took the first three places, with Pendry first, Goldsmith second and Jess Flynn third. A young English boy called Robbie Whittall, just 19 years old, placed eleventh, ahead of the Australian Master Steve Moyes and virtually every other member of the Australian World Champion team, guest flyers at the meet.

Pendry said some of the flying was aggressive ... 'until at one point a Russian and an Israeli got too close. The two collided and the Russian got flipped upside down. The (British-built) Magic he was flying stabilised upside down and he threw his chute, but before it had time to open he hit the side of the mountain. The landing was soft and he was unhurt. The Israeli was OK and continued to fly, and everyone else thermalled less aggressively for a while.' This was the first meeting at which the name Tomas Suchanek, a Czech flyer, appears, and it is probably where Bill Moyes began recruiting another honorary Australian.

The 1989 Worlds was another epic battle between the top nations in hang gliding, but new names were emerging, and the quality of flying reached new levels. I will return to this epic competition later.

Later that year Pendry won at Bassano for the fourth time. The Brazilians, gee'd up by Pepe Lopez, a cult figure after his 1981 World Championship win, organised a team competition, the Brazilian Cup, at a site called Governador Valadares. It was modelled on the American Cup for teams of four, but also included individual scores. Britain won, with Brazil second, USA third and France fourth. Pendry and Whittall were individually first and second, followed by Alex Silveira of Brazil, Larry Tudor of the US, Bruce Goldsmith and Jess Flynn of Britain, then America's Howard Osterlund, Brazil's Pedrao, France's Thevenot, and Pepe himself was tenth.

This competition became famous because one of Pendry's girlfriends, the inimitable Monique Amman, insisted on entering as the only woman competitor; it was her first contest. She was sucked up into a cloud to 12,000ft, where she froze nearly to death, and was carted away to hospital with hypothermia and suspected frostbite when she landed (she was terrible at landings). For the next three days Brazil's media, television and newspapers, carried breathless reports on Monique's condition. The following year she managed to blag her way into the World Meet ('Look at all the publicity I got you last year!'). Because she is so flamboyant, few people give Monique the credit she deserves for courage and chutzpa. (Pendry has had some interesting girlfriends, including Hilary Smith, who made such a first impression with a haymaker on Rich Pfieffer.)

In 1990, the European Championships were held in Yugoslavia (more properly, Slovenia). Three men had won the title twice – Gerard Thevenot, Tony Hughes and John Pendry. Hughes had moved on to microlighting, so Pendry faced Thevenot versus the rest. Suchanek was emerging, and Robbie Whittall was not going to be put off despite having had his shoulder recently dislocated. A new hotshot from Austria, Manfred Ruhmer, even younger than Robbie, was also tipped for the top. But Pendry grabbed the lead and kicked away anyone who got near to him, including France's Alain Chauvet, Britain's Peter Harvey and young Mr Ruhmer. Pendry won, with Ruhmer second and Whittall third. Gerard Thevenot had a poor competition, placing twenty-fourth. Tomas Suchanek, at thirteenth, had not yet found the form he was to show in the 1990s, though he was now flying a Moyes wing. Britain again won the team event, in a tight contest with France; Italy was third.

In the important Italian competition in Bassano, Britain's position in the competition side of the New Aviation was confirmed again. In

EVENTS AFTER 1980

hang gliding, the British took the first four places, with Bruce Goldsmith (his first international win), Darren Arkwright, John Pendry and Peter Harvey. In the paragliding event, Robbie Whittall won, in his first paragliding competition. In microlights, Angelo d'Arrigo of Italy won, but Britain's Old Etonian 1989 World Champion, Richard Meredith-Hardy, was second.

The year 1991 was when Suchanek emerged into his first real glory, at the World Championships in Brazil. He beat the best in the world, with two Brazilians, Pepe Lopez second, and Paolo Coelho third. Pendry was fourth, the great Jim Lee (168-mile flight in 1981!) of the US fifth, Harvey and Whittall sixth and seventh and Goldsmith ninth. Britain won the team event, with the US second, Brazil third and Australia fourth. Japan placed seventh, ahead of strong teams from Germany and Norway.

In this event, Gerard Thevenot treated spectators to a real thrill by climbing on to the control bar while the wing continued to sail smoothly away from the mountain. 'It looked like a stunt,' wrote his wife, Sherry, later, 'but it wasn't. Gerard had accidentally hooked his harness strap around a back wire, which made the wing completely misbehave, so he quickly unclipped and hooked in correctly without losing too much time and altitude.' This competition was also remembered for the large number of young women who milled around the take-off and landing areas in various stages of undress. It was not just the flying that was exhausting.

In 1992 the European Championships, held in Norway, featured another battle between Pendry, Suchanek and Manfred Ruhmer. By this time, class pilots like Whittall and Goldsmith had moved on to paragliding, and there were suggestions that, outside Pendry, the British were slipping. In the sense that there were no more 1-2-3s, and nor likely to be again, this was true. But the British – Pendry, Darren Arkwright, Robin Hamilton, Mike Stephens, Justin Needham and Steve Elkins – still won easily enough even with four relatively new names, with Norway second and Switzerland third (Hamilton was the Scots pilot sucked up to 22,000ft by the 1989 Great Italian Killer Storm in Spain that moved on the next day to kill five Italians at Como). Pendry was accused in Norway of being boring by Italy's Angelo Crapanzano for winning once more, for the fourth time, with Suchanek second and Ruhmer fourth after the Norwegian, Jens Krotseng.

(No one can accuse Crapanzano, one of the characters of hang gliding, of being boring. He managed, single-handedly, to wipe out the entire stock of spare uprights brought to Norway by Britain's Solar Wings company, whose glider he flew, by the 'quality' of his landings. Breaking an upright became 'doing an Angelo', and uprights were called 'crapanzanos'.)

In 1993, Tomas Suchanek became the first man to win the World Championships twice, and this in the American washing machine site, Owens Valley. Pendry had won the pre-worlds there, but the Americans, who had never had a winner in the mainstream Rogallo class of wing, expected in 1993 to redress this balance. A young pilot called Chris Arai carried the US flag ahead of the field all the way through to the last day, before Suchanek slipped ahead to win by just one point, though the Americans were compensated by taking team gold for the first time, with Australia in silver position, and Britain bronze.

Suchanek also, finally, beat John Pendry in the Europeans in 1994, to emerge as the world's number one pilot, with Ruhmer ranked second, and Pendry now third.

If you are not an Englishman reading these results, then I am sorry. If you are an Englishman, you could have gone through the whole of the 1980s and scanned newspapers like a computer, and you would not have known of the British triumphs. I have put the wins on record because, whatever advantage we had at the beginning of that great streak of wins has now gone. The rest of the world has watched and learned. Even after fifteen years of winning, in the end we remain in Britain a nation of amateur flyers, paying our own way, on a small island with poor weather and indifferent hills. There is less money coming into British hang gliding from the outside than there was when I ran the League, making the winning less attractive, and failing to stop the drift of superb pilots like Whittall and Goldsmith away to other sports or disciplines.

It is not as if journalists and newspaper editors did not know of the wins. It is that they did not care. With rare exceptions, such as Ronnie Faux of *The Times*, British sports journalists were fixed in a mindset about hang gliding established in 1977, and looked no further. Like King Canute (the sea, too, is indifferent), I tried to counter this by writing to all the sports editors in the country after the brilliant 1989 victories in Brazil, ahead of the World Championships that year. The background against which I sent these letters was that Frank Bruno was being praised to the skies for the way he lost to Mike Tyson in heavyweight boxing, and there was the usual 'sporting' behaviour of British football fans:

> Last weekend a British hang gliding team came home from the World Team Championships in Brazil. They competed against the current world champions, Australia, and strong teams from Brazil, the USA, France, Canada, Italy, the cream of the hang gliding world. The British won as if there was no one else in the competition. The Australians were sixth.
>
> No old ladies were beaten up. No one was killed fighting on the terrace. No official was head-butted. There was no mooning, no spitting, and the British did not come second in a two-man competition. Yet where is there a mention in the sports media of the British triumph?
>
> In a four-man team, the British individual places were as follows: first, second, fifth and sixth. The World Champion, Ricky Duncan from Australia, placed 49th. The current World Distance Record Holder, Larry Tudor from the USA, placed fourth.
>
> Not only did the British win, but they won on a British glider, the Airwave Kiss, built on the Isle of Wight. Of the top ten pilots, including foreigners, eight of them flew the Kiss. The two exceptions were Larry Tudor and the former European Champion, Gerard Thevenot, who came ninth. Gerard is proprietor of the biggest French manufacturer, La Mouette, and so could not be expected to fly Airwave.
>
> The British result in Brazil was the latest in a long line of British successes, none of which was celebrated by the British media. The Brazilian winner, John Pendry from Brighton, is the current European Champion, and the former World Champion. In the last European Championships in Italy, Britons placed first, second, third and fifth, and romped home with the team competition. In the previous Europeans in Hungary, Britons placed first, second, fourth and fifth. The only 'blip' was last year's World Championships, where Britain came third.
>
> It is not just one generation of Britons who dominate world hang gliding. Pendry will be restored to his rightful

number one place in the world rankings by the Brazilian win, and there are three other Britons in the top ten rankings. But a young flying genius, 19-year old Robbie Whittall from Leeds, current British Champion, was second to Pendry in Brazil, and won the FAI World Trials in Switzerland last year. He has to be a hot favourite to win this year's World Championships, held in Switzerland (he did!).

While the men were winning in Brazil, a stunning Englishwoman called Judy Leden went to the Venezuelan Championships. There, against the best male pilots, flying long cross-country flights at speed over 80km courses, Judy romped home an easy winner. She is the British Women's Champion, the European Women's Champion, and the World Women's Champion. She also holds the blue-riband British distance record, the European distance record and the World distance record. The only way she can go in women's hang gliding is down, and now she is taking on the men. But do you read about that in the British sporting media? She has to jump out of balloons and fly across the English Channel to really attract the press. Her sporting achievements are not enough.

Why does it matter? Only that hang gliding could have been an exhibition sport at the Barcelona Olympics, and has a chance to graduate to a full Olympic sport. Still, why does it matter that the British press ignore all the current British wins? Only that wins need encouragement and will not go on forever if they are ignored, because young men and women will leave hang gliding and go into sports which attract more attention, which will enable them to attract sponsors, and make winning pay.

If hang gliding had been possible in Ancient Greece, it would have become one of the most classical of all sports. It tests the best in a person; courage, stamina, nerve, physical fitness, tactical and strategy skills, and above all, character. If there is a Chariots of Fire era in hang gliding, this is it, but where is the body of British journalists to interpret this era to a wider public? Hang gliding is flying the way Leonardo da Vinci imagined it to be, clean, beautiful, sporting, free, but how would you know that from reading the British sporting media?

There is a cynical story going the rounds within the sport, the paraphrase of a conversation between John Pendry and a journalist after John had flown a record 130 miles in Britain.

'Was anybody killed?' asked the journalist.

'No.'

'Anyone injured?'

'No.'

'Did you crash into anything?'

'No.'

'What was the story again?'

'It was a record flight, further than anyone else in Britain has flown.'

'Yes, well, don't call us, we'll call you.'

One sports editor from one of the regional TV stations had the grace to phone up and ask what I wanted. I said, coverage, features, just attention. There was no other reaction, and certainly no feature coverage when Robbie Whittall went on to his great triumph, aside from a thirty-minute film I made for Yorkshire TV before the event predicting the win (which they prudently ran after the competition). And when you learn the manner and context of that triumph, you will understand my rage.

In all these triumphs, I have to say I played little part. In a couple of cases, I was on the other side. Approaching the story I have to write, I feel rather like 'I, Claudius' from the Robert Graves book, clearing away the work he did before turning to account for his faithless wife Messalina. There are similarities ...

In the summer of 1980, a pilot called Peter Hargreaves broke Robert Bailey's 50-mile British XC record. I was then editing *Wings!*, and threw out two pages of stories at the last moment to feature the Hargreaves flight. I also threw out two other pages to feature the 'War of the Roses', an XC competition between Lancashire and Yorkshire, in which big distances (for those days) were flown by pilots like Bailey, Calvert and the like. Hargreaves, a virtual unknown outside Yorkshire, had failed to get into the National League that year, yet in the same air as these champions he had flown much further. He was obviously a brilliant pilot, and I wanted to make him wider known.

Ever since trying to cross the Channel in 1977, I had been involved in a small sponsorship-seeking company called Flight Promotions. It was started and run by my wife Fiona Campbell and a PR man called Arthur Puffett, initially to raise the money for Ken Messenger and I for the Channel attempt (J&B Whisky, Olympic Holidays), then for the 1977 British Open (Long John Whisky), Len Gabriels' attempt at London to Paris by microlight (Bluebird Toffees), and the 1978 League Final (Atlas Express), but unlike other sponsorship attempts within hang gliding, I did raise some money.

That autumn I was very busy. My family had moved to Bristol but I could find no work there, so I used to commute 130 miles on Sunday to work at BBC Radio London, living in 'digs', and going home on Thursday evenings. I was a freelance radio journalist, the main source of stories to feed the current affairs programme *Rush Hour*. At the same time, I edited the monthly *Wings!*, attended all BHGA Council meetings, worked as Competitions Chairman and also flew in the League, and twice coached British teams abroad, in the Blériot Cup and the American Cup. One could say I was stretched to the limit, but I was so close to matters I did not see that.

The 1978 American Cup in Tennessee, which we lost for the first time to the Americans, was hard to take. They had produced a brilliant new wing in the UP Comet, another generation, but until they beat us in Tennessee that year, they would not sell such a wing to a Brit.

Three other events are relevant. First, the pounding we had received from the American UP – Ultralite Products – Comet made me alarmed about manufacturing in Britain. An agency, which later became Airwave Gliders, had already been established to sell UP Comets in Britain, and any pilot flying one would thrash any pilot not flying one ... so everyone was going to buy Comets. As I said earlier, I brought a Comet back to the company, Solar Wings, in which I had a 25 per cent interest, and told them to copy it. All over the country, manufacturers were working feverishly to sort out designs to cope with the Comet: Skyhook, Hiway, Flexiform, Southdown. In January, 1981, I organised a competition in which Airwave put in three Comets, to encourage manufacturers to meet the threat head on. A crack team came over from La Mouette in France, including the great Gerard Thevenot himself, to take part. This took a lot of time and energy.

EVENTS AFTER 1980

The second relevant event is that Fosters Lager, the Australian beer company trying to create a market in Britain, approved a budget – one magazine said it was as high as £1.5 million – to be spent on minority sports in Britain. Fosters went to the Sports Council to ask which minority sports were worth backing? Among others, the Sports Council told them, was hang gliding. This recommendation followed on naturally from our growing international competition success, for which we had already earned the 1979 Prince of Wales Cup, the highest British award in sporting aviation, presented to me personally by Prince Charles himself. But though I was competitions chairman, I never heard anything about this Fosters offer.

As my grip on competitions was well known to be firm, and strongly in favour of channelling most of the money raised through competition into competition pilots themselves, one has to ask why?

The third event was that Derrick Amoore, a brilliant and once powerful BBC TV executive, took over as Head of BBC Radio London. It is a big step downwards to move from ENCA, Editor News & Current Affairs, BBC TV, at 35, to manager, BBC Radio London at 45. But the BBC in those days was 'family' and looked after their own. One day Derrick called me into his office and told me I was spending too much time hang gliding. I replied, guiltily, that I did every job expected of me and more besides, and the programme I serviced was never short.

'I don't mean that,' he snorted. 'You are pouring your creative energies into hang gliding. I am paying for those energies. I think you should be editing Rush Hour.'

'But I'm a freelance!' I said

'Doesn't matter. I think you're the man for the job.'

Well, of course, it did matter. The programme was two hours a morning of current affairs, 7am to 9 am, Monday to Friday, serving the whole of London and much of the Home Counties. It already had an Editor, a staff producer who was bumped off elsewhere in the station but who remained in the newsroom and, frankly, was never going to be my best friend. Could you blame him? Other BBC staffers in the station, accustomed to asking me to do this or that story, now found I was editing the major current affairs outlet, and it would be my decision which stories would be used. I soon discovered that I had to rely on freelances myself, on a tiny budget, because there was no great rush to give me stories out of the newsroom. Derrick saw all this but let me sort it out, which, eventually, I did.

One problem about editing the programme was that I had to be up by four o'clock every morning, and in work by five o'clock. It was very intense until nine o'clock, and then there was a lot of detailed planning until two o'clock in the afternoon to decide what stories I wanted the following day. I spent many afternoons putting the monthly hang gliding magazine *Wings!* to bed, often writing articles myself, certainly compiling all the news, and then going back to 'digs' in the evening. I had a room with one of the First American Cup pilots, Mick Maher, in north London.

Roy was the first Chief Marshal in the National League, and he and I worked together for nearly three years. We were friends, and stayed in each other's homes. Roy was on the competitions committee, and once we agreed tasks he made them happen. As any chief marshal has to be, he was tough, rigidly enforcing the philosophy we agreed on, no flight, no score, your choice. That is just what I wanted and the League needed. Roy was first choice to be sent off as manager to teams at the Europeans and the World Championships.

Our first real difference of opinion was on selecting Bob Calvert for the 1979 American Cup team, in which, as I wrote earlier, I overrode his objections. But there were deeper differences, especially over South Africa. Roy came out of the mainstream gliding world, and like BHGA President Ann Welch he had little time for a boycott of Apartheid teams. If we lost Sports Council grants, well, that was the way of things, he thought, because there was also the principle of freedom of sport.

In 1980, two things happened that made things worse. First, Roy's son Andrew came into the League. It is one thing to hurl the rest of us hooligan League pilots into a howling gale, but it is entirely another thing when one of those pilots is your young son. Matters came to a head on a difficult Lake District site, when flying a task, 1-on-5. Once one pilot went into the task in the group, the rest were expected to go or score a zero. The task was a duration/spot, but the target was behind the hill in horrendous conditions and there were sail deflations and wobbly wings all over the place.

It was not pleasant, but then that was how the League sometimes was.

Tony Hughes, then still raw, his future titles in Owens and the European Championships ahead of him, took off into quite radical air. He wobbled around for a short while making loud alarmed noises, landed back on top instead of getting on with the task, and did a lot of shouting at Roy about how he was going to get killed. Roy came to see me to cancel the task. I was due to fly, and as nervous as anyone else, but went back to take-off to see what was happening. My friend Mick Maher, also due to fly, said quietly that Tony had made a hash of things.

He then pointed out the next pilot due to go.

It was Andrew Hill.

'No, we're not cancelling,' I said. 'Throw them off, please.'

I cannot remember if Roy himself did throw off the rest of the pilots. I know I flew and we completed the task, and we all flew and no one was injured. But at that evening's competition committee meeting, Roy resigned. At the time, the second factor was that he had also just become BHGA Chairman, so perhaps he would have resigned anyway. I know I spoke at that year's AGM in favour of voting for Roy taking hang gliding's top job.

I did not know then that, for months, he had been asking people privately, 'What are we going to do about Brian Milton?'

I accept that, in some matters, I have a reputation as a Marmite Man. That year was when I ran the series of Brothers in Law articles that so upset the mainstream gliding clubs by highlighting an organised campaign to drive hang gliding off some hills by whatever means possible. Roy and Ann Welch, both with a mainstream gliding background, caught the flak from this. Roy never really leaned on me to stop the articles, because he knew I wouldn't, but he wasn't very happy. Yet I also grew careless, under pressure from all that I was doing, and failed to make it to BHGA Council meetings on time or left them early. C.P. Snow's first rule of politics is, 'Always be there', however unpleasant or boring it is. I knew the rule, and did not comply with it.

I believe when the Fosters' offer came in, Roy knew what would happen if I learned of it. It was not that I would want Flight Promotions involved, but if we were going to run a competition to promote Fosters' name, then I would want at least 50 per cent of what was left over to go into competition funding. He was right. I would. As it turned out, he had other plans for that money, but what was he to do with me? He certainly needed my committee.

The Hargreaves/Abbott letter passed me by, but it came up at the first League. I did not really see the danger, and was surprised when the competitions committee passed a unanimous motion of confidence in me. At a council meeting before the AGM, I was late, and there was a motion to suspend me and appoint an investigator, Reggie Spooner, a former RAF wing commander and chairman of the BHGA. At the AGM I was asked what it was all about. It is, I told them, a fan dance, you have to sell something you haven't got for money, which, if paid, you have got. It must have sounded very dodgy, and I did not improve my case at all, even if it is all true, then and now.

I was suspended from everything.

Roy sent his personal friend and then BHGA Principal Officer, Barry Blore, to make sure I handed everything over. From his point of view, if I had anything left, BHGA Council, competitions committee, *Wings!*, then I would have a power base to strike back.

It had to be either him or me.

Reggie saw me, we went through everything together. Reggie produced his report, I think it was twelve pages long, and delivered it to Roy the night before a council meeting. Roy had a difficult task. He had to show it to BHGA Council and get them to agree they had no confidence in me at all. But it was important that I personally did not get hold of it until later, and even more important that I did not go in front of council to argue my case. He also had to avoid any resignations on council, or the competitions committee.

At the meeting Roy produced the report as if it was something very secret, led six hours of debate, and then asked for the report back from every member. When they left the meeting, none of the councillors had written proof of what they had been debating. I cannot understand why they agreed to this, and nor, years later, can they. Though I lived just down the road, Roy managed not to let me be invited in my own trial, arguing that I had put my case to Reggie and that was enough. I wrote later that Peter Sutcliffe, the Yorkshire Ripper, whose case was going on then, at least had the chance to make his case in open trial, even though he had chopped thirteen women to death … but it was too late then. I lost all my positions.

I think no one, probably even including Roy Hill, really expected it would be so absolute.

'Of course, you must go on looking for money for BHGA!' said Roy later.

'All you had to do was eat shit for eighteen months and then we would have you back,' said Robert Bailey.

I looked at him and thought, I set up a competition system so people like you could win and it could mean something. I worked all the months of the year to find the money to send you abroad so it cost you nothing at all, because I didn't think being poor should bar you from flying for Britain (not that Bailey was ever poor). I made you captain. We are now becoming the winningest nation in hang gliding and I had a great deal to do with it. I could do with some support while I am getting chopped off at the knees.

I did not feel like eating shit for eighteen seconds, never mind eighteen months.

There was a row, and a lot of debate over my case. Len Gabriels wrote a long letter of protest, as did Len Hull, and Charlotte Murchison from America. Tony Fuell, who took the lawyer's role in the Abergavenny Six Affair in 1977, this time took my side, writing a strong article in condemnation, labelled 'J'Accuse!' This was a play on Victor Hugo's historical castigation of the French Establishment in the Dreyfus Affair at the end of the nineteenth century. But the article was so mangled by *Wings!* Editor Mike Hibbit when it was published that it had no effect. It was a bit much to think there was a community within British flyers anyway familiar with the Dreyfus case or Victor Hugo in France. Judy Leden, then new to the sport, knitted a sweater with the words 'Brian Milton is Innocent, OK!' on it and paraded it on every occasion.

Looking back on it, Judy was right. I was innocent. I was as much responsible for getting stiffed as Roy was. It is tough at the top, and these things happen from time to time. I fought a very poor campaign to try and save my name. I was inhibited by the constant thought that I should not be having to fight anyway, and that there were enough people on my side for whom I had done so much that the least they could do was ride to the rescue. But I should have seen it coming, and should never have been careless enough to miss even a minute of BHGA Council meetings. Derek Evans, one of my most powerful allies, had left council the previous year and I did not cultivate enough other allies, not even a newly elected fellow League pilot, Colin Lark. Of course, I did not know then Lark's special role in the whole affair.

To complete that part of the story, the Fosters Open was run in 1982 on the Isle of Wight, and secured some TV and newspaper coverage. *Wings!* reported that £21,000 was awarded in sponsorship, for which Barry Blore took the credit, and he and Roy had a big say in its spending.

Building a test vehicle for hang gliders took £5,000, a project that had dragged on for years and about which I had whinged in editorials. The sum of £1,000 went to buying a hang glider in Foster's colours, and £15,000 was spent on the Fosters Open. Most BHGA Council members were at the Isle of Wight, on expenses. So far as I know, none of the money went to competition pilots, except as prizes.

Fosters put up a much-reduced sum the following year, but the event attracted only two radio mentions, one of them local. Fosters then lost interest.

Hargreaves' ally, Stan Abbott, went on to become editor of *Wings!* for three years, and was paid a great deal more than the £80 a month I took. He was an excellent editor, more tabloid than me but he covered all the stories. He wrote that he hoped to be half as good an editor as I was, and was always fair in his coverage of what happened to me. But it is a measure of how little he really knew about the affair he had helped to ignite that he ran an appreciation of my work when I eventually resigned from the League, written by Roy Hill!

Roy Hill and Barry Blore, chairman and chief executive, became a close-knit team within BHGA, and formulated plans to move headquarters from Taunton in Somerset to Swindon, near where they both lived. They were considered so close-knit that Roy was removed in a sudden coup d'état at the 1983 AGM, an event that seemed to completely surprise him. I was asked a week before if I wanted to be present, but declined. I was sick at heart. The big clubs took their block votes and turned him out 288–96 in favour of a nice mild man called Percy Moss (who was soon awarded the MBE that Roy might have felt he deserved himself).

It turned out that Hill and Blore had come to arrangements with thirteen 'sponsorship agents' (not including me) to try and bring outside money into BHGA, without a single success. Blore pointed to the success of Fosters two years earlier, but he and Hill declined to answer when asked if the initial contact had come from the beer company. Financial arrangements with the thirteen agents never emerged. No one asked if the agents were on a retainer, a standard practice. The two men always seemed to run into the same problem, 'the inability to guarantee TV coverage'. Blore left BHGA service not long after his mentor, but Hill became BHGA vice-president for a couple of years. Ann Welch, in whom I at no time had the confidence to appeal, remained as president.

EVENTS AFTER 1980

Two years after the council vote of no confidence, I was driving back from a flying site in Somerset in Colin Lark's van. Lark was chairman of the Frocester HGC, and I had published his story about problems with the local gliding club in *Wings!* in 1980. He had also run a League competition at the end of that year, and was then emerging as a good XC pilot. I remember using my last waning powers as competitions chairman to successfully persuade the committee to add Lark's name to the already-selected squad to fly against the French in the 1981 Blériot Cup. Lark made the final team.

He used that journey to apologise for having proposed the motion of no confidence in me on BHGA Council, at that meeting from which I was barred! I had been so sick at heart I had not even checked!

'I don't even know, now, what it was you were supposed to have done wrong!' he said. He must have made a terrific speech to convince the others of his case.

He's dead now.

In August 1981, Keith Nichols, US Competitions Chairman, asked me over to Nevada to commentate on their Nationals, sponsored by Blue Stratos. Fiona and I both went; it was her first visit to America. I was treated very kindly, and met socially many of the pilots I had led teams against. Back home, I had no more role to play in British hang gliding, and maintained an interest only through flying in the National League, in which I did poorly. Derek Evans changed the style of competitions, relying more on the top pilots, and aside from the flyers themselves, much of the success I detail in the opening part of this chapter is due to his work. We obviously talked – he remained my bank manager until he retired years later – and he said once that it would never have been any good relying on competition pilots to have come to my rescue.

'They are selfish, and only care for themselves,' he said. 'That's why they are so good, because they are so single-minded.'

The American Cup was not run in 1981, and it must be obvious now why Britain did not continue to make a case for running the 1983 Worlds. But Derek pressed for the AmCup to be run in 1982. Tracy Knauss had lost a lot of money in the 1980 competition, and it had only succeeded because Charlotte Murchison, mother of Dave Murchison, Meet Director at the first two AmCups, had put up $10,000 of her family's own money. Tracy couldn't run the competition again, so Derek Evans offered to run an American Cup contest in the Yorkshire Dales in June

1982. An American team was to bring the AmCup with them, and the other nations invited were Canada, France, Brazil and Switzerland.

I began getting queries from the Americans. Was I doing anything in hang gliding? No. Would I consider coaching an American team? I had been more than a year away from anything to do with British teams. Why not? I was bored, and understandably bitter. I said yes.

One of the problems with American hang gliding, apparent back in 1978 (and still apparent today), is team selection. The USHGA grew out of the Southern California HGC, and that is where most pilots are and where power resides. In Britain, we had broken the power of manufacturers through the League, and wrested the right to select teams of our peers, the best choosing the best. In general, it worked, and has been widely copied. But not in the US, despite Pete Brock's ruthless and successful selection for the 1980 AmCup.

I was sent a very good team of six pilots, but they were not the best in the US. It was widely felt in the US (and in Britain) that any American team taking on the British in Britain would get pounded, so Rich Pfieffer, for example, absented himself from selection. The best gloss put on that was that Pfieffer was not a team man; I've heard different. One could argue that Rich Grigsby and Joe Greblo could also have been chosen. There were superb pilots among those that came, especially Jeff Burnett and Stew Smith, and future stars like Bruce Case, Chris Bulger and Mark Bennett. The sixth pilot, Doug Lawton, was a bit out of his depth. As team competitions are essentially decided by how your fifth and sixth pilots fly, this presented a formidable obstacle.

There was obviously a frisson of irritation that I had appeared on the scene again, this time on the side of the Americans. In Bailey's mind I suppose I was to remain in shit-eating mode for a while longer. But I needed help, and got it from Mike Atkinson and Keith Cockroft, two other League pilots who felt I had not been treated fairly. Mike's son, Neil, also pitched in. I picked up my team early from Heathrow, took them to the Dales, and spent a week helping them understand English conditions. They had to learn never to leave a thermal until it is dying, and about gaggle flying, which they rather looked down upon (they called it 'leeching', letting other pilots take the risks to find thermals).

The British chose a brilliant team: Bob Calvert, Graham Slater, Tony Hughes, Graham Hobson, Robert Bailey – all experienced AmCup flyers – plus a newcomer, former British dinghy champion Mike Macmillan.

EVENTS AFTER 1980

Mike was an expert on micro-meteorology, and was related to me by marriage (his sister married my wife's brother). Very strong teams were sent by other countries, including Brazil's Pepe Lopez, France's Mike de Glanville and three superb pilots from Canada. But the two teams who really understood team flying were the British and the Americans. The British were understandably very confident.

The whole atmosphere of the meeting changed, and the stakes were raised, when the Americans won the first task.

On the advice of Jeff Scott, a very tall American pilot who was reserve for the 1980 US AmCup team (and who later died of cancer), I had told Stew Smith to stick with Bob Calvert throughout the competition, and only leave him when Calvert was on the ground. This unsettled Calvert (to put it mildly), and rubbed off on the other British pilots. Once, Mike Atkinson and I were out picking up pilots, we found Calvert alone, without Stew Smith, and offered him a lift. Bob was beside himself with rage, and shouted back, 'Go pick up an Argentinian!' (the Falklands War had just ended).

It was a very tense competition, and it was always going to be between two teams, because of the strength of feeling. We were often at each other throats while other nations went on to win the day, but so long as we were first and second, it didn't matter.

Britain won the second day, after five Americans had left the hill in a fully overcast sky, when a solitary blue hole came through for ten minutes at 3pm, and they (and Stew Smith) went back with the resulting thermal. On the third day, in very light flying conditions, the Americans won again, and it would have put them back into the lead except that Tony Hughes flew an absolute blinder; it was his distance that determined the points, so the US margin over Britain was quite small (Derek Evans' face that evening was a picture of frustration and pain). On the fourth flying day, in lashing rain and low cloud, the Americans flew 'paired' with the British, and the British deliberately landed short, protecting their lead. My mistake. The Brazilians won that day, with the Swiss second, then Britain, Canada, the US and France.

Only one more day was flown, again in light conditions, which Canada won, closely followed by the US, then France, with Britain quite a long way behind. After that, the weather closed in. While flying was possible, Derek Evans – running the meet – felt it would not be fair to run a competition, because 'somebody could get lucky, and skill wouldn't count'. This was a reference to the Americans winning very marginal days, the sort of days that were a British speciality. So Britain won the American Cup back. Stan Abbott reported, 'But it's no walkover', and Ronnie Faux of *The Times* said, 'Britain were perhaps lucky the weather closed in.'

While waiting for this painful (yet oddly satisfying) competition to come to a conclusion, I vividly remember one day parked on top of Semerwater, the British team at one end of a line of vans, and the Americans at the opposite end, with all the other nations in between. Johnny Carr came down the road shouting, 'Bring on the B-Team!' He was winding up his own side because they had not cruised to the expected easy victory. We all laughed. We needed a jester then.

Stew Smith stayed with Bob Calvert until the last full day of flying, and said later:

> For me Calvert is obviously the best pilot in the Meet, and I have learned a lot from him. I stayed with him when there were clouds moving through and we were fairly high at about 3,000ft, but I didn't go over the back because Bob knows the country and he made his judgement not to go. Eventually I saw that Bob had spotted a hole in the sky upwind, followed by a low cloud-street that was going to cut the sun off, and that's when we both went for it.

Just to tweak noses, Stew Smith left Calvert on the last day of flying and went with Jeff Burnett to score well. It left Smith as the top individual pilot, the first (and only) time an American was top pilot in the American Cup, and the first of a number of victories that took Stew to the top of the hang gliding tree after years when he was not considered quite the best. A nicer man was never born.

At the next League competition my honorary membership was raised and queried. Was I really to be threatened because other countries offered me work I loved in hang gliding, when there was none at home? Was Jack Charlton, an Englishman, a traitor for coaching the Irish football team, when no one in the English football establishment would choose him to coach the England team? I resigned. I think everyone was relieved, including me.

There it all might have ended for me. I still flew hang gliders, but on fewer and fewer days. Later that year I moved from BBC Radio London

EVENTS AFTER 1980

(now GLR) into TV-am, the new commercial breakfast station, and lived through the early 'bloodbaths' to progress from behind screen to become a reporter, then industrial correspondent, then a financial presenter. Like many people, I could have drifted out of the sport. My life would have been completely different if I had.

In late 1984, I had another request to coach an American team, this time in the 1985 World Championships. I was flattered, two years after disappearing into a virtual hole in the ground, and said yes. At the same time, the hang glider manufacturer Solar Wings was the subject of a takeover, and part of the price for my shares was ownership of the company's trike, on which I learned again to fly. From that, I wrote the brochure to fly a microlight to Australia, which led to Kerry Packer, the Dalgety sponsorship, the flight itself, and my involvement in microlighting, which would not have happened without the American invitation.

I was all set to go to Kossen in June 1985, when BHGA Chairman Percy Moss phoned one night. After the usual pleasantries, and a certain wariness on my part, Percy said the BHGA were creating a new award, the highest in British hang gliding, to be called the National Trophy. It was to be presented by no less a person than HM Queen Elizabeth to the person who had done more for British hang gliding in its first ten years than anyone else. Percy said I had the unanimous nomination of BHGA Council!

'But Percy,' I protested, 'in three weeks' time I am going to be locked in combat, coaching the American team against you lot at the Worlds.'

'Yes, we know all that, but no other name came up. You're it.'

I said it would not make any difference to the commitment I would give the Americans, and Percy said of course not ... and of course, it didn't. It must have taken a great deal for Percy to make that phone call, because he was on that 1981 council when Roy Hill got Colin Lark to propose the no confidence vote in me. But it was also an honourable decision, which I appreciated.

After I received the trophy from the Queen, and British team pilots and I had indulged in some cheerfully aggressive badinage, I was standing at the end of a line along with other dinner-jacketed pilots when the Queen went walkabout. I believe she has a collection of stories to put everyone at ease, and sure enough, she had a hang gliding story. It concerned her Scottish home in Balmoral, and had to do with having a quiet time one day when a hang glider pilot whistled past the window and landed in the grounds! Apparently, the gardener removed him.

I had taken three or four glasses of wine by then, but it still was not enough for me to step forward and point a trembling finger at Robert Bailey, four to the left of me, and roar, 'There, Your Majesty, is the dastardly offender!' Bailey had indeed landed on the grounds of Balmoral in 1978, on an XC during the Scottish Open. If Her Majesty chose to describe his flight as whistling past her window, then Bailey had better re-cast his story.

(Since I was the first recipient of the National Trophy, the next three recipients were John Pendry, Robbie Whittall and Judy Leden, all FAI World Champions of hang gliding.)

The 1985 World Championships at Kossen are almost worth a book in themselves. They were the first to get rid of targets, and concentrated on a beautifully simple scoring system. Pilots were set XC tasks, all ending at Kossen landing area, but if they arrived and it was still soarable, they could fly around a 25km triangle as many times as possible, increasing their score. Each kilometre was worth two points, so the faster you completed the main course, the more time you had to notch up a higher score. Just to make it interesting, the landing area was worth fifteen points, or 7.5km.

The Americans sent nine pilots, ranked 1 to 9 on the US scoring system, from which I was to choose a team of eight. I wanted the leeway to make the final choice because that is how we had always done it in Britain, and how Pete Brock did it when the US won the AmCup in 1980. But there was a deep cultural divide of which I was never really aware at the time, between my British methods and the American way. All the US pilots felt they had already earned their place, and felt, down deep, that Mark Bennett, ranked ninth in the US, was the natural candidate to be dropped. I did not see it that way.

The US squad, aside from Bennett, was Rick Rawlings, Larry Tudor, Rob Kells, Steve Pearson, Rich Pfieffer, Stew Smith, Kevin Kernohan, and Chris Bulger. The US manager/coach was Jeff Burnett, and the support team was Walt Dodge and Luigi Chairani.

These were all very good pilots, but most of them achieved their scores in California, flying in what was called at the time 'fishbowl racing'.

'Out there,' Pfieffer told me, 'I am not concerned about the next thermal, or even the one after that. It's the third thermal I want to find!'

EVENTS AFTER 1980

In Kossen flying, thermals are more difficult to predict, there was a more complicated tactical game to play in the huge gaggles that formed over take-off, and essentially being aloft in the last gaggle with Moyes and Pendry was going to be the way to win. Again, Jeff Burnett and I went through this learning process, and early on, an embarrassing fact became obvious; Burnett was better than all the team pilots, except perhaps two, and yet he was merely the coach. I could not select him as a competitor.

We had other peculiar problems to overcome. The two latest Sensor 510s flown by Rich Pfieffer and Stew Smith had not gone through the US certification process. If this fact came out, both pilots could find themselves disqualified. We had to do the qualification tests actually at Kossen, using Rob Kells and Steve Pearson of Wills Wing, rival manufacturer as well as team pilots, and liaising with Mike Maier in California, also from Wills Wing. By a superhuman effort, especially on Pearson's part, we got the process completed, but it ate into our practice time, and also filled me with admiration for Pearson. He deserved that admiration, but it clouded my judgement of him as a competitor. I *wanted* him to be selected.

There was great effort to make the team work, again complicated by the fact that in the intense atmosphere of southern California flying, Rob Kells and Rich Pfieffer had not spoken a word to each other for three years! In such circumstances, Kell's efforts to certify Pfieffer's glider were even more extraordinary.

Right up to the time of deciding which pilot to drop, the favourite to go was Steve Pearson. He had not really come to terms with the peculiar Kossen conditions, and I think he knew it. But the day before the decision we met up with the British team, and I wanted to see how the American pilots compared with them. Derek Evans was managing a team consisting of John Pendry, Bob Calvert, Robert Bailey, Michel Carnet, Graham Slater, Johnny Carr, Ronnie Freeman, and Darren Arkwright.

Incidentally, this was the day that Rich Pfieffer had an unexpected response to the constant wind-up games he loved to play. He had met John Pendry at a previous competition, in which Pendry had a local girlfriend. Pendry's more permanent girl, Hilary Smith, was with the British team. Hilary has green eyes, long hair, and an unreconstructed accent right out of Thomas Hardy country, completely unaffected by the effects of twentieth-century media. She also has a formidable personality.

When Rich, who is no gentleman, called out in front of everyone that Pendry was not with the same girl he had been with previously, he obviously hoped to disturb Pendry's judgement. Instead, Pfieffer was fiddling with his harness a couple of minutes later when he was tapped on the shoulder. He stood up to face Hilary.

'Are you Rich Pfieffer,' she said in her rich regional tones

'Yes,' said Rich.

Hilary hauled back and walloped Pfieffer a perfect haymaker on the jaw, shaking him rigid. She then smiled sweetly.

'Well, I'm Hilary Smith, and I'm John Pendry's real girlfriend,' she said, and walked off.

Later that day one of the pilots asked Pfieffer, mock-innocently, if he had met Hilary Smith.

'We have,' he admitted, without conceding anything else, 'been introduced.'

I wanted to see how three of the American pilots, Rob Kells, Kevin Kernohan and Steve Pearson, flew against the British, one-on-one, because that was the only way I saw them making the final against the sort of opposition Kossen provided. I asked Pearson if he would stay with Bailey, but he said he would rather 'pin' Pendry. If he could succeed, that sounded great. I asked Kells to take Bailey, and Kernohan if he would fly with Calvert.

Of the three tasks, Kevin Kernohan's was the most difficult. Calvert hated being pinned, and was brilliant at scraping pilots off him in any number of ways, like coring sink to put his opponent low and then finding lift to get away to leave him on the ground. Calvert actively retaliated, whereas other pilots try to fly away from those pinning them.

Pendry set off, closely followed by Pearson, and I watched them both reach a big column thermal at the same height. To my delight, Pearson climbed through Pendry and sat above him, going a lot faster in the sky but *pinning* him. Calvert and Kernohan set off soon afterwards, as did Bailey and Kells.

It took time getting down the mountain to chase the three pairs we had set off (I wrote later in my report to the USHGA), so neither Jeff nor I was able to monitor developments. But we drove along the route, looking to see where our 'pairs' had ended up. Their brief had been simple. They would be judged solely on the distance that separated them from their British target. If they were ahead on the ground, that would be fine, but they should not be behind.

We found Rob Kells soon enough, with a thunderous-looking Bailey. Kells had put Bailey on the ground and still had 250ft in the air. He had maintained for a while and might have made the next designated landing field, but he had followed instructions, and won. At another field we found Pearson, to our delight, with Pendry. We were given to understand Pearson had pinned Pendry right into the field. But Kevin Kernohan had landed alone.

Kernohan was very honest about it. At one time, he was 50ft below Calvert, and the British pilot had flown low across a hill, with Kernohan unable to follow. They both circled on opposite sides of the hill, first one and then the other up. Kernohan said he had the chance to join Calvert at one time, but judged that the British pilot had no chance, so he flew on alone over the course and soon landed. Calvert, as he has done so many times, climbed out and flew another 20+ kilometres.

That night Jeff Burnett and I discussed who was to be dropped. Kells was definitely in, but our views changed on Pearson and Kernohan. On the one hand, we had – or thought we had – a pilot capable of staying with the favourite to win the World Championships. All we had to do was make sure he was in Pendry's heat, pin him on Pendry every day, and he would piggy-back through to the final. On the other hand, we had a pilot not very much better (in training) who did not follow instructions.

So we dropped Kevin Kernohan.

He did not take it very well. Kells, Bulger and Tudor took him off to Munich for a day in one of our buses to cope with his pain. I heard later various threats were made. Strangely, Steve Pearson also did not take the decision well, either. It was only in the final week of the competition that Walt Dodge was told (and told me) that Pearson had lost Pendry and landed, and that five minutes later Pendry had chosen Pearson's designated landing field to come down.

There was a possibility, unspoken but there, that Kevin Kernohan made a pact with himself that day. If the American team, without him, went on to produce a winner, he would accept it. But if not ....

At a team leaders' meeting while Kernohan was in Munich, the German leader, Manfred Moos, raised the point of landing in another country. Kossen, in Austria, was about 2km from Germany. Manfred had been Meet Director in the 1983 World Championships at Tegelburg, and in that competition, landing in another country scored zero. Karl Petutschnig, 1985 Meet Director, made an instant decision from the platform, and said landings in another country would give a pilot a zero. I told the US team the news, and warned them of the consequences, but did not conduct map sessions nor raise the point that Germany actually began within yards of one of the turn points.

The Austrians, being Austrians, wanted 1983 World Champion Steve Moyes to take an oath of sportsmanship on behalf of all the pilots. I cannot remember why or how I was drafted to write it, but I drifted around one night, asking a lot of pilots what they expected from the competition. It was the first time I talked to John Pendry. I woke up the following day with something representative of what they hoped for. In the light of what happened, there is a certain irony in my authorship:

Oath
Let this be a contest between man and man,
One to one,
Fair, free, friendly, open to the best of all who fly.
Let there be every quality of flying,
Except the going-down kind.
No stumbling, no falls,
Nothing broken, no loopholes,
Great flyers together,
And the best man and team to win.
Let the only friend any one of us has in high places
Be the One who opens the sky for us.
Let the contest reflect talent, genius, soul,
The ability to stay in the air,
The gift of reading the wind,
And not a paragraph of words that no one else has noticed.
Let this be a contest about the one who thinks best in the sky
And not the one rich enough to buy a better wing than others.
Let us go into this meeting agreed
To find one of us better than the rest
At staying the course
And covering the distance
In the only place any of us want to compete –
The sky.

EVENTS AFTER 1980

And let us be what we all want to be,
God's own children,
Closer to Him than others.
And may all of us stay that way,
And live to fly again another day.

About 180 pilots were divided into four groups, each with two pilots from each country, and each group self-contained for the first week. Then a cut was made, the top ten pilots in each group going into the final, with the scores from each group 'normalised', that is, the top score in each group is added together, divided by four, and then halved, with the half-score carried on into the next week. In this way, the organisers hoped to ensure that the competition was tight right to the end ... and it was.

My main story concerns Rich Pfeiffer's group, where he came head to head with John Pendry. This was rather like showing a hungry dog a large piece of meat, and Rich Pfieffer had a brain lock. In what was to be the longest (and therefore highest-scoring) task of the first week, Pfieffer raced Pendry around 138km, trying to establish dominance over the Englishman. On the final glide, Pfieffer watched Pendry land, flew further on himself, and was terribly pleased with himself until he tried to make a phone call. He found the phone box wouldn't take his money. He had landed in Germany!

We only gradually realised that despite the longest flight of the day, Pfieffer was on a zero. When I did, I fought tooth and nail against the decision. Every day I sent out two-man teams to various hills, and each day Pfieffer beat Pendry in the air while I wrestled with other team leaders to get Pfieffer's first-day score restored. The competition organisers, especially task setter Dr Jo Bathmann, were urging me on, because they thought Pfieffer a sublime flyer. Ironically, after what I wrote about 'Let the contest reflect talent, genius, soul, and not a paragraph of words that no one else has noticed', I found a paragraph in the FAI Sporting Code that prohibited new rules being introduced to FAI competitions within six months of that competition occurring. 'A zero for Germany' was obviously a new rule, actually published two days after Pfieffer's fatal flight, so I had a watertight case in law. But not in politics.

It should have been a very straightforward matter, a ruling based on the FAI code, but in the end it went to a vote, where a two thirds majority was required. Naturally (as I would have done), the British and Australians voted their national interest against the re-instatement, and I failed by one vote to get the required majority. A later attempt by the organisers to allow Pfieffer back by saying the top thirteen could go into the final (Pfieffer had clawed his way back to thirteenth) was neatly parried by Derek Evans threatening to withdraw the British team from the competition. A wonderfully Roman Italian team manager began calculating his national interest if that happened, but by this time the organisers threw in their hand. Pfieffer was out.

When the smoke cleared, I had lost, not only Pfieffer, but also Stew Smith, who lived in the same room as Pfieffer and whose flying was affected by all the attention we were paying to Rich. Five Americans made it through the cut, including Chris Bulger, who led his group, plus Rob Kells, Rick Rawlings, Larry Tudor, and Mark Bennett (who would have been out had I got Pfieffer's score reinstated, as he placed tenth in that group). Steve Pearson flew his heart out on the first day and landed in a terrible physical state; he never really showed for the rest of the week. Both Jeff and I had felt Pfieffer and Smith were our best pilots; we had lost them both.

The British team took seven pilots into the final (only Ronnie Freeman failed), while the Americans, Australians and Canadians took five pilots through. Adding up the scores, Bill Moyes threw a party to celebrate Australia winning team gold, on the dubious premise that the four best Australian scores (the first four counted) were better than the British could produce ... 'and we won't lose that lead in the coming week'. This euphoria lasted for twenty-four hours (I don't know why Bill does that; it doesn't dishearten anybody, but just makes his opponents more determined than ever to beat him).

The contest was essentially decided on one day's flying, the so-called Zillithal Run across a deep valley from a 6,000ft mountain, through a narrow neck and then out into the 'Racing Valley'. This was a straight 10km to a house on a mountain, and then back 135km at 10,500ft over Hitler's 'Eagle's Eyrie' at Berchtesgaden, and into the Kossen Valley to start making triangles.

My Americans lost Larry Tudor in the Zillithal Valley, and though Bailey, Carr and Arkwright also went down here, the British could afford to lose three so long as the other four scored highly, as they did. Two of them, Pendry and Carnet, actually made it to Kossen. The Canadians and Australians lost no one in the 'Zillithal Hole'. We found Chris Bulger on the ground halfway through the Racing Valley, and that effectively put the US out of contention for team gold.

The US pilots said later I had been too intense, put too much pressure on them, and had not enough sympathy when things went wrong. Kevin Kernohan, who had left the meet to go to Italy with his girlfriend, came back and expressed his own view on America's loss. One night, while I was sleeping, he kicked the door in and I woke to the unpleasantness of a systematic beating up. The following day, nursing a swollen fist, which he had smashed into a wall afterwards, he could not account for why he had done it.

John Pendry won the Worlds, with four British pilots in the top ten. Steve Moyes was a very close second, and Randy Haney of Canada third. Australia won team silver, and after an appeal on Haney's photographs, supported by Derek Evans, Canada were awarded team bronze over the USA. Ironically, the only US pilot who made the top ten was Mark Bennett, the so-called reserve, who placed tenth.

Afterwards, there was a private ceremony in which Rich Pfieffer was awarded a trophy that read 'Weltmeister im Hangegleiten', which reads 'World Champion of Hang Gliding'. Pfieffer had beaten Pendry on every day except one, but that first day's task remained a zero. But Pendry was a worthy World Champion.

Later that summer, I was appointed Meet Director of the US Masters of Hang Gliding, invited as a form of atonement for Kernohan's behaviour by Hugh Morton, owner of Grandfather Mountain. Most of the competition was rained out. Stew Smith, resident flyer there, said I took too much of the blame for the US defeat on myself. But a coach has to take the brickbats if he takes the plaudits, and once upon a time I had received the plaudits.

After that, I concentrated on microlighting, eventually raising the money to fly a microlight called the Dalgety Flyer to Australia, for years the longest, fastest microlight flight in history. It included being wrecked on a Greek island called Kythira but gluing the aircraft back together and flying on. On Christmas Day I landed in the Persian Gulf in the middle of the Iran–Iraq war, but rescued the aircraft after six hours in the sea and gluing it together again and flying on six days later. In both situations, my mechanic was Mike Atkinson, making the journey on a first-class airliner seat to the capital of every country I flew through, ready to help me if things went wrong. Michael had been a key part of the team I put together in Yorkshire to try and win the American Cup for the American team.

On my return from Australia, I heard about the young Robbie Whittall, and sold Yorkshire TV the idea of a half-hour feature on him, to be screened before the 1989 Worlds in Fiesch in Switzerland.

Robbie is the son of another hang gliding pioneer, Noel Whittall, who, while not as distinguished as Bill Moyes, still had a big part to play in British hang gliding. He was, for a time, BHGA Chairman, and though never a real competition pilot, followed British teams abroad as a supporter. He was the first British pilot to settle in a tree in the 1978 AmCup. Noel must have been delighted when his second son, who left school at 16 to become a printer, was three years later one of the favourites to win the World Championships. Most hang gliding champions are in their early 30s, and take years to discover the mixture of guile, knowledge and physical skill to win against the best. Robbie, a raw force if ever there was one, flew whenever he could with John Pendry, and spent some time with the Moyes Boys in Australia.

Most pilots know why they are good, and can explain where they find lift. Robbie, like a genuine artist, had a fantastic gift, but never formulated it in words. Asked why he flew to one place to find lift, he said he just expected it to be there, and it was. Other pilots look at brown fields, or cloud formations, or the shape of hills. Robbie just seemed to know, in the way a great artist knows how to paint. He knows how to fly, and one day would become the first man to win two Royal Aero Club gold medals, and he would still not be 25 years old!

British sports journalists will not recall the 1989 World Hang Gliding Championships. It was during a particularly bad period for English cricket, playing against the Australians, and the journalists were vying with themselves to see who could most wittily dismiss England as a land full of wimps. Some of them were very witty indeed.

About 600 miles away from those green English pitches in Switzerland, blood was being spilt. The weather had been highly unsuitable all the way through the World Championships, with strong northerlies. To imagine the effect of such winds in mountains, think of a rushing stream over sharp stones, and look at the eddies and whirlpools that are produced. The same thing happens with air. Before the competition began a Brazilian pilot was killed and a Korean broke his neck in accidents, being whacked into the ground. Neither were competitors, but neither were novices either.

There were at least four tumbles and parachute deployments. One was by Jess Flynn, 1989 British Champion, flying in apparently smooth air with one hand off the bar adjusting the radio, when he hit severe turbulence and barrel-rolled. He hit and broke an upright on the triangle control bar on the way over, and while lying in the sail contemplating the damage at about 400ft AGL, had the presence of mind to throw his parachute.

'I lay in the sail,' he explained later, 'and had a look around to see if it was worth flying down, but decided against it and threw my chute.'

Flynn, who looks like an eighteenth-century pirate with his flaming red hair and beard, landed unhurt halfway up the mountain. He had transmitted a message on the way down, but because he sounded so calm no one took very much notice. After de-rigging his glider and bundling up his parachute, he climbed over the mountain, only to find that the cable lift had closed. Unable to convince the operator to restart it (you have to do something serious to merit that), Jess spent the night in a hotel and travelled back to competition HQ the following day.

Despite the radical conditions, including thunderstorms, the competition got to a cut, and four of the six British pilots – Pendry, Whittall, Goldsmith, Flynn – got through. Five Australians also made it, and five Americans. Peter Harvey, one of the two British pilots who failed to get through, was later awarded an International Olympic Committee medal for outstanding sportsmanship. On one task he saw a Japanese pilot who had thrown his 'chute and landed in a tree. Harvey spiralled down, sacrificing time and several thousand feet to check that the pilot was OK. The Japanese pilot was fine, but Harvey was unable to climb out and continue. His absence and that of Darren Arkwright meant the Australians had a team advantage, which, in the traditional way of Australians, they rubbed into the British at every opportunity.

On the last day of flying, conditions were terrible. The north wind continued to blow over mountains and hit a north-facing slope on an east–west valley, along which pilots were expected to fly to complete a 126km out and return task. Individually, Robbie Whittall was leading the competition, just a few points ahead of the brilliant emerging young Czech, Tomas Suchanek, and Pendry was lying third. All four British pilots were in the top twenty, but the Australians were flying tightly as a team, and had established what looked like an unbeatable 400-point lead. Bill Moyes was backing Suchanek for all he was worth to win the individual title, because Suchanek was flying one of his wings ... and anyway, the alternative was a Pom winning (if it is very heaven for Englishmen to beat Australians, the reverse is also true. Foreigners may think Australians are actually Englishmen who have been six generations under another sun, but *they* don't actually acknowledge that).

The problem with the wind direction is that, with a northerly, it gave ridge lift on the shadow side of the valley, while the sun was popping thermals on the opposite south-facing side. But the south-facing side was in rotor, with air tumbling down the mountain, punctuated by thermals popping up, rather like a hot plate boiling water inside a washing machine. At the briefing, pilots were told the northerly winds were 'quite strong'. 'How strong is quite strong?' asked a concerned pilot. 'Quite strong,' came the reply, 'is very strong.'

When the 'window' opened and pilots were allowed to fly, the German team took a collective decision to fly 10km into the valley and land. It was, they said firmly, too dangerous. Larry Tudor, the distinguished OV Racer, also landed for prudence sake; the US team was lying third in the competition, with no hope of catching the first two, Britain and Australia. The two leading nations were virtually at each other's throats, waiting to pick a time for take-off. The tactics of the Australian team – Steve Moyes, Drew Cooper, Mark Newland and Steve Blenkinsop – should have been obvious, to stick, man for man, with the British. Bill Moyes was watching like a hawk, with sharp instructions to cover every British move. Jess Flynn rigged among the Australians to let the rest of the British team know what was going on, much as I had put Stew Smith among the British team in the last American Cup, to discombobulate them. But the Australians did not follow the classic tactic.

In this fraught atmosphere, Robbie Whittall, John Pendry and Bruce Goldsmith moved to the front of take-off. A few words on the radio and the Australian gliders were shuffling forwards. A thermal came through. Off went Jess Flynn and the Australians. Ten minutes later, Whittall said, 'I think we've blown it, boys.' Just then a bird started circling, and off they went, the words of Bill Moyes on the radio to his team fading in their ears, 'All four Poms in the air now.' The scene at take-off became serene with the draining away of all that tension.

EVENTS AFTER 1980

Most pilots went down about a quarter way along the course, though fighting all the way, unlike the Germans. They chose the north-facing slope where the wind provided ridge lift, but it was of a fickle and turbulent quality. Except for Steve Blenkinsop, all the Australians went down at 30km, along with Jess Flynn. Goldsmith and Pendry set out to fly along the north-facing side, while Robbie, who had to beat Suchanek to have any chance of the title, took the much more risky south-facing slope, on which the sun shone.

The rotor was terrible. Once, over the Aletch Glacier, Whittall was tumbled so strongly, rotated head over heels, he and the kite together, that the bar was torn out of his hands. The tumble was so fast that he just had time to grab the bar as it went by. There were sail deflations, he banged his heels repeatedly on the keel, and at one particularly dreadful moment a tip-strut broke and dangled from the leading edge, which meant Whittall's wing had lost one of its means of pulling naturally out of a screaming dive. Unbelievably, he continued.

All this time Whittall was in radio contact with Pendry and Goldsmith. They could hear his strained and heavy breathing, his curses and groans, and every now and again his wild shouts, 'I'm getting killed out here!' But they also noted that Whittall kept in the air and was struggling past where most pilots had been sent to the ground. They could hear Whittall's agony, and Jess Flynn was now on the radio to say that most of the Australians were on the ground.

There was only one way they could beat the Australian team, and that was for Pendry and Goldsmith to retreat back up the valley to take-off and take the route Whittall was being half-killed on. That is what they did!

What were they going to gain from this decision? Money? There were no cash prizes. Fame? Given the lack of interest among Britain's sporting media, that is a joke! Honour? Yes, I guess so, certainly other top hang glider pilots would know what they had done. The Australian team would know, and so would Bill Moyes. There was a strong element of, we are not going to let Australia beat us, and if we have to take this route and risk being thrashed into the mountain to stop that happening, that is the way of it. They had also been deprived, by distance, of reading in British newspapers that morning about how wimpish the British really were.

Bruce Goldsmith said later that he and John Pendry did little talking to each other. For hour after hour, mutely, they flew for their lives, sails rattling harshly above them, heels crashing on to the keel, hand-standing on the bar as rotor and rough thermals threw them around the sky. They fought their way for five murderous hours over the course ... and landed just short of goal. But they finished fifth and seventh on the day. Tomas Suchanek also fell just short. Robbie was one of only three pilots to make it to goal; the others were Paulo Coelho of Brazil and Markus Mittelberger of Austria.

Robbie Whittall became, at 20 years of age, World Champion. These were the other top ten in 1989: Suchanek (Czech), Pendry (GB), Coelho (Bra), Blenkinsop (Aus), Goldsmith (GB), Haney (Can), Cooper (Aus), Bostik (US) and Steve Moyes (Aus). That flight, as Goldsmith and Pendry knew better than anyone, was enough to overturn the Australian 400-point lead, and leave Britain world team champions by a margin of 1,400.

Bruce Goldsmith, my protégé, weary but with deep satisfaction, told me most of the story that night. Then he gave the phone to Bill Moyes. I could hear the sounds of drinking and laughter in the background from the bar where they had found a place to call me. We discussed the formation of a Superleague, a World Series of hang gliding, on which I was later to lose $55,000 trying to get started. Bill admitted then, fair and square, that his boys had been out-flown by the Poms. There were no excuses.

'Your boys did well,' said Bill Moyes.

My boys!

Chapter 7

Deaths, and All That

Now, let us consider the deaths.

In the mid-1970s, the death label was pinned on hang gliding by a media that nearly convinced the public that merely to get into a hang glider was to die. Wherever we have gone since, however high we have soared or far we have flown, the question always has been, 'Uh, yeah, but did anybody die?'

And the answer is, yes, they did. What enrages me is that no one asks what they died for, and why. They made mistakes and paid the ultimate penalty, but they were not fools to dream of flying.

Look through the list of flyers who died in the 1920s after the heroic first age of aviation and the First World War. It goes on and on: from France, Nungesser, Coli, Begrin, Casal, de Precourt, Manyrol; from the USA, Rodgers, Stinson, Bettis, Sperry; from England, Brancker, Thompson; from Australia, Ross Smith, Mackintosh ... some of the hundreds who died violently in the air. Historians write of the 'long struggle to achieve the Conquest of the Air', and the sacrifices made.

There were, of course, no sacrifices made. Men risked their lives. And lost.

They did not give their lives. Their lives were taken away, by chance, because of an error in the air, poor manufacture, the weather. But though each death was mourned, it was judged worth the effort because of what was being gained, the so-called conquest of the air.

In the New Aviation, we don't want to conquer the air. We want to live in it.

Why are our deaths so much less honoured than deaths in the mainstream, or even honoured at all?

And let us be reasonable about death, anyway. It is just the end of life. It will happen to us all. Like taxes, it is eternal. Look across the tube train, walk down a street, fall in love, ride your bike, get promoted, lose your job, and you know that all around you will die. You, your mum, your dad, your child, one life and then it ends. Life is not a rehearsal. You don't get a second one.

I think the Victorians lived with death more closely than we do, and understood it better. They were shy about sex, which we are not, but not about death, which these days we try to avoid talking about. Have you noticed the slang we use to say someone has died? Bought the farm, popped his clogs, turned his toes up, gone west, pushing up daisies, copped it, had his chips, passed on – as if to pretend it hasn't happened?

There is a temporary alternative, of course. It involves finding one day that your son can beat you in a hundred-yard sprint, as you once beat your dad the same way. You can lose your hair, become hard of hearing, feel your eyesight failing, get used to your teeth falling out. You can watch muscles once round, smooth and efficient, wrinkle up and weaken. You can puff to the top of a hill and stagger a few yards before stopping to mumble, well, it wasn't worth catching the bus anyway. You can speak and hear your words fade into the ether, where once they were hung on. You can peer, frightened, through a half-open door secured by a chain at whoever might call. You can spend most waking hours filled with apprehensions, your mind full of events of forty years ago, and those memories fading anyway.

You can have all this to look forward to! Don't smoke, lay off the drink, be careful crossing roads, don't over-exert yourself, always be moderate in your tastes, put aside your savings for a rainy day or to 'enjoy the twilight of your years'. Why, if you do all this, never take a risk and you're lucky, you might get to be 85 years old!

These delights are denied to those who die young. Those whose luck, for that one fleeting second, runs out on them while they are stretched to the limits, invigorated, everything working, going over the top, reaching for the sky, just over that next peak … and they are killed. These unfortunates miss an old age.

Do you know of Enoch Powell? Greek scholar, Cabinet Minister, 'Rivers of Blood' speech, maverick, denied a peerage, once asked his ambition, replied, 'To have been killed in the Last War.' One wonders how many old men feel the same?

Do you recall the words of Rebecca Ridgeway, on that canoe adventure with her father?

DEATHS, AND ALL THAT

'You feel so alive you think you can never feel it again. So you want to go back to see if you can find that aliveness once more.'

Like anyone else, pilots in the Mainstream as well as the New Aviation, I do not want to die. But risking death is the price we pay if we want to fly.

It is, after all, an ethical equation. Lawyers will tell you otherwise, but you cannot get something for nothing. Not even in America.

To achieve the pleasure, the sheer surging charge of flight that happens each time we lean forward to run into the air, the risk we accept is that something could go wrong and kill us. It is because of the price we could be charged for our daring that our flying life is so much sweeter.

Aside from Alvin Russell, I have avoided until now focusing on the deaths in the New Aviation. They are too easily, in too facile a way, fecklessly brought up by journalists.

Unless you are able to understand where we are trying to go, I don't think we really accept your right to ask us about the risk. You cannot say to us, 'isn't it dangerous?', without knowing what 'it' is. And as we move from ground-skimming 196ft to Larry Tudor's 300-mile flight, and the poetry and wonder and awe in between, I think we want you to understand that those we lost on the way are mourned. But we all know that can be the price any one of us might pay.

Mainstream Aviation coined the phrase, 'There are old pilots, and bold pilots, but no old, bold pilots.' Well, there are.

Most of the people whose accounts of flight you have read here are still alive, and still have the dream. By our very nature we will not be able to betray that dream by turning flight into mere transportation. The end result of a hang glider will never be a Jumbo Jet. It is the experience of getting somewhere, rather than arriving, that we want from flying. We are going the other way to Mainstream Aviation, to turn what we know into an even purer form of real flying. But I wish you to know something, outside of what passes for journalism and media images about the New Aviation, about how many have died to get us to where we are, and who some of them were when they were among us. It would be shameful if you did not know that, because you would not know, as we do, who paid the price for us to get where we are. And there is still a price to be paid for where we want to go ...

No one pulls together the worldwide fatality rate in hang gliding or other branches of the New Aviation. About the best accident accounts, covering the most flyers, are those from hang gliding in the United States. The nearest we get to world figures came from Robert Wills in California, father of Bob and Chris Wills. Robert kept the records on those in our world to die. Tragically, one of his statistics was his eldest son.

Taking the twenty years from the First Lilienthal Meet in 1971, when there were two hang gliding deaths in the United States, to 1991, when there were nine, we are able to see where the risks were and which were the worst years for taking them. These are the US hang gliding fatalities in detail:

Year	Foot	Tow	Tandem	Total
1971	2			2
1972	4			4
1973	9			9
1974	40			40
1975	32			32
1976	38			38
1977	24			24
1978	23			23
1979	30			30
1980	22	1		23
1981	16	5		21
1982	11	1		12
1983	11	3		14
1984	4	4		8
1985	6	1	2	9
1986	5			5
1987	17	1		18
1988	10	2 (2)		12
1989	6			6
1990	5	3		8
1991	5	2	2	9

The worst years were in the 1970s. For two thirds of that decade we did not have parachutes. The fastest development out of steerable 'chutes and into wings also occurred during that period. When Roy Haggard's Comet arrived in the middle of 1980, a real wing with high performance, fatalities, with the exception of 1987, started to fall. Mainstream Aviation also produces isolated poor years when a string of fatal accidents happen for no logical reason. France had a dreadful year for microlight fatalities, for example, in 1988.

Taking a year at random, because Robert Wills chose it to compare US fatalities with deaths outside the US, sixty-three people were killed in 1979, thirty-three non-American. In his investigation, Brazil, with 500 pilots, reported one death in 1974, one in '76, one in '77, eight (!) in '78, and one in '79. Yugoslavia (most of the country's 150 pilots lived in Slovenia) reported four deaths to '79. Australia, home of the Moyes Boys with 1,500 pilots, lost eleven in '77, four in '78, and three in '79.

Looking at British figures for hang gliding alone in 1983, separated from microlighting and with paragliding still a distant dream, there were 106 reported accidents and four deaths among 4,000 flyers. The four died in the following way: one landed in the sea after losing lift, and drowned; one clipped into the wrong part of the hang strap so his weight rested on the stitches, which came apart in a high banked turn and he fell 300ft; one was a wire-man helping a pilot on a cliff launch, but he fell over the cliff himself; one didn't clip in before take-off and could not hold on.

This is how Doug Hildreth, who took over from Robert Wills as USHGA Accidents Reviewer, reported on the year 1991:

> There were nine fatalities in 1991 among an estimated 11,000 US flyers. It should have been better, but it wasn't. Unfortunately, two fatalities were tandem students. The last tandem student fatality was in 1988.
>
> I almost subtitled this report, 'The Year of the Dumb Mistake'. There were 10 – yes, TEN – reported failures to hook-in. Two of these were fatalities. And in the same vein, there was a fatality because the pilot failed to put his feet through the leg straps of the harness. There were three incomplete assemblies of wings, or inadequate pre-flights, with a very near-fatality. There was one fatality from aerobatics at 200ft. The pilot purposely (for better performance) left the 'remove before flight' cover over his rocket parachute deployment handle. A pilot 'crashed safely' into a cliff, where his glider was firmly stuck, then

unhooked to climb the cliff and fell to his death. The two towing fatalities were directly related to fundamental errors during the early phase of the towing process.

Pilots continue to launch, slow down, and turn back into the hill. Or launch, look down at the harness, stall and turn back into the hill. We keep flying into things (27). There were three mid-air collisions, one with a paraglider.

Crashes on landing are still double those on launch. My biggest hope is that the new sure-flies-real-slow-and-lands-sooo-easy gliders will help the crash on landing problems, and reduce the number of broken arms.

Parachutes are still saving lives – 10 reported deployments. Twenty-three per cent of pilots have a ballistic (rocket-propelled) parachute. Only 5 per cent of pilots do not have parachutes, and virtually all of them are on the training hill. It still appears that early deployment is best. The injuries relating to deployment and descent under canopy remain few.

(Hang glider parachutes descend with both the pilot and the wing together. The majority of parachutes are kept in a bag on the pilot's chest or stomach. To deploy, the pilot grabs a handle, rips the 'chute out of its pouch and throws it as far as he can in a deployment bag. At full stretch the bag springs apart, the 'chute opens and pilot and glider swing underneath, so the pilot lies on the upside-down wing. The wing hits the ground first, absorbing the energy of the descent. The pilot normally just has to unclip and stagger away, considering whether or not to take up the priesthood.

Rocket 'chutes are fixed to the keel and can deploy in half a second so long as the pilot activates it quickly enough.)

Those are the numbers. How did they die? This is Hildreth's full 1991 US fatality list, following investigation:

Lynn Smith, 37, novice, 70 flights with 11 from mountains. Flying Lookout Mountain, GA, hooked in, did a hang check. Straps not straight, so he unhooked, straightened them and re-hooked. Reportedly, at least three different hang checks were done, with at least one un-hook. Pilot launched, popped the nose up slightly, dived to recover, and about halfway through the pull-out the pilot fell from the glider. Was either not hooked in, or hooked into something other than his hang loop.

Harold Austin, 37, advanced, 23 years' experience including 400 tows. Flying at Mt Pleasant, Michigan, foot launched behind a tow-truck with high nose angle, as was his habit. Immediately after launch, a lock-out occurred to the right at 90 degrees, which the pilot corrected. During this correction, with the pilot's hands on the left side of the control bar, the lower bridle (on the tow line) hooked over the left stub axle (on the control bar) which was an extension of the base tube (wheels were absent). The pilot was unable to correct the left turn or release the line, and dived in from 75ft.

Karen Schenk, 26, advanced hill-launcher, 7 tow launches. Flying at Big Spring, Texas, her truck tow-launch was hurried because others had been able to go XC and she was anxious to follow. Immediately after leaving the truck bed, the pilot asked for increased winch pressure (a technique usually reserved for greater than 500' of altitude). She then asked (by radio) for a second increase of winch pressure. At 75ft she entered a lock-out, released from tow, stalled and dived into the runway.

[If you have ever flown a child's kite you will know what a 'lock-out' is, when the kite dives off right or left and whacks into the ground – BM].

Mark Kerns, 41, advanced. Flying Wasatch State Park, Utah, he forgot to put legs through leg straps of cocoon harness. In flight, slipped through and was able to hold on for several seconds, but then could hold on no longer and fell 200ft.

Eddie Hunter, 31, novice, returned to launch after first flight in Marlboro, Kentucky. He had desperately wanted to soar, but agreed with advanced pilots in the LZ (landing zone) that he should not return to the launch alone. But he did, and utilising an inexperienced wire crew, he attempted to launch into a 20 mph wind, stalled and turned back into the cliff face. Glider impacted the cliff, and hung there firmly. Pilot called up to spectators that he was OK. A short time later the pilot yelled 'help!' and then silence. Apparently, he had unhooked and tried to climb the cliff unaided, and fell to his death 200ft below.

Leonard Rabbitz, 55, intermediate. Flying Elizabethville, Pennsylvania, pilot's hang straps were draped over the keel. To be hooked in, the carabiner had to go through four loops. He only hooked into two (on one side only). Right after launch, pilot fell on to base-tube, glider dived into trees and he was thrown to his death.

Jan Jefferson, student, 35, first flight, tandem at Montague, California. Experienced tandem tow pilot towed up and then released. The pilot dropped a teddy-bear with a six-foot diameter parachute. The pilot lost sight of the bear, turned back to where he thought it should be, and as he levelled out the glider flew into the bear, with bear and parachute catching on the right lower flying wire. The parachute initially deflated. But at 300ft, as the pilot turned on to finals, the parachute re-inflated. The glider instantly rolled to 90 degrees and side-slipped into the ground. Passenger was killed instantly. Pilot sustained severe injuries.

John Powell, advanced, flying at Waikee in Hawaii, was performing wing-overs past 90 degrees at about 200ft altitude, stalled and side-slipped into vertical dive. He had to remove safety cover on his parachute before pulling the firing handle. The rocket fired 20ft before impact.

Michael Elliott, 27, novice, at Lookout Mountain, GA, went tandem with experienced tandem pilot in preparation for first solo altitude flight. Passenger was nervous prior to the flight. On base leg of landing approach, flying crosswind over the tree-line, the attempt to turn on to finals was unsuccessful. The inability to make the turn may have been caused by thermal activity (warm bubble of air under one wing), the passenger interfering with glider control, or both. The glider continued straight, hit a tree and side-slipped 60ft. The novice passenger died, the tandem pilot seriously injured.

DEATHS, AND ALL THAT

None of those fatal accidents occurred because of a failure of the airframe or wing. They can all be attributed, one way or another, to pilot error. In the early 1970s when we bodged things together to get into the air, there were failures of the airframe or design faults in the wing. But there are so many tests nowadays before a hang glider gets out on to a hill that equipment failure is rare. You can get wings broken up in radical conditions, as Liavan Mallin discovered, but she knew before she went into the Owens Valley that she could meet conditions like that, and the pilot who tried to help her threw his 'chute and landed safely. Back-up parachutes have saved hundreds of lives (I threw mine during my 250ft fall on my Soarmaster-type accident in front of TV cameras in 1978, but I was too close to the ground for it to deploy in time. It is likely to have been caught in the propeller, anyway. I still have it, but have never used it since. Search 'Brian Milton hang gliding accident' for the YouTube pictures of the event.)

From the beginning all accidents were thoroughly investigated and design faults in our wings were written out. Each of our national magazines carried these reports, and lessons to be learned. In Britain, the BHGA accidents investigation officer was John Hunter, who used to go out on to the lonely hills and pick up the pieces after things went wrong, and painstakingly work out what happened. Teaching methods, in particular, were monitored, through the work of Alvin Russell, Keith Cockroft and Bob Harrison, a succession of flying and training officers who policed every school in the country, and withdrew permits to teach if standards were not high enough. As the years went by, it became rare for an accident to occur except for one reason, pilot error. And the only sure way to get rid of pilot error is for pilots not to fly in the first place.

Looking at a 1977 report in *Hang Gliding* magazine about the first National Championships – 'Annie Green Springs' – in 1973, of the thirty-six competitors and standbys, within five years six had already been killed. These were the best and the brightest in the US at the time. Among those who survived are famous names like Dave Kilbourne (first man to soar), Chris Price, Dave Cronk, Chris Wills, Tom Peghiny and Peter Brock.

The most famous of the competitors to die, and the news stunned the whole world of hang gliding so we all went into mourning, was Bob Wills, brother of the 1973 Champion, Chris Wills.

WILD ADVENTURES OF THE NEW AVIATORS

Bob Wills was the first hang gliding superstar; no one since has reached his stature. We all knew him, or knew of him, or even thought we knew him. He was tall, California cool, and a superb flyer. He did the flying stunt work in four movies, including *Sky Riders*. Sequences like 360-ing at 600ft, hanging upside down with his legs draped over a trapeze, 6ft below a hang glider. Well, who else could do that? He stood in for film star James Coburn, and the sequence where Coburn 'learns' to fly, acted by Bob, is a complete delight to watch as he nonks the wing all over the place, looking as if he knew nothing, while in complete control.

Bob Wills came to England only once, in 1975, immediately after shooting *Sky Riders*. He and his brother Chris and their friend Chris Price turned up at our national championships at Mere in Wiltshire, a 200ft bowl with targets at the bottom. Of course, he won the competition, but as Tony Fuell, a future League pilot who was marshalling the target, will tell you at the drop of a hat, in what style!

> Since every pilot was allowed three goes at the spot, it wasn't surprising that a huge queue developed at the takeoff. Or that there was a fair amount of pushing and shoving in the queue. It was then, at that rather fraught moment, that England became aware the Yanks had arrived.
>
> At the back of the queue appeared three gliders. But not ordinary Rogallos. These things were, like, exotic! They had huge control frames for a start. They stood high off the ground. They were all black. And strangest of all, next to them stood some HUGE pilots.
>
> I stand about 6ft nothing, and as I walked through the seething mob of kites to look at these new arrivals I felt like a midget. I was grabbed by one of them and found myself looking at his chest as a voice from up above somewhere inquired, 'Say, Mac, howja make a score in this crummy comp anyway?' Patiently, I explained the rules for the 25th time and went on down to the landing area.
>
> Gliders were bombing out of the sky in all directions. Some were getting on the spot and some were not. Some pilots were accepting the marshal's decision and some were not. Some people never even made it to the damned field and still wanted points for their stand-up landings!

DEATHS, AND ALL THAT

All in all it was pretty busy down there, and it went on and on. And ON and ON and ON. Lunchtime came and went, and I was still there. Hours passed by. On the radio, 'Next one!' 'Here he comes' 'Look out – duck!' 'Get his score' ... on and on.

At some point in that endless afternoon, I became aware that one of the big black Swallowtails was taking off. It flew over our heads. What the hell was going on? Most gliders were desperately trying to conserve height just to make their landing approach, yet this guy looked as if he had plenty to spare. He set up his approach, smack-on, skimmed over the ground towards the circle, pushed out, down, a stand-up landing about two feet away from the centre.

I took the tape towards his feet. 'Really good!' I said, 'Only 2 points – 24 inches – off a maximum'; we were giving everybody 100 points for the landing, minus the number of feet (and inches) they were away from the centre. 'What's your name?'

'Baab Wills' (At least it sounded like that). 'Say buddy,' he continued, 'howja make a max?'

'A what?'

'Ya know, a Max. Max-out the score. High points, all that?'

(I got the feeling he was treating me like a nice, but stupid person ...)

'Oh, well, max is 100 points, see, and we knock off one for every foot away from the centre stake, and count inches in decimal places.'

Silence.

'Can ya make a Max 100 points?'

'Well,' I said, thinking fast, 'you'd have to be real good. I mean, you'd have to do a stand-up landing, under control, and land on one foot on top of the centre skewer.'

That'll fix you, you Yank pillock, I thought. Now get out of my hair, and let's get on with the rest of this charade ... I had had enough of hang gliders at this point.

'Oh yeaaah?' (God, is he still here?)

'Yes, now PLEASE get off the spot!'

'Waal, maan. Ah guess it's possible at that.'

And with that Bob Wills disappeared from my perception, and we got on with our separate lives, him to de-rig and walk up the hill, me to carry on measuring throughout the long afternoon.

The next time I saw him was when the black glider approached the spot for a second time. A little higher now, but still flown impeccably, very smooth, lower, lower, over the edge of the circle, a HARD flare, six feet up, the glider stuck its nose way up, and stopped ...

A swooshing sound, and a hard SLAPP! Bob was standing in the centre of the circle. On one foot. The control frame was off the ground. He wobbled a bit and then got it under control.

I ran in with the tape. One giant (and rather dirty) sneaker had obliterated the skewer in the dead centre of the circle. It was so central that the skewer holding the tape was under the ball of his foot. The other foot was waving violently in the air as he fought to keep it off the ground, and the glider balanced.

Just for a moment, neither of us could believe it. We looked at each other. I felt a grin break out on my face.

'I did it, right?' he said.

'Yes, you did!'

All around us, other marshals were running in to look. I said to them, 'We'll have to give him a max score for that!'

No one disagreed. We got on the radio and told the commentary box. Soon the sound of distant cheering floated down from the hill-top, as the crowds got the message.

I never saw Bob Wills after that. We passed by later in the competition and I watched, awed, while he and Chris Price put on the very first aerobatic hang glider display ever seen in England, but I didn't speak to him again.

Of course, it was a fluke. No one could have been that good, could they? To land, on one foot, under control, dead centre of the spot? Well, it happened. All of us in the landing area were aware that we had just seen something magic happen. One man's concentration, ability and courage had put him EXACTLY where he wanted to be.

DEATHS, AND ALL THAT

I was in the commentary box that year when Tony Fuell passed up the message about Bob Wills's one-footed bullseye, and at the prize-giving afterwards. I never spoke to any of the American flyers (what could I have said to demi-gods?) but that day they confirmed the myth of American invincibility that we found so hard to shake off.

On 24 June 1977, Bob Wills was blown into the ground from 80ft by a helicopter while filming a Jeep commercial. The helicopter broke pattern and left a wake of lethal turbulence, into which Bob flew. Chris Price, the man who stuffed his hang glider up Rich Pfieffer's bum when Pfieffer tried to scare him out of a thermal, was Bob's lifelong friend:

> I can remember when I was 8 years old, arguing with Bob Wills about whether or not animals went to heaven. He argued then that all living things went to heaven. I can remember spending the night at his house, and when his mother Maralys tried to kiss all of us good night, each one of us threw a huge fuss. The trips to Disneyland and the beach in his mother's Cadillac. The orange fights in the groves. Underground forts. All the filters and equipment for his asthma.
>
> Once one of his rabbits had worms growing out of its head and looked terrible. I wanted to whack its head off with a shovel and put it out of its misery ... and I did just that. Bob could not believe I had killed it because, he said, I had no way of knowing whether it might have gotten better.
>
> Bob was a forgiving, optimistic person who never held a grudge. He would always look for the best in people and would refuse to accept the worse.
>
> Once, a dealer who was already copying one of Bob's gliders showed up from out of State on the pretence of learning as much as possible about Bob's newest model so that he could sell them better. I knew the guy was just going to copy the glider. I wanted to physically throw him out of the shop. Bob believed him when he told Bob that he would not copy it. Bob even let him stay at his house. Bob felt that if we threw him out, it would make it much easier for him to copy it, in his own mind. Bob also pointed out that he could always just order one and copy it anyway, but he

could never copy the attitude that went behind the glider. I was right. The glider was copied. Bob was right. The copy was missing some things that made Bob's glider easier to fly … and the attitude.

A pilot had redesigned a glider in Bob's shop and had taken it to another manufacturer to see if they wanted to make it. When the pilot started flying Bob's gliders again, Bob was excited over the fact that the pilot had come back. He had completely forgotten the circumstances in which he had left.

One evening I wanted to make some modifications on my glider. Bob told me he wanted to make changes on the sail floor and asked if I could come back first thing in the morning to work on my glider. When I left the shop he was sitting in a chair looking at the different patterns he had laid out on the floor. When I came back the next morning, he was still sitting in the same chair. I asked if he had been sitting in that chair all night. He said yes. I asked, what for? He said he was considering all the possibilities. Ten years from now we will realise the significance of Bob Wills.

The last time we spoke I tried to talk him out of doing the Jeep commercial, and to come down to win the Palomar Open. 'It's going to be hang gliding's first one-on-one contest. I'm doing the rules and you will win for sure, Bob!'

I have seen the footage shot from the helicopter filming him. Most of his last two flights are on film. How did Bob end up flying unknowingly into the wake of a helicopter?

He was to take off from the 1,500 foot hill at Escape Country, and fly right over a Jeep driving along the top of a 500 foot hill. On his second flight, after the Jeep slowed down and Bob flew over it, the right wing tip hit a wooden pole at the top of the 500 foot hill. The pole supports a flag to show pilots the wind direction. The glider yawed about 25 degrees.

The film crew saw this and then saw the glider tumble to the ground later in the same flight. They assumed the impact of hitting the pole weakened the glider. The film crew knows nothing about turbulence caused by the wake of a helicopter [which logically displaces its own weight in air – BM]. They could not see the wake. Newspapers gave the film crew's account of the accident.

Footage shows both leading edges clearly before and after hitting the pole. There was no change or damage. He hit the pole about 18 inches from the tip. Hitting the pole was about equivalent to hitting a bush on take-off and getting yawed about a bit.

Right after Bob completed his last 270 degree turn, he crossed under his own flight path and levelled wings ... and hit the wake of the helicopter which had taken a short-cut across Bob's intended path of glide. At this point the helicopter pilot, perhaps realising that disaster was imminent, tried to 'back away' by swinging around and flying backwards, pointing at Bob when it came into Bob's view. That was perhaps the worst thing it could have done.

As Bob hit the turbulence, the glider's sail crashed negatively against the frame. The glider pitched nose down. Bob went flying into the keel. The film stopped with Bob a third the way around his first tumble. The leading edges were bending negatively but had not failed yet. Witnesses on the ground said that he tumbled more than once from about 80ft before he hit the ground. He died two hours later from massive internal injuries.

Bob had flown with the helicopter pilot on maybe a hundred flights before (in *Sky Riders* and the Smithsonian film *To Fly*). Both were aware of the dangers involved. Basically, because of the helicopter's speed and manoeuvrability, a hang glider pilot has to trust the helicopter pilot. The helicopter pilot has to keep his wake out of any possible flight path of a hang glider.

Hang glider pilots are not the suing kind. We know the risks we take, and accept them. But Bob Wills' death was, in our view, so obviously the helicopter pilot's fault that Robert and Maralys Wills sued for damages. Three years later when the case came to court, the jury found the helicopter pilot innocent. No one in hang gliding believes that verdict. I should think the helicopter pilot has woken up at four o'clock in the morning many times since, and knows what he did. I won't fly with helicopters without a hang glider pilot in its co-pilot seat.

Bob Wills was more than just a pilot. He was an attitude of mind.

Nearly two decades after his death the company he founded, Wills Wing, is the biggest manufacturer of hang gliders in the United States, and its gliders hold many of the world's distance records. It was on a Wills Wing that Larry Tudor made his great XCs, and that Kari Castle flew her 210 miles in Owens. Judy Leden often flies one.

George Worthington was another huge American character. At 60 years of age he held virtually every hang gliding record there is, for open distance, height gain, and distance to goal, in both rigid wing and Rogallo classes. In the summer of 1980, one of our most brilliant pilots, Keith Cockroft, only half George's age, went out to Owens Valley to try and take George's records from him. There was a day when they both flew a storm front, and Keith went beyond where George had previously flown to make his open distance record. But George was in the same air and entered the storm to go 10 miles further and see the young English challenger off.

George spent two months in every summer of his later 50s, 1977–80, in Owens Valley, with its 'killer' canyons, 'boomer' thermals, flights above 15,000ft, heat, dust devils, silence, sheer overwhelming size ... the Scareyergordoff site. He put in for every record there was, and because he knew the procedure, he drilled it into the rest of us ... no barograph, no witness, no record!

John Hudson, another Englishman and a great fan of George's, did more than anyone else in Britain to make certain British pilots always entered the OV Classic competitions that George started with Don Partridge in 1977. Hudson acknowledged that George, the tough guy on the block at the age of 60, used to enrage people, but said there was another side to him:

> I was driving for George Worthington at Cerro Gordo. It was blown-out on top, and believe me it was really honking! George insisted on driving 500ft down the mountain and rigging up where the wind was slightly less. We helped him assemble his rigid Mitchell Wing, and after a wait I noticed him sitting in his car, doing nothing. I walked over, leaned on the door and asked, what was up?

'John', he said, 'I'm scared. The wind is strong, maybe too strong. I'm very nervous about it. But I'm going to sit here a while longer and think it out.'

I just didn't know what to say. Here's the great George Worthington telling me, a punter from England, that he's scared of flying. He eventually flew off, making a very clean launch and disappearing into the distance, but it was then that I realised that here is a man who didn't hide behind anything, least of all a reputation.

I met George Worthington at the American Cups. He was always interviewing people, writing articles, getting up the noses of younger pilots. He felt the loss of the first two American Cups very deeply, and was keen to wind me and other Englishmen up as soon as it was apparent the Americans would win. And why not? Why should the aged, if they can resist it, move over for the young? George showed none of the normal signs of growing old, and he displayed his young wife proudly to prove it. He was always strong-minded. He *believed* in things. He would champion his causes with as much certainty as David Cook, even if he was in a minority of one; they were often the same causes.

As he lived, so he died.

In July 1982, George wrote enthusiastically about a new, twin-boomed, powered ultralight called a Wanderer, made by a pilot, Mark Smith. It had a fully enclosed cabin, and an engine that could be switched off in the air and the propeller retracted to give better streamlining. George described it being flown in turbulent conditions, by a 72-year-old mainstream glider expert, Tasso Proppe, and he was due to fly it himself when Mark Smith went up again:

> Ten minutes later (George wrote) there were frantic gasps and moans from a dozen throats. I looked up and saw the Wanderer at about 400ft, spinning towards the earth with one wing gone. As I watched I saw a 'chute come out and fully blossom about 150ft above the valley floor.
>
> The aircraft landed upside down. The steel construction above Mark's head had acted like a roll bar and he was only bruised. I felt as though I had seen a miracle.

We pieced together the explanation of the wing failure; Mark had been in a steep turn and had, at the same time, unknowingly allowed the speed to get too low. The aircraft stalled and then spun. Mark found himself pointing straight at the ground. He didn't want to build up too much speed and so he unwittingly pulled a little too hard and a little too fast back on the stick. A wing broke off and the rest was inevitable.

George's amazing faith in the aircraft was not dented. It was, he thought, Mark's fault, not for his design but for his flying: 'The fact that a wing came off does not mean that the ship is flimsy, weak or under strength,' he wrote. 'In any light, clean soaring machine you can pull the wings off with a combination of high speed and an abrupt or sudden backward movement of the stick.'

These comments, as many of George's did, caused a row. A Mainstream Aviation designer, Kevin Renshaw, commented, 'He will not live to be an old pilot if he makes a habit of flying brand new aircraft designs without adequate ground testing, and static loading in particular. I have seen many cases of a critical part being analysed very carefully only to have a failure occur in some other area than that which was expected. Six hundred feet above the ground is not the place to find out that the wrong area of the wing fitting was analysed.'

But George had the bit between his teeth, and was adamant. He always put his money where his mouth was. There was a competition coming up, and George loved competitions. This one was for soaring ultralights, powered hang gliders, on long XC with pints of fuel. He wrote:

> I must admit to a habit of flying gliders and ultralights without first checking into the area of 'ground testing' and 'static loading'. But I would like to make it quite clear that I do have self-imposed rules: (1) I will not fly any machine in the role of a test pilot; (2) I will not fly any machine owned by another person unless that person flies it first just prior to my flight; (3) I do try to evaluate the designer-builders and have been known to go on the principle of faith.
>
> I am 62. I love to fly and have flown over 300 different makes of flying machine during 43 years of everyday flying. I fervently believe I will not die as a result of an aircraft-

related cause. If I have a fault regarding safety in general, it is in the area of being overly-fearful and overly-cautious.

Mark Smith rebuilt the Wanderer, strengthening the centre sections and beefing up the fastenings where the twin tail booms met the fuselage. George made one flight in it, of less than an hour, before the competition began. First task was a 70-mile out-and-return on 2 pints of fuel, using the engine to get competitors up into thermals and save them close to the ground. George took off safely and climbed to 400ft before he and another aircraft hooked into a thermal. Scott Rutledge, a veteran hang glider pilot described what happened then:

> The air was mildly lifty and relatively smooth. I was intently watching the Mitchell Wing and the Wanderer to see if they were going to catch anything. It looked as if both of them were starting to work a thermal, except they were both extremely low to the ground. My whole attitude is to get as safely as possible to 1,000ft and cruise. I would have been at parachute-effective level before I started to 360.
>
> They were working something that had a fairly good size to it. George wasn't banked up at all. Not even 30 degrees. And for a thermal, that's keeping a pretty flat and wide turning circle. They were making clockwise turns. Then George's inboard wing broke. It broke right in the air. And it looked like there was a puff of smoke that came off it.
>
> It's on fire, someone cried.
>
> We stood frozen, our breath stopped, as George began his fall.
>
> 'Oh, no! George.' It was Mark Smith, screaming, 'Throw the chute, George, throw the chute!'
>
> When the wing broke George entered what looked like a spin with the wing that was intact still at a flying attitude for a half-second or so. It didn't take but a second before that wing was straight up in the air, matching the side that was broken. The fuselage was on its side. It continued a slow spin with both wings straight up in the air ('clapping hands'), plummeting toward the ground. It impacted going straight down from maybe 500ft.

I would say the whole thing, from the breaking of the wing to impact, was five or six seconds. I don't think he had enough time, I don't think he had enough altitude, to effectively do anything. George was killed instantly.

Commenting on the accident later, Kevin Renshaw said of George Worthington and Tasso Proppe, 'What kind of bugs me about them was their attitude: "We're older. We know better. We know everything there is to do and we're not going to get hurt. It's you new guys coming into it that aren't going to survive." And that kind of thing. It's not really a good example.'

Wherever it happens, it only takes an instant. In Britain, Guy Twiss had come second in the Nationals in 1976 on a Rogallo with what looked like a large flattened biscuit tin as a steering rudder, taking advantage of a poorly set course and rules. He was due to be selected – by me, who had not written the rules, but inherited them – to go to that year's World Championships in Kossen, and was testing the very latest Gryphon I, an early version of the wing under which Johnny Carr made so many long flights. Twiss had even fewer hours on the Gryphon than Worthington on the Wanderer. After half an hour flying the South Downs near Brighton, he flew back over the top of the hill, apparently stalled, and because you cannot turn a stalling aircraft, hit the ground downwind, killing himself.

That same year a keen young woman, Barbara Jones, having done some training, took delivery of a brand new wing. She was told conditions were too rough for her to fly, so she went off on her own and rigged. When she put her seated harness on, just two straps with a seat, she put the straps behind her body instead of in front. After take-off there was nothing to stop her falling forward, pushing the bar out, so she descended in a series of stalls and dives, unable to control her machine. The days she lay in a coma before dying intensified the media frenzy in England about 'poisonous butterflies'.

If you were careful, hang gliding was safe. Work out a routine, make sure all your checks are done, don't fly in weather that is too strong, think about what you are doing. And yet …

There is something about the intense experience of the flying we do that allows a mind to wander from rational sense. We know mistakes can kill, and we resolve not to make them. Then we do.

DEATHS, AND ALL THAT

John Amor was flying prone at the coastal site of Rhossili. He was wearing boots with hooks, instead of holes, for his laces. On one of his flights, making a turn, a hook on his boots caught in the back rigging, but he was able to shake it free before the kite spiralled in. He was unhurt, but he did not change his boots, and carried on flying. A second time, when the boot hooked on to the back rigging during a 360-degree turn, he could not unhook and the kite carried on its turn into the hill, where he died.

Clive Bissett wanted to fly seated off the hill, after flying prone all day. His seated harness was not long enough so he found some rope on the hillside and lengthened his harness. He weighed 165lb, in all. The breaking strain on the rope, sash cord, later tested, was 185lb. Soon after take-off the sash cord broke and the pilot fell 600ft.

Tony Jones spent Sunday morning in late 1976 looking for a place for Graham Driscoll and me to take off dangling under a balloon. We were going for the World 2-Man Balloon Drop Record, and the first attempt the previous day had been called off because of low cloud. On Tony's way back over the Long Mynd, heading home for lunch, he stopped to chat to friends rigged up to fly. One friend had modified his McBroom Cobra by putting on deflexers (then all the rage) but was unhappy with its flying characteristics. In fact, he had made it divergent, so that when put into a dive it would not naturally come out, but had to be forced out. He asked Tony to do a test flight, saying he would drive Tony's car to the bottom. Tony clipped in, took-off, flew out, did a 360 in which he lost a great deal of height, and hit the ground with the control bar, heavily bruising his chest. His lungs bled, and he drowned in his own blood before an ambulance could arrive.

Dan Racanelli was the most famous aerobatic pilot in hang gliding. Cartoon strips featured his stunts, scarcely more amazing than what he could do with a wing. His great friend was Rick Rawlings, one-time US National Champion. Both were flying in the Australian Nationals in 1986 at Mount Buffalo, in New South Wales. On one task, Rawlings landed badly, his glider caught up on electric power lines, so it was suspended, swinging in the breeze. Racanelli landed to help. When he touched Rawling's glider, he was electrocuted and died immediately. Rawlings freed himself from his harness and dropped to the ground, without injury.

We last saw Paul Maritos a mile high over Snowdon with Graham Hobson, and earlier exploring weak wave in South Wales, also with

Hobson. Maritos went into manufacturing, making the Flexiform Wing, and for one season was a League pilot before dropping out to concentrate on research. Though there had been talk for years about a BHGA test vehicle, there wasn't one in 1979, so like all British manufacturers Paul had to suck it and see. He developed a cross-boomless hang glider like the Gryphon, and took it to 800ft above Mam Tor in Derbyshire. He had said he would put the wing through some radical manoeuvres to check its handling. He was seen to stall the glider, and then go into a steep, almost stabilised dive, during which he built up a lot of speed. When he pushed out of the dive the glider folded up. Paul then threw his emergency chute, but it tangled in the wreckage, and failed to deploy before he hit the ground and was killed.

The first time I saw Pepe Lopez was in 1980 at the third American Cup, flying for Brazil, when he took off with a great surge from Crystal launch, turned to 360 immediately and stuffed his glider into the trees. The next time we met was two years later at the Yorkshire Dales American Cup, when I found him in a field ahead of every other flyer and where he wondered aloud about the wrong done me that I should be coaching Americans. With him was a dishevelled little man called Willy Metcalfe who owned half of Wensleydale, and who said proudly, 'D'ye know he's t'World Champion? An' he's landed in ma field!' Pepe had beaten Rich Pfieffer and Graham Slater to win the Worlds in Japan in 1981, and became a cult figure in Brazil, where he was also national surfing champion. Jeans and sports clothing were marketed with his name. He organised the Worlds in Brazil in 1991, renowned for its poor weather and the number of good-looking women who cheered pilots on and comforted not a few. Pepe placed second behind the brilliant Czech, Tomas Suchanek, and went off to Japan for his first visit since becoming World Champion ten years earlier. On the second last day of the Shima Seiki competition, Pepe, lying second and going for big prize money, flew into a dangerously turbulent area and was forced down in extremely inhospitable territory and killed landing.

In 1978, Paul Renouf flew a cliff site out to sea with no bottom landing except the beach at one end. He flew to the other end before realising that the lift was not strong enough for him to soar. He tried to make it back to the beach, but failed, landing in the water. The sail, with him underneath, immediately adopted the profile of the sea surface, but Paul could not unclip his harness because the cloth hang loop had swelled up and there was not enough room for the clip to break free. Paul was found, six hours later, under his glider at the bottom of the sea.

Stew Smith was one of the most gentle men in hang gliding. A former US gymnastics champion, the 1982 American Cup in Yorkshire was where he first showed his brilliance as a top pilot. He went on to win silver medal position at the 1983 Worlds, and win the 1984 US Nationals. He was resident flyer at Grandfather Mountain in North Carolina, and almost a son to the mountain's owner, Hugh Morton, who sponsored the yearly US Masters of Hang Gliding competition. Stew flew a Sensor 510, in common with his friend Rich Pfieffer, a very high-performance wing that Rich always wanted to wind tighter to get better performance. Stew also tightened up his wing, so tight that in a racing dive quite close to the ground, when he pushed out it didn't respond as it had always responded in the past and it failed to pull out. Stew hit the ground and died. After his death, Hugh Morton had not the heart to run another Masters.

By the time Chris Bulger, from Seattle, was 20, he had won both the US Nationals and the US Masters, and flown in the 1985 World Championships, won by John Pendry of England. Later that year, when Pendry was in America, the two decided to do some towing, Pendry on a hang glider, Bulger on a trike. It was meant to be a short trike flight, up, drop off Pendry to find a thermal, and down again, so fast it wasn't worth Bulger wearing a helmet, not that it would have made any difference. What did make a difference was that there was no weak link on the tow rope, so it did not break when Pendry locked out and Bulger tried to release. Because of a design fault, the release jammed. Bulger and his trike ended up dangling from John Pendry's harness, until they broke free. Bulger's trike started to tumble, and continued to tumble down from about 1,000ft. John Pendry landed safely.

Dave Jones, 30, was a 1980 League hang glider pilot, but dropped out halfway through the season to concentrate on flying trikes, then a new phenomenon in England. He set up a microlight centre on an old RAF training station at Bovingdon, with, among others, Dave and Kay Simpson. Jones had been a relatively cautious hang glider pilot, but loved to throw around his trike combination, a Hiway trike with a

Solar wing. His speciality was doing 140-degree wingovers. The trike made three flights the day Jones died, and he took it up for a series of wingovers, each more radical than the last. He looked to be preparing to land when he made another wingover, apparently to come into wind. Halfway through, perhaps hitting his own prop wash, he stalled, sideslipped, started to luff, rotated the nose and then the right wing distorted. The right wing boom broke, and the left leading edge. The nose went down, and with power still on, Jones spiralled in from 200ft and was killed instantly.

Paolo Coelho, known as 'Paolinho', or Little Paolo, a Brazilian, was one of ten children of a gardener. Paolinho could not read, but spent every spare moment in Rio helping pilots pack up their hang gliders. Pepe Lopez's uncle bought a French 'Atlas', and when he stopped flying, he gave the Atlas to Paolinho, who, without lessons, rushed up the mountain carrying it, rigged and took off. He figured out how to turn while he was on his way down. In 1981 Paolinho entered his first competition and placed tenth. Two months later he entered his second competition and won! In 1985 he was the only Brazilian to make the cut at the Kossen Worlds, and placed sixth. Though he was poor, other pilots helped him, giving him equipment and rides. Bill Moyes gave him gliders. Paolinho was tipped as a future World Champion, and when he went to fly Torrey Pines in southern California in 1993, he can have had no forebodings. Torrey Pines is to hang gliding what a 500ft hill would be to the great mountaineer Reinhold Messner. But Paolinho went further along the cliffs at Torrey than anyone else and disappeared from view. He was later found dead in the wreckage of his wing.

Steve Hunt had been in hang gliding since 1974, as the bubbling, Australian partner to John Ievers in setting up Hiway Wings. Hunt always had a tape measure, an opinion on why a wing would fly, and an absolute desire to fiddle with things. His tutor at Sussex University, Alan Marsh, remembers dragging Steve to a gathering of Sussex sophisticates:

> Talk of Heidegger, Tawney and Kant buzzed idly in the air. Steve was unconcerned, not that he cannot deal with such stuff when it seems relevant. But our hostess mentioned that the room was cold because the electric heater was bust.

DEATHS, AND ALL THAT

> Steve seized the offending appliance with both feet, tore out its innards, replaced them, and sophistication proceeded in a warmer atmosphere. Everyone remembers Steve doing that; no one remembers my views on Heidegger ...

Steve Hunt's Hiway Superscorpion, his refined version of the Moyes Maxi, was one of the best-performing and handling gliders of the 1970s. But when trikes arrived, Hunt broke away to build them, to head the BMAA and design and build his own microlights. He had thrown a punch at me once in an argument (and missed), but the last time we met he and his wife Joan were going to see Reinhold Messner, the man who climbed Everest without oxygen and a mutual hero; I had given them the tickets, Messner was a guest on a radio programme I edited. Steve took his new rigid-wing Pathfinder II microlight to a race across southern France in the summer of 1983. He ran into exceptional turbulence near Carcassonne, possible a *Foehn* wind off the Pyrenees, so bad it broke his machine and dashed it to the ground from 600ft, where Steve Hunt died. He was not carrying a parachute because he believed microlight pilots should not fly in conditions where one might be necessary. A French competitor, also flying a Pathfinder II, was killed 10 miles further along the ridge in the same way. Twelve microlights made forced landings that day, fearing for their safety.

The Great Italian Killer Storm in 1988 haunts mountain pilots in Europe to this day. It is hard to piece together what actually happened, only that six pilots died and there was hysteria in the Italian media about 'more controls'. It was, as Gerard Guerrier wrote, hang gliding's greatest individual tragedy:

> Northern Italy, Como, on the slopes of Mont Cornizzolo (1,240m, over 4,000ft), 40 kms from Milan, and 10 km from the Swiss frontier. This is the most popular of the Alpine sites, with 3 clubs, 200 active pilots, and in 1987, more than 7,000 flights. It is the site of the Lariano Triangle, one of Europe's biggest annual international competitions. Como is one of four large industrial cities at the base of the Italian Alps, looking down into the Po Valley, encircled by mountains. The Alps are to the north, and Apennines to the south.

Normal weather features stagnant lower levels, with the mountains forming a screen, and high humidity because of the Po, and the lakes of Maggiore, Como, Ises, Garde and the Adriatic Sea. In general the area has high atmospheric instability whenever a cold front arrives to clash with the region's stagnant humid air mass, causing mist and fogs. Local pilots know this condition well, and in spring enjoy flying where the two air masses meet, between mist and storm. One can then fly along the whole Alpine range, such as from Como, 120 kms to Lake Garda.

As for the local pilots, French and English readers should have no illusions of superiority. Do not imagine them to be moustached windbags, petty crooks with gold medallions and lots of pizza. Naples is light years away from Como. We have hardened mountaineers, upright and courageous. Hang gliding is well-developed. We fly Moyes GTRs, Airwave Magic Full Races, Colts, Hercules, Wills Wing HP2s. These are pilots used to hard conditions, to storms, to landing on mountainsides to avoid valley power lines. If some are less expert than others, they always try to follow the best.

A day before the Killer Storm hit Italy, it was in Spain on July 23. At Ager the cold front passed over Catalonia. In the evening a Scottish pilot, Robin Hamilton [the best hang glider pilot Scotland has produced – BM], entered a cu-nim and emerged at about 7,000m (22,000ft), severely frost-bitten on his face and hands. But he survived the experience. So much for the overture.

The Met Office at Varses in Italy anxiously records the tightening of the isobars (the tighter the isobars, the stronger the wind). Pressure is falling rapidly. The hot air (30C, 86F at ground level) is ready to be activated by the arrival of cold air. A warning is sent to the safety authorities.

On Sunday, July 24, the front moves very quickly, at least 50kph, over France (and St Andre, a famous hang gliding site). Then it is blocked by the Alps. The isobars draw tighter. Meanwhile, on the southern side it is a summer's day, with a few clouds and a nice soarable southerly wind.

DEATHS, AND ALL THAT

Met offices in Italy see the potential danger and alert airports. Bergamo stops all flights. Sparks are going to fly. Suddenly, the ramparts of the mountain give way and the cold air rushes into the valleys. Turin is first affected at 2pm, just 150 kms from Como, and then the peaks of Mt St Gothard (2,112m), as the cold air sweeps towards Belinzora.

As the crow flies, we are only 30km to the northwest from Cornizzolo, when the final act begins.

At take-off on Como, everyone is in high spirits. There is old Memo, Felice, Raimondo, all enjoying the lift from the 20kph southeast wind. The local instructor, Giussepe, thinks, 'Strange ... is this a sign of a warm front? With this heat that will be no danger.' But high up in the sky the wind is strong. One needs the penetration of a GTR, and 15 gliders are airborne. The temperature falls gradually. Giussepe gets anxious.

Alto-cumulus appears, and then moving very rapidly, alto-stratus. Then far away to the west, a mass of black clouds. Giussepe stops all flights. It is 4.05pm.

Little by little the wind eases and veers towards the south. There is now no doubt. A curt message over the radio. Some gliders have the time, 3,000ft above take off, to get back to the official landing area. But a group of 10 gliders still circles.

Giussepe calls out, 'Land please!' The monster is now a few kilometres from take-off. Its base is about 1,500 m. Below it, a curtain of rain. This is decidedly not an ordinary storm.

But wait, here is Felice with 11 years of experience, an international pilot, and also Mario, 10 years' experience, Director of the Lariano Triangle. They are readying their harnesses ... for take-off?

Later Felice was to say, 'We took off then so as to have a flight that was a little different.'

He certainly had that.

Once in the air Felice realises the danger. The wind is gale force. He forces his glider towards the plains below, his bar stuffed to his knees.

Mario does not seem worried. He circles slowly to within a kilometre of the giant. Unconscious? Defiant? Everything is waiting. It is too late. It was too late as soon as they took off!

In a few moments the storm strikes. Mario is sucked up helplessly, pulled into the entrails of the monster. Later, he is thrown against the side of a mountain called 'La Grigna' 30 kms away. The impact was tremendous, judging from the pitiful remains of pilot and glider picked up next day by helicopter.

Several pilots die in a panic to land in the official field near their friends, so close to safety. Alas, there is no time to descend before the wind reaches 100 kph and the hail is upon them. Antonio, a pilot for 4 years, heads into wind and dives towards the lake, then turns around and, in rotor from the mountainside, is thrashed to the ground. His uprights crumple. He is killed.

Angelo approaches the landing area and gets low. Alas! The suction is too strong. He struggles, but all is black. He is lifted like a speck of dust, pulled up to 5,000 metres. Miraculously, after an hour of horror, he is ejected above a deep valley. With frozen hands he manages to land at Valteline, 60 kms from Como. All ten fingers will be amputated.

Guido has less 'luck'. Like Mario he is dashed against the rocks, but close to take-off. Was he trying to land there?

Ezio took a bad direction. He found himself above Lake Galate with nothing he could do. He fought to the edge. Flying over boats he cried, 'help!' A gust prevented him from getting to the bank of the lake. The glider fought and swung. He was hurled into the water. Holiday-makers saved him.

The tragedy continued. Mario had also decided to escape, but too late and too slow, and not far enough in the direction of the plains. He disappeared into clouds. When his glider broke up he threw his parachute, which pulled him upside down and he was unable to get upright. He landed head first and died after two days in a coma.

DEATHS, AND ALL THAT

What happened to Memo? (10 years' experience, 'old' Memo?). He had enough time to find shelter. Did he also wish to make a flight that was 'a little different'? Like Mario and Guido, he was covered in ice, and then thrown by the wind on to a factory building at Lecco. Death was instantaneous.

Roberto, with two years' experience, fled from the front but what looked like the wrong direction, straight towards the Alps around Bergamo. His speed and his relative caution, however, enabled him to avoid the worst. Cornered by mountains, he came down in trees 70 kms from take-off.

Luciano and Alberto, two other novices, fled in the same direction, but with less time and landed not far from where Mario was killed. Alberto pulled his parachute and – a gift! – only broke his collarbone.

The sun set. Later that evening a pilot lost his life in the Italian Tyrol.

Those killed were Memo La Rocca, Antonio Legranzini, Guido Baruffini, Marco Liette and Mario Maspero. We never learned the name of the pilot killed in the Tyrol.

Play with large clouds at your peril. Please learn from those who have gone before us.

John Hudson served on my competitions committee for at least four years, and long after I left. He was a northern businessman, a fan, if you remember, of George Worthington and the man who insisted we fly against the Americans in 1978 in British gliders. He was a man who fought every inch of the way for what he believed in. If he lost the argument, and it was a committee decision, then he threw himself into making it work.

Hudson was a League pilot from the first year it started, and he was in awe of the sky in the sense that he could be moved deeply by his experiences. He wrote about everything: concerned letters about where the BHGA was going, stern letters on safety, urgent letters saying the British had to take the Americans on in Owens. He was a great patriot, not just 'a punter from England' as he described himself.

John Hudson had the capacity of a poet in his descriptions of flight. He and Bob Calvert flew a lot together. One day in May in 1978, something unusual happened to them. They had driven to the Lake District in search of lighter winds, and Calvert and a flyer called Phil Robinson teased John Hudson about carrying a parachute weighing 8½lb up a hill 850ft high in a temperature of 30°C:

> Hudson: I was absolutely shattered by the climb, and since the day had practically zero thermal activity, no sign of bad weather and little chance of aerial collision, I argued for the merits of owning a second harness, without a parachute. How wrong can you be?

By 6pm they were the only three left on the hill, with almost no wind, so they decided to compete against each other, longest in the air the winner. Robinson went first and when the other two saw he was not going down, he was maintaining height, they clipped in and ran off to join him:

> Hudson: Phil had started lazy, slow 360s. Bob Calvert took one look and ran to launch. It was obvious to me that since both were holding their own, we must be right in the middle of a large gentle thermal. I launched, running quickly into the now zero wind, and found that by flying dead slow and creeping around the turns I could also stay up. Looking forward to winning our duration contest, I was surprised to see that Bob Calvert had top-landed and that I was about 50ft above the top.

Calvert elected to land to watch the other two fly, but as they kept climbing, and knowing he was the best flyer of the three of them, he then took off again and started climbing steadily. Robinson kept going forward and fell out of the lift and headed out for a landing. Calvert reached Hudson and asked how high they were. Hudson did not know:

> In fact, I had forgotten to set my altimeter, and since I thought we would be flying down anyway, paid little attention to it. When Bob shouted about 1,000ft above take-off, I misheard him and next heard him shout 1,100ft. That is how fast we were rising. I could feel the suppressed excitement rising in me at a similar rate. We shouted to each other about the lift, and Bob said it could be ridge lift since the wind may well have risen. I just could not weigh things

up, since at one point I wound up at least eight consecutive 360s in 4-up (+400 fpm) and gained about 500ft without drifting back more than 100 yards.

They found lift everywhere and came to the conclusion they were not flying in a thermal, or in ridge lift. When he looked up he saw lenticular clouds all over the sky. These are cigar-shaped, and marked the presence of 'wave' lift. Calvert estimated they were at 2,000ft when he flew over to tell Hudson what he thought:

> Wave! What an evocative word! As soon as Bob said it and I looked up, I just couldn't believe the number of clouds around with typical wave form. Apprehension immediately grew. We were in steady and smooth lift. I had no idea how high we were, but my Thommen altimeter kept adding on the feet, and I could see that the dial was starting to show a small section of blue, indicating 6,000ft. Wow! What the hell are we doing up here? How soon would it be before we flew into the huge rotors and massive turbulence that one associates with wave lift? I kept fingering my parachute to make sure it was still there. I looked for Bob but he was about ¾ mile back from me and about 200ft higher. That's the answer, I thought. Follow The Calvert and if he gets tipped upside down, I will be able to pull out immediately and fly down. Well, Bob must have cottoned on to this because before long he flew over and started shouting.

Calvert suggested they split up, the lift persisted, and though his hands were cold they decided to go XC and head for Keswick. He decided to fly along the wave, and set off north, to his left, weaving to gain height every time his vario told him the lift was strong. It was some time before Hudson saw what was happening:

> I was in a world of my own. I have never been so high above take-off in a hang glider, and the feeling was magical. The whole of the Lake District was wrapped in a haze, and as we climbed higher the sky got bluer and cleaner. I watched the Skiddaw range as it seemed to melt into the landscape, and

very soon found it hard to make out the ridge from where we had launched. I then got a shock seeing Bob miles away, and wondered what on earth he was doing in the opposite direction. I soon found out as I gained about 500ft, pulling in to try and catch him. I remember thinking 'this guy knows what he's doing'.

The two flyers reached 6,250ft before the 'magic' lift disappeared, and they headed downwind, flying first by the sun and then by compass. Calvert had flown the area before and recognised where he was. Hudson followed, and they circled in zero sink, hoping they would catch the next up elevator of the wave pattern, but this did not happen and they headed downwind again, as he recalled:

I think we flew out of the wave because 2-up gently became 4-down, and after searching around at a cost of 400ft, I decided to fly off and call it a day. Bob was above and behind me and seemed to be flying over the mountain into an area of lovely fens and moors. I had not a clue where we were and so carried on out over the flat land towards a more populated area. I soon realised I was making a mistake and turned around to follow Bob, who was steering a positive course downwind. A blip on my vario had me 360ing around and as I turned I could see Bob above me doing the same.

They both relaxed and enjoyed the scenery from 3,000ft in the late summer sunshine. Once they did find gentle lift but it did not develop into anything, and eventually Hudson found a field and landed there, to be surrounded by a herd of cows. Calvert thought he had found one more source of lift and started climbing but it did not develop and he, too, elected to land among the cows. They were full of excitement, jumping around, and lucky enough that the farmer handed them two cold cans of beer:

As we sat on the grass waiting for Phil to pick us up, we watched the sky. Lenticular clouds were everywhere, and the evening was fine and dry. We talked about the lift, about the argument we had had about the necessity for parachutes at all times, about the cows which surrounded me quickly on landing, and about the thrills and beauty of this sport of ours. I felt deeply satisfied and at peace. It had been a remarkable experience and one which made five years of top to bottoms, thermal and ridge soaring flights, all worthwhile. We had soared on that magic invisible lift, miles wide, generated not by the sun but by the sheer power of nature.

John Hudson was 32 when he wrote that superb account of the first high wave flights in England. He had started Mainair in Rochdale, Lancashire, which became (and still is) Britain's premier New Aviation supplies shop, and supplied finished aluminium to hang glider manufacturers. He began building trikes when the idea arrived in England in 1981, with wings made by Len Gabriels and the body and engine configuration designed by himself. Mainair 'Flashes' won many microlight competitions; it was one of John's Mainair machines that Richard Meredith-Hardy flew from England to South Africa. But when a fast single-seater was developed elsewhere, John had to respond by trying to build a faster, flatter wing. In 1989, at the age of 43, he was testing a prototype near Newhey, Manchester; it didn't work, possibly because the floating cross-boom was so tight it pulled through, folding the wings, and he crashed to the ground and was killed. His prototype, ironically, was not fitted with a parachute, which were banned on British microlights at that time because of their propensity to open accidentally.

Why am I telling you all this?

Because there is no memorial to them. I am haunted by the fact that they might be forgotten.

My list is a version of Ernest Hemingway's account of the values in his beloved bullfighting, which he wrote about in *Death in the Afternoon*.

It is the verbal equivalent of all those photographs pinned up in the bar at Pancho's Place outside Edwards Air Force Base in America, when pilots, *who had the 'Right Stuff'* according to Tom Wolfe, were dying in droves test-flying for the USAF after the Second World War. The photographs of the dead, taken when they were at the peak of their powers, were displayed around the bar, and wuffos of the day – Chuck Yeager called them 'weenies' – would ask daft questions like, 'Say, how can I get my picture up on your bar wall?'

'You have to be dead first!'

To quote Patrick Davis, a young Gurkha officer in Burma in the war, who wrote *A Child at Arms*, 'The dead had no life but in us who survived. If we forgot, they were nothing. If we forgot, where lay all the effort and courage of their lives and ours?'

Our deaths are reported as four lines in national newspapers, whatever the country, and then dismissed: 'hang gliding!' Unless it is the Italian killer storm, and then the usual happens, calls for 'tighter controls'.

But our deaths happened for particular reasons, as we search for the means to fly. If our deaths – and I have remembered only a few of those I knew – are forgotten, who would risk anything?

There is no roll of honour to these pilots. There seems to be no historian to look after their interests and place their flights in context. There is no museum commemorating their amazing exploits. In thirty years we have moved so far in the New Aviation, and spread across the world in the face of attacks – sometimes, shamefully, from our own flying kind in conventional gliding – or indifference.

But there has been no *understanding*.

It could so easily have been someone else who died, as every pilot will acknowledge. I went into the sea trying to cross the English Channel by hang glider with the same killer hook as Paul Renouf. I did it a few months before him, but my hang loop was metal, and though I had a frightening struggle to get unclipped I did so before drowning. When I hit the ground in 1978 after falling 250ft, I knew as I was lying there, hardly able to breathe, that my friend Tony Jones had died because his lungs filled up with blood the previous year. For about ten minutes, in a dream, I thought that was happening to me, too, but it didn't. John Amor caught a hook of his boot in the back rigging at Rhossili and 360'd into the hill at 40mph and died, but when I hit the hill on Dunstable trying to 360, it didn't kill me. It bloody well hurt, though. Lynn Smith rigged badly at Lookout and was killed, but I once secured the bottom rigging of my kite with just two turns of a wing nut, intending to tighten it later but failing to do so. It held and the wing didn't collapse, so unlike Lynn I was not killed.

It could have been me under Alvin Russell's wing on Christmas Eve in Ireland in 1976. It was my turn to fly it. I just didn't.

In each case, my luck held and their luck did not. Every pilot has a secret store of such stories, and it is not confined to the New Aviation.

DEATHS, AND ALL THAT

A mistake in aviation can kill, be it with a Jumbo or a paraglider. But you are not destined to die if you fly hang gliders.

I feel that I am writing to you directly. If you are old, George Worthington should be a hero to you. If you are young, well, you can't have a brilliant singing child molester like Michael Jackson as a role model all your life, however fascinated journalists and editors are by such people.

It is possible the media reflect the real values of modern society. If so, they are poor values. I prefer those personified in the New Aviation, old-fashioned values like courage, stamina, honesty, loyalty, strength, judgement, style, character. None had them more than Keith Cockroft, the man who took up the job that Alvin Russell created in 1976 before he was killed in Ireland, of making our training safe for newcomers.

There are many physically beautiful men in hang gliding. I cannot think why this should be. Keith Cockroft was one of them. He was tall, lean, dark, with black curly hair, very white teeth and a lazy Yorkshire charm that disguised his commitment to flying (and anything).

I first saw him when he was 1,000ft above me at the Skirrid in South Wales in 1976, when I was running trials to choose a team for that year's Worlds. Keith, seated, was out-flying everyone on one of Len Gabriel's then unfashionable wings. He did not join the League in 1977 because he was playing himself into the job that Alvin had started, but drifted into the League a year later. On a hill, when we ran cross-country tasks and a thermal came through, all the 'animals' set off first to get in it, then the less daring (like me), and forty pilots would hack around trying to get up and away. At the other end of the hill, all on his own, sniffing around like some absent-minded greyhound, would be Keith Cockroft. He hardly ever went where everybody else went, and the quality of the lift he was looking for was often more important to him than whether it took him further than anyone else.

He often flew without instruments, trying to train his nose to determine where the lift was. He did not want to hear the beeping of a vario, but to see with his eyes, feel with his body, and sense what was happening in the air.

We took him to Tennessee for the First American Cup in 1978, where he briefed pilots on the hills and worked like a demon to make sure we won. He never said, 'what about me?' He did things without a fuss and you found out later that he had done them, and we would have been worse off without him. I would not want you to think him quiet and retiring, because he wasn't at all, but he was selfless. And he had his own values to which he was always true. Four years after Tennessee, in the cauldron of the Yorkshire Dales American Cup when I was coaching the Americans, Keith joined Mike Atkinson in supporting me. It was a personal gesture, and like Mike, he could only suffer grief for it, but it didn't bother him. He offered local advice in difficult flying (and political) conditions to any team, US, Brazil, France, because he wanted it to be a fair competition.

He was a hero in Spain. One summer he turned up there and flew away from sites where locals had never gone XC, and Keith disappeared over the mountains. 'Ooo-aye, lad, I'll tell yer if yer like,' he might have said to them. And he did, and they loved him for it.

Keith set up his own flying school near Hebden Bridge in Yorkshire. He concentrated on Rogallo hang gliders, and not paragliders, despite the huge surge in paragliding in recent years. Keith did not want to take that easy route. I phoned to ask him to an important birthday; he said he couldn't, but I think he just didn't want to leave, even for a short while, his wife Annette and two children. He mellowed.

In the Easter holidays of 1994, Keith took the most advanced students in his school to the south of France to teach them mountain XC. The weather was dreadful for most of the time he was there, and then one day it wasn't quite as bad. Keith took his students to the top and briefed them.

'If cloud comes in, you will land there,' he said, pointing to a landing area at the bottom. They rigged and took off, and Keith joined them. Cloud did come in, low and threatening, and one by one his students spiralled down and landed. They looked up and there, thousands of feet up, circling as the wisps of cloud went by, was Keith Cockroft, still looking for his own private source of lift, doing what no one else was doing, listening to a different drum.

Keith disappeared over the back of the mountain. They found him two days later amid the wreckage of his wing where he had hit the mountain. He must have been in cloud, totally whited-out when it happened, because he was Keith Cockroft, and if he had had even a two-second chance, he would have flared out and survived. Yet I have to say that, when my time comes, there are worse ways to die than the way Keith died.

DEATHS, AND ALL THAT

Lines Written on the Death of Keith Cockroft

Snows melted
the other day
over green springland,
fresh snows
on great Dormillouse,
ever sleeping mountain,
where you overtook
a raptor's limits,
with the Mistral blowing
on the fifth of April.

I drove down to Digne
where you lay eternally
silent, your face, living
pink and blueish,
your black curls, for once
combed and an unusual silence
around your frozen captivity.
We dressed you in a flying suit
red socks and a pine cone
to travel with.

Today, we will lift our glasses and drink on your eternal voyage!
Life was an instant,
love everlasting.
The snow is whiter today
the green, greener
and after my visit
I saw a black hawk
turning a thermal,
the almond trees flowering
underneath, getting smaller.

Frans Pannekoek
Mison, 4 May 1994

Chapter 8

Migration

In the great imaginative tumult of forces released by the First Lilienthal Meet in 1971 we have come a long way, some of which we have marched in lockstep with sailplanes. Though the majority of New Aviation pilots foot launch from a hill or mountain, there is a growing use of the tow winch. Flatland flying, with its more predictable thermals and the possibility of greater distances, is like the song of a siren. It is forgivable to go, to explore the new distances possible, but it lures us away from our unique roots.

Our winch gear can be kept in a small garage, along with our wings. We do not need the ancillary equipment that sailplane pilots have built for themselves around their airfields. Our equipment can be pulled out, we can drive to a suitable take-off, rig, winch off, and be gone, winch as well as wing. But it should also be recognised there is a quality difference between foot and winch launching.

Given our origins and our aspirations I say a foot-launched flight is better than a winch-launched flight, in the same way that one wine is better than another wine, because the quality of the foot-launched flight is more pure. When a flyer rigs on a hill, having dumped his equipment off a car, he is then independent. He can achieve flight by his own efforts, as a bird does.

He does not need the winch man or anybody else, really.

At the core of the New Aviation is the idea of independent flight. That is flight without any back-up, no cars to follow, no winches, just the skies and the urge to fly. And the ultimate aim is to learn how to migrate with the birds. In the middle of all the tremendous energy and force and movement of the New Aviation, there is a small band of poet-pilots who are looking in a singular and pure way to devise ways to test themselves against the birds and then to fly with them in their sky pathways. In this, they are going where Mainstream Aviation, despite all its early dreams, can never go, and being truthful to the deepest of our urges to fly.

If I add up my contribution to the New Aviation, I can say creating the British League was worth tuppence, another tuppence for my role in creating the American Cup, tuppence for helping British women to fly well, and perhaps another fourpence elsewhere. Being the first man to fly a microlight around the world in 1998 has to be worth something. But the best tuppence, and possibly the most lasting, was an editorial I wrote in early 1981 at about the time Peter Hargreaves and Stan Abbott were planning their letter to British clubs, complaining at the way I had lost the Newton Aycliffe sponsorship deal.

Half an idea had already been formed by reading an account by a Dr Pennicuick in *Scientific American* years earlier, in which this American scientist had used a motorised glider to study the flight patterns of vultures in the Kenya Rift Valley. When I took over *Wings!* I republished that account in March 1980. It had struck me that we now had the glide angles of Rupell's Gryphons and other vultures written about by Dr Pennicuick, so we should be able to fly the way they did. Could we not migrate?

There was no response in Britain, but the Pennicuick paper seemed to ignite in France, where the editor of *Vol Libre*, Hubert Aupetit, ran an article on migration habits of the big birds. In the US I struck a chord with the cross-Channel man-powered flight ace Bryan Allen, hero of *Gossamer Condor* and *Albatross*. We chewed over the idea one evening at the First American Cup, and tried to plot some rules. My 'tuppence' was to be the first to formulate such rules.

Milton's Migration Rules

1. **Length of Flight** – Should follow migration pattern from Latitude 51N to 10N. The northern limit of 51 degrees in Europe is just south of London, north of Cologne, and about level with Dresden. It is south of the Central European summer nesting place for most birds. In North America, 51N is north of Vancouver, up in the high BC Rockies. The southern limit, 10N, is north of Addis Ababa, south of Kano in Nigeria, and about level with the eastern Horn of Africa. In North America, 10N is just above the Panama Canal, and about level with Caracas in Venezuela.

A crude measure of the distance between the two latitudes is 2,600 miles. In Europe, that is the distance covered by a migrating bird in the autumn, on one of the two most-used routes, via Gibraltar and the Western Sahara, or via Turkey, Syria, Israel, Egypt and the Sudan.

2. **Duration of Flight** – Should not exceed 120 days, about four months, giving an average southerly distance of 22 miles/day.
3. **Ethics** – If you come down on a flat plain, you must launch from where you land or walk back over your previous route carrying your glider to find a launch point. All launches must be made by foot, and no use is allowed of a winch or any kind of engine.
4. **Glider** – You may only use one glider, although it can be extensively repaired.
5. **Sporting Spirit** – Flyers are expected to take all sensible steps to certify their flight. They are also expected to conform to the sporting spirit of the challenge.

It was a measure of my Englishness – an Irish sort of Englishness – that I set 51N rather than the more logical 50N, so that a migrating pilot could set off from England. On reflection, 50N is a better starting point.

Looking at the map, the most popular route in Europe for birds is down from the great German plains through the Balkans, over Turkey, and then the politically difficult route via Israel and Jordan into East Africa. Of course, birds don't give a twopenny toss about politics. But the route via Spain is hardly less popular with birdlife. The sea crossing at Gibraltar is about 11 miles, and in the autumn birds thermal up every morning in huge columns north of Gibraltar, before setting out over the sea to Morocco. Some fail to make it.

In America, I think a migration flight would be a lot easier than in Europe, basically finding launch and landing sites in the Rockies down through southern Canada, the US and Mexico. The hard bit is the last part to Panama.

I had hoped the editorial would provoke a discussion in Britain, that perhaps we would link up with the RSPB (Royal Society for the Protection of Birds) and examine mile by mile the best migration routes, discover where birds tended to congregate, where they found the best lift, where they stayed overnight. The project would have had to go through the Royal Aeronautical Society (RAeS) to have the loose ends

MIGRATION

tied up, and one would need a sponsor as generous as Henry Kramer had been to set a decent financial prize. But the Newton Aycliffe Affair was much more interesting, and I thought that editorial had been just a lonely little thought thrown into the wind. And despite a number of attempts to even elicit a response from the RAeS, there has never been a reply. But I was wrong about the lonely thought and the wind.

Mike and Caroline de Glanville are as English a couple as you would ever meet, but they have lived in France for years and both flew in official French hang gliding teams. In 1979, Mike was European rigid wing champion, and, curiously, he won the French title in the 1980s on Rogallo wings in the same year as French-born and bred Michel Carnet won the British League title. Both de Glanvilles are excellent pilots, and in 1983, they became the first to actually try a form of migration flight, though they took their family with them by car; Mike wrote about it later:

> The idea of bird-like migration on a hang glider is one that has often been tossed around between pilots in cafe discussions, but very little actual experimentation has been done. These days, with XC distances pushing the 100-mile barrier, the recovery drive can often extend into the early hours of the next morning. Migration could be a step towards cutting down on recovery drives.
>
> Let me tell you about a little migration that Caroline and I flew, to give you an idea of how this can be achieved. We flew from Lachens in the South of France to San Sicario in Italy over three wonderful days in June to discover that, with a little help from your friends, migration is already well within our capabilities.
>
> With a few days set aside for shaping up before the XC Classic in Owens Valley, we decided that a good way would be to try a migration. Our friends Nick and Leila were quite happy with the idea of driving in the southern Alps so we signed them up as our recovery team. We checked out the CB radios – one in the van and one for each flyer – loaded up the gliders and camping supplies, persuaded the children that we were off on an adventure of considerable importance, squeezed everyone aboard and set off for Lachens.

Now as anyone with a young family knows, all this takes a little time to happen. When we arrived at the take-off we were a bit late in the day for a long XC, so we settled on St Andre (30 miles) as our first goal. It would give us a pleasant warm-up and an easy start for the following day. Caroline rigged her 13 square metre Bullet (weighing only 23kgs, 51 lbs), excited to be trying a new glider, and I set up among a mass of gliders and vehicles parked on the grassy summit.

We launched around 3pm and climbed to cloud-base in the sea breeze before turning north and gliding off towards the Teillan Mountain. On the way across the plain, over La Batie, we ran into some fairly hefty turbulence as we crossed the convergence line with the westerly wind. Caroline came out rather low on to the south slopes of the Teillan and after some desperate scratching, she went down at the base of the mountain. I managed to squeeze around on to the west face and work my way back up to the top. From there I was able to contact Nick in the van, pinpoint Caroline's landing for him, and confirm the rendezvous in St Andre.

Two speedy glides along well-orientated south-westerly-facing ridges took me through to the goal. I circled down to land in a freshly cut hay-field just outside the town. When I was breaking down my glider, another wing appeared high over St Andre from the north. After a lazy cruise around the valley it circled my field, set up an approach and came in to land beside me. It turned out to be Pierre Bouilloux. He had just completed a 70km triangle flight, having left St Andre earlier in the afternoon, another good solution to the recovery problem.

Soon afterwards I heard Nick calling on the CB as he approached St Andre and I was able to guide him to our field.

We set up camp for the night in a grassy meadow next to a glade of pine trees. The night sky glittered with a thousand stars, promising some fine flying. We dozed off to the sound of crickets in the grass, and owls hooting in the trees with the scent from the pines drifting slowly across our camp.

MIGRATION

True enough, next morning was sunny and clear, and after a swim in the lake and some breakfast we broke camp and drove into town. The bustle announced it was market day and we found ourselves some good cheese, pate and olives among the brightly coloured awnings of the square. The met forecast from the nearby glider field at St Auban promised 'surface wind light and variable, westerly, increasing with altitude to 2,000m. Good lapse rate with cloud-base around 3,000m.' It sounded just right for pushing on to Barcelonette, some 60 kms to the north over the Col d'Allos Pass at 2,240m (7,350ft). We chose a south-westerly launch point on the mountains near St Andre, and set off up the forest road.

At the take-off spot, to our delight, the wind was fresh and blowing straight on, so we wasted no time rigging. The launch would put us directly over a huge natural rock bowl 200m below. At regular intervals, the pines over our heads would whistle and sway as a good thermal came dancing through.

Hurriedly stuffing a lump of cheese, some baguette and an apple into my ballast bag, I stood up to announce through a mouthful of delicious black olives that I thought it was time to go.

For simplicity, we had chosen a route up into the Alps which stayed close to a road that Nick could sweep. It would be our responsibility to land close to the road if we wanted a quick pick-up. We also had a telephone number to use as an information depot in case our plans changed radically. After we launched, Nick set off down the valley to take Leila and the children for a swim in the lake before setting off after us. We were going to fly a short detour around the Cheval Blanc Mountain 15km to the west before turning north in order not to get too far ahead of the van while they were swimming.

In fact, after an easy start, we were pinned down on a low ridge just before the Cheval Blanc and had to return towards St Andre without making our turn-point. The change of plans – thanks to the CBs – caused no problems.

We changed course to the north and headed off towards Allos. At this point the lift became stronger and more easily workable, and we were soon both at cloud-base near 3,000m ASL, with the alpine cumulus lined up before us like stepping stones over a series of southwest ridges.

We made good progress up the Verdon Valley, staying high under the dark grey bases. But it was cold and our battle to stay up on the low ridge behind the Cheval Blanc had tired Caroline. She told me over the CB that she was going down to land at Allos. I heard Nick giving her wind strengths and directions from the valley floor as she set up to make her landing.

As I approached the col it became apparent that the wind, locally deviated by the high summits around me, was now blowing from the other side. This meant I would have to catch a lee-side thermal off the sunny slope facing me, in order to get over the col. If I missed the thermal I was sure to get drilled by the down-slope wind coming off the col.

As I approached the slope, the turbulence and sink let me know I had not misread the situation, but the lee-side boomer was there too, and I was popped up into the strong north wind above the col. Cloud-base in this new air mass was a good 300m higher, and the lift was energetic enough to allow me to penetrate upwind over the col and into the Ubaye Valley.

Leaving the tension behind me with the col, I began to relax and enjoy my cruise around in gentle thermals getting a good look at the area, and picking out likely launch spots for the next morning. Eventually I flew down to land beside Barcelonette, having contacted the van on the CB and radioed my intended landing spot. Shortly after I finished folding up, I was picked up by Caroline and Nick and we were soon retracing our flight on the map over a steaming cup of tea.

It was so nice to look forward to an early evening meal and relaxation, instead of the long winding night road back to St Andre.

MIGRATION

That evening the campsite was in the woods, a few kilometres north of Barcelonette. We drove up a forest road that our map indicated would continue up to one of the spots I had picked for the next day's launch. We parked the van in a clearing within earshot of a rushing stream. In the morning the icy stream-bed was the scene of some very rapid washing but the sun was already warm as we cooked up our breakfast and watched early morning cumulus develop on the east-facing slopes behind us.

Later a short drive up the mountain track brought us to a reasonable launch spot, right on the road, where the wind was already westerly. Caroline decided to stay in the van as the wind already looked pretty strong out in the valley. We set the glider up on the dirt road and by the time I was ready to launch, the wind shadow behind the spur to the west had deepened and only a light slope breeze persisted. Launch went well, however, and after getting quite low for a while I finally latched on to a good thermal and spiralled back on to the spine at about 2,800m. The west wind was strong and my progress down the valley was slow. I ended up in a large cirque with the way ahead seemingly blocked. So much for plan A.

I had intended to fly west to the Lac de Serre Ponçon and then turn north into the Durance Valley which runs all the way to the Italian border past Briançon.

Plan B was to go 'over the back', glide down 10kms of uninhabited snow-covered valley and come out at the ski resort of Les Orres. I can remember wishing it was plan Z, and that plan B was to glide out and go swimming, but after some encouragement over the radio and a reminder that the rendezvous was Briançon, I decided to try it out. It took a while because cloud-base was not far above the ridge top and I had a healthy fear of going over the back into the different aerology that was bound to exist on the other side.

I was well above the snow line, and landing out just over the other side would mean a long walk out. However, a good strong thermal got me slightly above and to one side of the resident cloud from where I saw my way clear into the next valley, so I squeaked over. To my surprise there was no dreadful sink, no appalling headwind, just smooth normal air. In fact there seemed to be no wind at all.

The sky was completely covered by cloud, and I glided silently down this empty, endless, snow-covered valley towards Les Orres, wondering why it had got so smooth. Flying over the granny ski slopes, a patch of sun appeared and was soon followed by weak lift.

It took me about half an hour to work my way back up to cloud-base again, but then I was able to glide out towards Embrun and the Durance Valley, and get on the Autoroute to Guillestre and Briançon as planned.

The combination of west-facing slopes and the strong valley wind produced classic Alpine XC conditions and, due to my high ground speed, I again lost contact with my chase crew. At Briançon the main Durance Valley splits into three separate valleys and the wind-flow is always rather complex. As usual I lost a lot of height before I managed to sort out the change in wind direction. Having landed in this triple valley junction several times before after long flights, I was anxious not to fail again.

Determination and persistence paid off, however, and I slowly worked my way back up to the top of the spine from where things became clearer.

There was a standing bar of cumulus about 4km away to the east, over the Cime de la Charvie, indicating convergence. Perhaps the westerly wind was backing up against the northerly coming down from the Italian plains? Gliding over towards the cloud I found a huge area of lift that soon had me back at cloud-base, freezing again. By this time I was thinking in terms of my final glide. To the north the change in visibility down in the Susa Valley betrayed the presence of an inversion. To the east the high mountains were not very inviting at this late hour. I decided on a long glide down towards Susa and set off over the Italian border (sensa passaporto).

After a 10km glide I was over San Sicario and dropping through to the murk below. I found my glide deteriorating fast due to the north wind rushing up the valley. I selected a fine-looking field on the side slopes of the valley as the wind strength made me worry about possible turbulence behind houses and trees.

But a gentle upslope landing finished the flight off perfectly. I laid the glider down flat in the grass and took off my harness to stretch away the stiffness of the long hours of flight. I set off down the path to the village accompanied by a young boy who had seen my landing.

I found out that Caroline and Nick were waiting in Briançon with the van, and would soon be on their way over the Col de Montgenèvre to join me near Oulx. Our plans for the following day were to drive up to Monte Fraiteve from Sestriere, and try for the Col de l'Iseran via Mont Cenis. The evening bubbled with excitement as we made camp near Sestriere, and collected dead wood for our barbeque. As night fell we grilled merguez and potatoes over the brazier and discussed the possible route we could take back into France over the Col de Mont Cenis. We were really pleased with the way our migration was going. What finer way was there to discover the Alps? Day after day, unravelling kilometres of breathtaking scenery that would take a hiker months to travel on foot.

I had twice flown in close company with golden eagles, once above Barcelonette and again near Embrun. Our passion for hang gliding was getting us where we loved to be, close to nature. But next morning, on waking, nature reminded us that we were not yet in the same league as eagles. A light snow was falling all around our camp. Our dreams of migration shivering in the chill reality of a cold front at 1,800m, we sadly packed camp and set off back down south to Grasse, this time on four wheels. Next summer, things will be different!

The year 1983 was the period when the British – almost entirely English, rather than Scottish or Welsh – had established themselves as the best competitors in Europe. Our traditional rivals, the French, were wondering what to do about it. It may be forgotten these days, but in the nineteenth century, French primary school history books opened with the line: 'Never forget, France's eternal enemy is England'. Mike de Glanville's flight seemed to act as a prophet for a new type of competition devised by the French and the Swiss, called the Trans-Alpine 500, on migration principles:

> The French hang gliding federation's competition committee has approved plans for an international experimental meet with the Swiss federation which has been invited to participate in the 500km Trans-Alpine Rally.
>
> The proposed start is in the French Southern Alps near Digne, with the finish at the end of the 'Owens Valley' near Chur in Switzerland. Minor hurdles such as Mont Blanc at 4,800m (15,750ft) and the formidable Furka Pass at 2,400m (7,670ft) lie across the route, but the two teams will fly the five consecutive 100km fixed-goal tasks to see who can achieve the fastest average speed over the course.
>
> Recovery hassles have always been the big drawback to long-distance flying. The Trans-Alpine 500 could prove the value of its new format by cutting recovery down to a minimum. Instead of driving back to their initial start-point after each task, pilots will stay overnight at the goal and be fresh to fly the next day. Pilots achieving the goal would face only a drive to the nearby launch the next morning.
>
> The density of good launch spots all over the Alps facilitates this type of Trans-Alpine XC. Plan your landing at the foot of a popular launch site each evening and you can even do without transport all together. Sleeping bags and iron ration to be carried inside the double surface of the wing, please.
>
> Rumour has it that this is an elaborate plan to put an end to British domination of hang gliding in Europe. Once the cunning Continentals have got the whole route sorted out 'comme il faut', they are going to invite the 'Bloody British' down to see if they can't teach them 'une chose ou deux' about Trans-Alpine flying! We shall see ... Mike de Glanville.

Sadly, the Trans-Alpine 500 did not ignite into life, and it seemed the flame of the dream of genuine bird flight was close to flickering to death. Across the world, big distances were being flown – it was in 1983 that Judy Leden took the women's XC distance to 146 miles, and Larry Tudor crashed through the 200-mile 'wall'. But pilots used whatever means they could to do distances, drove to the toughest mountains, found ways to make Trikes tow, developed winches. The idea of man as bird, not just for hours but for days, not just waiting overnight at launch sites, but for day after day, flying further and further, the Holy Grail of the New Aviation, could quite easily have been forever lost had it not been for a group of people, the New Aviation's own Knights Templar, determined to make it happen.

Two of them, Didier Favre from Switzerland and Hubert Aupetit from France, formalised the idea in a self-policed competition (Aupetit, you may remember, wrote that beautiful account of walking and paragliding across Scotland). A pilot was on his honour not to lie in trying to win, and this competition laid down the first rules to enable us to migrate. Favre and Aupetit called this 'Bivouac Flight', and the competition the Cap 444. By 1989, no one had won it:

> Still not achieved since it was initiated in 1986, the CAP 444 is a special challenge to the individual XC hang glider pilot. The competition was conceived for the promotion of 'Bivouac Flying'. The regulations are intentionally simple and flexible, relying basically on a code of honour:
>
> 1. The winner of the CAP 444 will be the pilot who completes a distance of 444km by hang glider, by foot launch, with no outside assistance whatsoever for the transport of his wing (including vehicle, chair-lift, man or animal, etc)
> 2. Distance is calculated each day by straight-line measurement from one bivouac to the next, from take-off to landing.
> 3. The pilot is free to choose his direction for each bivouac flight, except that he may not fly over any portion of his itinerary twice in the same direction.
> 4. The first take-off must be within a European country, and by foot launch.
> 5. A pilot must supply proof of his flights. Every take-off and landing must be documented with photographs, and

if possible, attested by witnesses. It is equally necessary to photograph key or recognizable points during each flight. The use of a barograph is highly recommended.
6. Any displacement on the ground with or without a wing is authorised, but does not count in the total sum of mileage in flight.
7. From the first launch to the last landing, the total time allocated for the CAP may not exceed the sum of its three numbers: $4 + 4 + 4 = 12$ days. A pilot partaking in the challenge is engaged entirely at his own risk and is on his honour to respect the spirit of the CAP 444.
8. The jury is the single and final judge on the acceptance or rejection of a pilot's proving documents. Its decision is without appeal, and a reason does not have to be given.
9. Once a CAP 444 is achieved, CAP 555 will be inaugurated ...

A shower of prizes awaited the winner of the CAP 444, an indication of the force and energy of the originators:

1. A trophy from *Vol Libre* Magazine;
2. The sum of 4,444FF from Didier Favre;
3. A 'Citizen' computer printer, from A. Delavy CPI;
4. A Skywatch anemometer from JDC Electronique;
5. A paragliding weekend in Verbier, all expenses paid, from Ailes de K;
6. One week at Hotel Jolimont in Les Marécottes, Switzerland, including free food and lodging and tour of the Valais, from Roland Delez;
7. A hang gliding 444 harness, from Pierre Bouilloux;
8. Pair of Racer gloves, from Jean Marc Boivin;
9. A gigantic pate, from renowned chef Yves Meynard;
10. One year's subscription to *Cross Country* and *Vol Libre*.

The rules for the CAP 444 evolved over three years, and were pertinent to the mountain flying on Continental Europe.

In England I saw the challenge in a slightly different way, more concerned about distance travelled over the whole of the journey rather

MIGRATION

than treating each day separately. I tried for a straight cash prize, which I hoped would make the event self-financing. These were my rules.

The 444

Hang glider pilots in Britain are capable of migration, flying in the same way birds do. To encourage migration, I have initiated a competition open to all.

I will pay a thousand pounds (£1,000) to the first hang glider or paraglider pilot to fly more than 444 kms (275.89 statute miles) in 9 consecutive days, subject to the following rules:

1. All flights must be foot launched with no external sources of mechanical or physical power at any time, although wiremen are permitted;
2. After the initial qualifying flight, no means of travel other than free-flying or walking are permitted, and walking may take only a maximum of 5 per cent of the total distance covered;
3. No ground crews are allowed;
4. All flights must begin in Great Britain or Ireland;
5. The measured distance shall be from the beginning of the first flight of the 444 on day one to the end of the last flight on day nine (or earlier);
6. Every competing pilot must be registered prior to making any attempt; registration with the organiser is annual and covers a calendar year; registration costs are £20.00; there shall be no retroactive registration;
7. All pilots must inform the organiser each time an attempt on the 444 is made, within 24 hours of the start of that attempt; any number of attempts may be made, each beginning with an extra £20.00 payment within that calendar year;
8. All pilots must give adequate proof of the competing flights, including witnesses to take-off and landing, witness address and phone numbers, time, date and co-ordinates of take-off and landing (the organiser must be satisfied of a pilot's bona fides if witnesses are not produced); after the first day's flight, photographs are mandatory and additional to witnesses;

9. The 444 is open to any pilot regardless of age, creed, race, nationality or sex, so long as they comply with the rules;
10. The rules will be interpreted in the traditional spirit of sportsmanship, in the same way flights are expected to be made.

If no pilot completes a 444 in any one year, then I will pay two hundred and fifty pounds (£250) to the pilot who flies the furthest, complying with the 444 rules, so long as five consecutive nights are spent on the attempt.

Only a dozen people in Britain over a ten-year period registered to make a 444; some of those did it because they were friends. The first paraglider pilot signed on in 1994, and one signed for 1995, but no one has yet made even a qualifying attempt. There was once, in a club magazine in the north of England in the late 1980s, a learned article on how a 444 could be completed in Britain; I have been unable to track it down.

I cannot think why the English, the overwhelming core group of pilots in Britain, did not respond to the sheer romanticism of the 444 challenge. It is in the English tradition, exemplified by the Alpine Club of mountaineers, say, or Mallory and Irvine going for the top of Everest in 1924, or 'Blondie' Hasler and Francis Chichester sailing single-handed across the Atlantic in 1960. Aesthetically, it should have struck a deep English chord ... but it didn't. Is it our history teachers? Or are the 'damn dull fellows' who write our newspaper leaders now truly representative of us?

When the rules were framed for the CAP 444, and my 444, we were thinking of hang gliders only; paragliders were only just beginning to appear on hills. Over the last few years there have been, as we have seen, big distances flown by paragliders, ideal aircraft for bivouac flying. Hubert Aupetit thought he would launch a CAP 111 for paragliders, only to find it beaten in one flight! A Cap 222 was set, and then easily won.

Pierre Bouilloux, a Frenchman, was one of the small group fascinated by bivouac flying. He offered prize No. 7 for the original Cap 444, a '444' harness, and was the pilot who spiralled out of the sky to land at St Andre with Mike de Glanville in 1983 after a 70km triangle hang glider flight. Bouilloux's true and sweet account of completing a Cap 333 on a paraglider is so much different than the distance gobbling needed to make an Owens Valley flight. In an odd way a 444 is a seduction, rather than the masterful overwhelming of nature:

> I had a chance to complete the dream of a season, the Cap 333, during ten days in August. Like the Cap 111 and 222, it was a fantastic adventure and equally as fulfilling in the air as on the ground, with magnificent flights, long hikes in the wilderness and warm generous people who nourished my body as well as my courage to continue.
>
> To describe the flight in brief, the Cap began at Dormillouse in France. From there I reached Thorenc in 2 stages, then worked my way up to Orres in 4 flights, before making a nearly straight crossing to Maurienne via Guillestre and Navache. Within the next four days I reached Sion in Switzerland, passing over the Tarentaise, Neaufortain, the valleys of Chamonix and Verbier to make a total of 385km. It was certainly not as easy as describing it, but absolutely unforgettable.

It began on Sunday, 2 August 1992, but the start was not brilliant. Pierre Bouilloux raced off to St Andre, his intended starting point, with a Katana 51 paraglider. But the north wind and local pessimism sent him on without hesitation to Dormillouse, where a rather awkward launch from a roadside saw him sink rather than climb, in a sky full of other flying machines playing among the cumies (clouds). Finally out of his hole, he made a beautiful flight late in the day to Cordeil and capped it, in his journal, with his usual positive outlook:

> As always I get a tremendous pleasure from this welcome
> of the Southern Alps and its incomparable ambiance ...
> where I can finally relax and breathe in the wonderful air of
> the pines and resign myself to peace and quiet.

The next days were hot and sweaty with a sequence of 'flea jumps' (8–30km), interrupted by storms, followed by treks to new launch sites. Often anxious to get away from the suffocating heat and into the air, Pierre carried a 3-litre water bottle with him to avoid the 'nightmare of dehydration'.

He continued his joyous aerial tramping from ridge to ridge, often wondering whether to fly on quickly, or stay and marvel at the magic moments and incredible views ... 'to think that there are so many undiscovered peaks'. He usually ended his day under a neat blanket of stars, but occasionally in a bed of hay, a mountain hut, or even better, the inn of a flying friend who rubbished any doubts he had about continuing.

Once, after a 54km flight, he met an old sheep herder who told him of a hut higher up the mountain, with a spring and a shepherd. Pierre emptied his water bottle and slowly hiked up in the evening sun, but by nightfall had found neither the hut, the shepherd nor the water. He spent a sleepless night with a very dry throat, swearing, 'never will I empty my water bottles again!'

The longest flight was seven days into the CAP, a race of 86km from peak to peak between Le Méale and La Tarentaise. The following day he flew over a small village and was invited down by great shouts, as a group of boys waved to him to join their celebrations at their newly acquired driver's licences (in what other form of flight would this happen?). Arriving at Chamonix, he was shocked after ten days of silence by the delirious crowds, but amused by a 72-year-old flying friend. Fatigue, stiffness (next time he says he's going to jog for three months to prepare) and thirst were constant enemies, but tourists on mountain launches were the bane of his adventure. Their incessant questions and misconceptions prompted him to take-off too early in the day ... 'anything for my cherished solitude'.

The peaks and rock faces, lakes and waterfalls, accompanying eagles and occasional chats over a hot meal, all wove a rich pattern into this new bivouacing activity, which otherwise is a tale of more lift than sink, in foreign and sometimes familiar places. Ten days into his log book, Pierre was able to claim the Cap, according to new rules that take into account the distance covered on foot as well as in the air. Although entirely in accord with the idea of the flight or hike kilometre, as opposed to pure performance in the air, he was not entirely happy. He still wanted to do his 333 in the air alone. It was a satisfying decision, and his next and last leg was a good one:

> Fatigue is getting the best of me. Today I had to finish. I climbed to a refuge, Albert 1st, without doubting for an instant that the view would be spectacular. Enthused, I kept climbing, and at 3,000m (9,850ft) I was surprised

to discover a group of people on the terrace of the refuge, 300m below me, awaiting my takeoff. I decided to wait for the best conditions to get enough height to cross over the Col de Balme. It worked! I sailed over the most indescribably beautiful scenery to 3,200m, then turned a little uneasily towards Switzerland. Breathe slowly, I thought, and consider for a minute the best route in this labyrinth of huge rock walls. I arrived close to Verbier where I hesitated about going towards Valais, because of the terrible valley wind. A veil seemed to be drawn over the sun. Bad weather coming. No more lift. I landed at the Croix de Coeur, and soon took off again after a little mishap, with a key getting caught in my lines (I blush to think of the article I wrote in 1988 warning about the risks of hurried take-offs!).

Over Inserable, I got a good 300m climb, then set off on a long final glide into the middle of the valley, crossing Sion and its airport to land at the base of Val d'Herens. That is 41kms today, which makes it 385 in all, including 30 by foot! This time I have clinched it. I am too excited to even think straight, after 12 days in an incredible time zone. I am hitching home to my family as fast as possible.

OK, OK. I have to admit to over-doing it about the magic of bivouac flying. I can only encourage you to try, just once, even for 2/3 days. It is like bathing in nature, an unforgettable adventure. Travel light, with a minimum on your back and on your mind. Ten days of life in the wilderness is Spartan, but what a purge, psychologically and physically! As someone quite correctly remarked, 'You must have had an awful thick layer to remove!'

Bouilloux, like Favre, was a committed bivouac flyer, ready at the drop of a hat to get into the mountains and go. Hubert Aupetit, French guardian of the concept, worried that other pilots would think bivouacing was for supermen only. He searched in print for the essentials of this type of flying:

> I know Didier Favre and Pierre Bouilloux well. I would not call them mutants, but only just! Each is an exceptional

individual in his own right, in terms of character, motivation and perseverance. I feel unable to do as they do, or do it as well. However, I don't think that bivouac flying benefits from being exclusively associated with such extreme acts of prowess.

Uphill landings at 3,000m on a hang glider with not a soul in sight, downwind parapente launches with a blocked vario; I wouldn't measure up, nor would most pilots, yet my love of 'free flying' and the mountains and my way of expressing it abides, although differently, during periods when personal affairs keep me occupied.

So I would like to defend a different approach to bivouac flying, one more open and accessible, less hard-core, and compatible with a normal lifestyle. The only conditions; to love nature, expect the unexpected, and to feel at ease, alone under a starry sky.

Itinerary: One night outdoors is the minimum unless you're very badly equipped and have to abandon everything to avoid catching pneumonia. Two or three nights are necessary to reach the desired state of trampiness in the first outing.

Available time determines the length of the itinerary: 15–30km a day is a good gauge. It is not a test to be passed but a journey made in a most original way, with time given over for a nap, an encounter or a whim.

By hang glider, a closed circuit itinerary is 'de rigueur'. Nothing is worse than having to hitch back to the car after a long flight, then drive back to the landing spot to pick up your wing.

It is easier with a paraglider. Train and bus schedules help determine the departure and arrival locations. As for which direction to take, eventual difficulties such as hills to be climbed, stretches of aerial freeway which make the trip easier, and of course, the weather conditions on departure day, are all determining factors.

With an open circuit, it is simpler than a closed (triangle) circuit. In general, if winds and breezes from the west are favourable, we opt for a west to east direction, with the added advantage of a flight each morning. A good way to start the day. The vagabond is easy-going. If it rains, he walks. If it is windy, he flies. This is one of the great things about a total experience like bivouacing; there is always something to do (from now on I will refer to paragliders, given the practical limitations of hang gliders). Obviously a long journey is to be avoided when snow and storms are forecast. Yet there is nothing so grand as a good late-afternoon summer storm, viewed from the shelter of a shepherd's mountain hut.

Ethics: The problem is to define what is acceptable or unacceptable in one's own mind. In certain flight disciplines, one imposes a strict limit beforehand. Pierre Bouilloux explains it very well: 'An ethic provides indispensable motivation to avoid giving up when the going gets tough.'

In the more flexible framework which I am proposing, I will admit I am not always completely consistent. In principle, I like the idea of getting off a train, doing the whole journey on foot or by air, then getting back on another train ... but I would not ruin my day, trudging along a boring national highway, without trying to hitch, if I couldn't short-cut across a field.

Here the ethic is to rely on oneself, but not to refuse the help of others every once in a while, in order to spare yourself the really tedious bits.

Nonetheless, it is a great feeling when you scrutinize the map and think you've done it all under your own steam, with your legs, your arms and your head. Wouldn't it be a shame to deprive yourself of that pleasure?

Never hesitate to land or continue on foot if the idea of flying is too daunting. Just don't do the whole trip with your paraglider wrapped up in your backpack.

Flight Precautions: As soft-core as my idea of bivouacing is, it calls for lots of self-confidence. You have to be experienced in launches, in all flying situations and conditions, landings on all sorts of terrain, and above all, doing it alone. One has no idea how much a place can change when it is deserted. It is hard to describe the mixture of fear, confidence and euphoria. One thing is certain, you don't fly in the same way. You are more cautious in some cases, and less in others. You are always more attentive and more intuitive. For me, it is almost a completely different sport. Some call you irresponsible. But reproaching someone for being imprudent is usually done to make oneself feel more prudent by comparison.

Gear: Back to Didier and Pierre, whose check-lists are incredibly detailed. This is to say that from trip to trip it is a real pleasure to put together your own gradually perfected pack. Some prefer a hot meal but care less about a good book. Others get nourishment from William Faulkner and fill up on granola. Those who fear the cold take a down-feather sleeping bag. But the Spartan makes it his code of honour to take only the bare essentials. What is indispensable is a water container (at least 2 litres) and above all a wing that doesn't give you any trouble. Reliability is worth a little loss of precision.

Rest assured that no joker is going to pass overhead and sneer, unless he's a bird. Whatever the flight, for once you will be 'King of the Skies'.

So these are among the Knights Templar, nurturing the vision of bivouac flying as a prelude to the Holy Grail of human migration flight: Pierre Bouilloux, Hubert Aupetit, Roland Delaz, Jean Marc Boivin, Mike de Glanville, Sherry Thevenot, Yves Meynard ...

But if there is a Galahad among them, a Victorian 'Beau Ideal', it is the man dubbed by a shepherd in the Alps as the Vagabond of the Skies, Didier Favre.

Chapter 9

Didier Favre – Vagabond of the Skies

There is said to be a theory by Carl Jung about unfulfilled ambition, that children are loaded with the responsibility to do what their parents dreamed of doing, but never did. These unfulfilled ambitions can go down the centuries, passed from one generation to another, often unarticulated, perhaps wrapped up in myths, a ball of codes of behaviour, waiting for one person in one generation to unravel it and make it happen.

There is no blood link between Icarus and King Bladud of Bath and England, between Eilmar and the Saracen of Constantinople, Armen Firmen and Leonardo da Vinci, Sir George Cayley and Alphonse Penaud and Lilienthal and Rogallo and Dickenson and Miller and my friend Alvin Russell. But if they are all Children of the Wind, passing the essential dream of flight, one to another, generation after generation, then none of them should feel disappointment at where their dream came to fruition, in a man steeped in all the thrusting, aggressive, contradictory, sensitive and wild virtues of Western culture, Didier Favre.

I only met Didier once. It was in late 1985, and I had recently returned from Switzerland where the President of CIVL, a Swiss called Tomas Boshard, had used me as a sort of battering ram to change the way his countrymen organised their competitions to try and produce the winning ways of the British (I am pleased to say that, years later, they have succeeded). When Didier Favre phoned to make a date for dinner at a restaurant in Charlotte Street in London's West End, I thought he wanted to continue the discussion about Swiss competitions.

My memories of Didier all through that evening were that he seemed to bounce off the walls! He could hardly contain the energy driving him. He was not interested in competition – 'puhhh! puhhh!' – it was *migration* he wanted to talk about. I had written my forlorn editorial on the subject nearly five years earlier, but Didier was taking me to dinner that evening because, he told me, he saw it as the 'trigger' for the sort of flying he cherished, and he wanted to thank me.

Didier told me about the Cap 444 he was setting up with Hubert Aupetit. I knew Hubert from Lachens in France in 1980, when he made me nervous by flying too close to me; he gently explained later he was trying to get a photograph of me in the air for *Vol Libre*, of which he was the editor. I was always afraid of flying too close to other hang gliders. They had not come up with the term bivouac-flying then. Contrary to reports later, I had nothing to do with originating the Cap 444; the version I set up in Britain was a straight copy of Didier and Hubert's event. If he saw my editorial as the trigger for his Cap 444, his phenomenal energy was a trigger for my own 444. If there are kindred spirits, Didier and I were brothers.

Didier was a Swiss businessman, an entrepreneur, first selling bicycles, followed by an import-export company dealing with the Middle East. He then moved into electronic security where he stayed for ten years. Judy Leden wrote of first meeting him in 1982:

> I was thermalling in the Alps when a bright yellow glider flew in a thousand feet below me, banked up at an impossible angle and began to corkscrew his way upwards. Everyone moved aside to let him through. Here was someone whose determination was so strong you didn't want to stand in his way.

Didier became Swiss hang gliding champion in 1983, and once held the French distance record at nearly 200km. He won the French XC Cup in 1984, and said that at one point he was possibly the best pilot in Switzerland. He was a tough competition pilot; in a feature in *XC Magazine* called 'Pilots on Pilots', there were no illusions about his will to win:

> He trains a lot. Takes the sport very seriously but not competition. He's got a big mouth. Always trying to prove something. He wants to win, or rather, beat the others.
> - Direct. Has no tact. He's raw. He provokes others intentionally.
> - In flight he's aggressive, resistant, a fighter. He hangs in there.

- He's an exhibitionist, but also extremely generous. He'll give the shirt right off his back.
- He enjoys playing macho in the air and on the ground.
- In thermals, he butts in.
- He conceived the 444. That's his thing, a big challenge without a competition.

Taken together, such qualities are those lauded by the famous cartoon characters based on Uderzo's Asterix and Obelix as the essential qualities of an Ancient Gaul. Didier was like that, physically not very big, but there was a feel to him, like the best of Fred Quimby's *Tom and Jerry* cartoons. If he was playing a character in *Winnie the Pooh*, Didier was Tigger. He had what the British call 'a Marmite quality'. You either loved or hated him.

His energy ran, overran even, all over the place. He started a museum in Switzerland to cover hang gliding:

> I started it because it's our responsibility to leave something behind for future pilots. We are still the pioneers of hang gliding today, so we should collect everything while it's easy rather than wait 50 years from now. I proposed this idea to the Swiss Federation with a budget, and was put in charge of starting it. We collected many gliders, a lot of material and set up a theatre. We are also conducting exchanges with Eastern European countries. It is interesting but I am not involved any more. Still, I am proud of the fact that because of the museum there will be 50 more pilots flying in Eastern Europe.

Didier was born about three years after Alvin Russell, but lived a great deal longer. The path Didier chose for himself echoes in my mind with memories of Alvin, who, had he lived, could have chosen the same way to go. At the age of 44, with a wife and two grown-up children, Didier finally became ratted off with business. He had always been torn between work and flying, describing work as a lot of money and a lot of trouble, but in 1991 he told his partner: 'I'm sick of it. To talk about freedom is easy, but to be free is another matter. Give me one French franc – ten English pence – for all my work, and I'll leave.'

And he did, for the American equivalent of 15 cents. He felt he could make enough money, through talks and articles and photographs, to stay alive. He made and marketed video films of his 444 attempts. He could not be bothered trying to find a big sponsor, though the hang glider manufacturer ICARO 2000 gave him two gliders and pin money.

The urge to be a prophet drove him to speak out. He saw hang gliding as something holy, a whole step further than Richard Bach's gift of wings and *Jonathan Livingstone Seagull*, with deep responsibilities as well. He told 'Spanish Joe' Hayler, then editor of *Wings!'* in England, that he did not see throwing in his job to become a full-time flyer meant he was a bum, a hippy, or even a holy lunatic:

> We live about 80 years and fly for about 30–40. To go through life just thinking about flying and nothing else is stupid. Flying is not a goal, it's a means. I discovered nature through flying. Before, I did not care about nature. Now I see we live in such a fantastic world. Anyone who lives in the wild knows it has to be protected. I am giving back what nature gave to me.
>
> Between the South of France and the Alps, the war left a lot of debris. I wonder how people can leave such rubbish in the mountains? To help solve the problems of the world, like pollution, we have to act ourselves. Why don't we get 1,000 people to come and clean up the mountains? Pilots can help a lot by observing and reporting. It is good for the mountain, it is good for the pilot too.
>
> If you speak loud enough, people listen. Five or ten sincere people are enough to get results. More and more will become conscious that something must be done. To be truthful, it will take years. There should be more about ecology in hang gliding magazines.
>
> I am not an extremist. If pilots make a ramp or cut down 3 trees, it is not a problem. You have to be careful to strike the right balance, not to become too extreme. As ecologists gain power, free flyers are coming under attack. Sometimes rightfully. Look at all the cars you find at a site! If we can walk, we should. Hubert Aupetit and I have launched 'Marche ou Vole' (Walk or Fly), a new kind of

contest where cars are not allowed. The first one was held in Verbier and was very successful. We have to change our way of thinking.

Judy Leden felt that Didier was one of the world's few truly happy people. His decision to leave the rat race to pursue his dreams was a conscious one. It could not have been easy with the usual pressure from society, especially in Switzerland, to conform, and he had a family to support. He made a success of the 444 through hard work and the ability to tell good stories and take superb photographs. His chosen path epitomised the reasons why Judy and many others fly – freedom, excitement, the beautiful scenery. Who can know what joys he experienced in the pursuit of his long-distance serial safaris? The sunsets he must have seen, the birds he flew with, the suppers he shared as an unexpected guest of mountain shepherds? He never seemed to lose track of the big picture, remaining fiercely independent and refusing to acknowledge limitations.

Didier became one of the running stories of Sherry Thevenot's superb *Cross-Country* magazine, the true chronicle of the New Aviation. There were always snippets of information about what he was doing. Not enough people were trying the Cap 444, he thought, and threw himself into doing it himself. He ended the first attempt in a hospital in Nice after misjudging a landing. Didier finally completed a Spartan, self-imposed Cap 444 in 1991, but only after disappointments that would have stopped almost everyone else:

> Everything was planned so that July would be mine, an entire month to reattempt, and this time finally succeed in the Cap444. Ever since my first fumbled attempt in 1989, not one day had gone by without my pondering on this fateful liberating act. The closer I got to goal, the more my obsession grew. Fours were everywhere! I took it as an omen, especially the morning I woke at 4:44! But on the eve of my departure I still had not united all the psychological and physical ingredients necessary to venture off anew. My mind was turning over professional laundry. I was being treated for back problems and general fatigue. Yet I have always said that to be totally sound in body and mind is an absolute requirement for this kind of undertaking.

Thank God my old motivation was still intact and would accompany me right to the end.

The Chamonix/Planraz chair-lift was out of order, which left me one alternative to get to takeoff, by jeep. Because of turbulence and scrappy thermals, it took me 3h20 to make 35km to Verbier, where, for safety's sake I landed at Champsee, the official LZ. To ease myself into the mood of the Cap444, I walked and carried all 45kgs (101 lbs) of my equipment up 1100m (3,600ft!) at La Chaux, in two separate trips. I was fed up with machines and people, the perpetual circus. All I wanted was to be alone. At least I knew where I was, and where I was heading.

Sarrayer was asleep while I ambled off to lay my head in some hay, serenading the night with my harmonica.

Next day I joined up with some friends in a blood-curdling thermal that hoisted me to 3,000m and then eased me into the Rhône Valley, where there was nothing. Two hours later I was with the cows near Sierre, borrowing a car to get back to the start, and setting the 444 mileage counter back to zero.

July 2nd: The inversion layer persisted at 2,100m, my wing needed tuning and my harness zipper had broken in mid-air ... enough for one day.

Grounded, I witnessed Heren cows clashing horns to determine who would lead the herd. It was a real show, with a magnificent backdrop of five peaks over 4,000m high, among which were the proud Matterhorn, topped with little puffers, and Mont Blanc with a lenticular halo in the distance.

July 5th: I finally managed to rise above Mt Bonvin, Fiesch, the Eggishorn, the magnificent Aletscher Glacier partially shaded by the 3,700m high cumuli, but in spite of all my proddings it was impossible to cross the Furka Pass.

In rough dynamic lift my right wing rose and threw me practically against a rock face. Woooah! Before long I was prone under a starry sky, satisfied but a little unsettled about not being able to tune my wing correctly. Regretting the lack of a sleeping bag, I woke to a cold morning that warmed as the sun peered over the peaks. Suddenly the Oberwald chairlift began to rattle and a local innkeeper surprisingly appeared with provisions and hot coffee.

It wasn't until 3.30 in the afternoon that I took off under a bona fide cumulus that guaranteed 4,000m, more than enough to get over the Furka Pass. At Andermatt, the resident 'old faithful' thermal failed me so there wasn't enough altitude to attempt the Oberalp Pass. Instead, I landed on top of it.

Things were looking up. Physically, I was in good shape, and psychologically too. The professional laundry was drying! Also, my fly-on-the-wall landings, the greatest invention of XC flying, were improving. Starved and stinky, I decided it was time to descend the mountain-top for a good scrub up. The road meandered all the way to a hotel filled with bawdy weekend fishermen. No women. I opted for the other side of the street where a colony of young jovial boys offered free lodging and good humour.

July 6th: An eagle guided me in centring lift to cross the pass. Circling above the unfriendly fishermen's lodge, I sent off a good spit, but the joke turned on me – I had forgotten to snap the chin strap of my helmet and got it right back in the face!

Above Muttenstock, an ibex observed my landing, and a shepherd offered me his hospitality, thank the Lord. My feet were hurting from all the climbing. At sunset I watched an eagle, the sixth one encountered today. What ease. No tuning problems for him! Hmmmmm. How can I find an acceptable compromise to make centring in thermals easier?

Next day was unflyable. I went in search of mountain goats that are so hard to spot from the air because their coats are camouflaged and blend in with the rocky terrain. I tracked them down by the sound of their hooves on the rocks, and butting horns. The north wind, which kept me from flying, became my accomplice since the animals could not smell my presence. Before long I was confronted by a magnificent herd of males with huge horns. Unforgettable moment!

For bedding, I hiked in the thickening fog to a hut where there was a profusion of drinks: beer, wine, but nothing to eat and I was starving. Fortunately, two students from Liverpool, novice Alpiners with an assignment to gather geological specimens, happened in. Conveniently, they had some spaghetti!

July 8th: My goal was to return to the Valais, westward, although turning back made me waste two hours of good thermalling. Over Mount Hochwang an eagle adeptly entered lift at the base and quickly overtook me to fly out at the top while I was forced to land. After four hours of circling in a harness that would not close, I was bushed.

A 70-year-old inhabitant of Spondeca, a mountain hamlet, offered me his chalet for the night, and woke me the next morning by placing a pan of greasy battered potatoes under my nose, a local speciality smelly enough to wake a dead man. His generosity was hard to refuse.

The area has a reputation as being difficult to fly, but I easily found good lift which carried me to Davos, where a huge cumie ignored my prayers. As a result, I landed at Jakobshorn and waited for the sun to reappear. Then a parapentist, like a fly on a cloud, showed me the way to Val Susauna en Engadin, where I landed again on a 2,600m perch.

There were hundreds of untended sheep and a little cabin basking in the sun next to a small lake. Was it a dream? The door was open and on the table lay a note. 'He who is here thirsty is himself at fault', and a spread of drinks and food. Thank you, anonymous friend. Of course, I did not depart without leaving something. Such a pleasant surprise did wonders for my morale.

Conditions were strong. I got a free ride to 4,000m right off launch and flew over the lakes of Livigno in Italy. But my wing was giving me trouble. Hell, you would think that after flying for 14 years I would have learned to tune it properly. At least I was able to close my harness to my knees.

Scrappy lift got me to rainy Bormio, then a cold front took me up to 4,200m, a nirvana compared to the desolate country below. I crossed the Stelvio Pass and the Etsch Valley to land above Monte Croce on the Austrian border. In another little cabin, tea, coffee and sugar with a 'For You' note were waiting.

I ran down to Schluderns to buy film, call my wife for the first time since my departure, and take a good bath. It was odd to be parachuted into a town without knowing whether to speak Italian or German. Thank goodness I had remembered to take some foreign currency.

Thirteen days into my log (although only 7 days into my Cap for having used a car at Aminona), I had about 300kms under my belt and was feeling pretty good. My next goal was Zillithal in Austria, via the Brenner Pass. Cap444 here I come!

July 13th: Stormy weather had me grounded. I found a mountain hut enveloped in high, untrampled grass. There were cows in the fields but no one around. A ray of sunshine on the village in the bottom of the valley, and two intersecting rainbows, accompanied my solitude. Difficult to tell if the animals appreciated my harmonica serenade. A straw mattress on the wooden bed, and my carry-bag as a cover, made a perfect niche for the night. On the wall of the hut I left my mark, like many others: 'Volare e vivere' – To Fly is to Live.

The morning rain led to reflection, rest and wisdom. It was like a bird cage that dissolves with the sun.

I met Raphael, another breed of solitary individual. A flyer of sorts, thanks to a certain weed. He was on a hillside in this stark wild region, among a multitude of sheep, troubled over the day's loss of seven animals. His passion was hybrid plants, an interest he pursued methodically. Although his artificial paradise did not tempt me (thinking so as I cling to my bottle of wine!), his self-taught scientific approach to nature did.

July 15th: The storm passed but left a howling wind that chilled my optimism. Nevertheless, I left Schluderns and climbed up to find my wing, abandoned for two days, flapping in the sun in a bed of wild rhododendron. Flapping?

Yes! My pace slowed down. I did not want to face the catastrophe. A whole section of the undersurface was waving like a flag in shreds. The undersurface was torn as well. How was it possible? True, I had used the carry-bag as blanket, but I had taken precautions to protect the wing. It must have been the cables that wore the sail right through, or an animal that ripped it before the wind got the better of it.

It was too much to bear – completely unjust! In 1989 a shoulder injury kept me from making the Cap. In 1990 it was bad weather on the first attempt, and theft of my equipment on the second. And this time, a storm! I was too sick to even blaspheme!

'Didier, clean up your professional laundry before attempting something as noble as the 444. Don't fly with all those strings attached!'

But all that I had worked up to, day after day for over a year ...

It took me a good ten minutes to get a grip again. Then I did not waste a second. Grabbing up my equipment, all 45kgs of it, I threw it on my back and headed for the nearest road. A kind Schluderner agreed to take care of my wing. I hopped on a bus to Austria, and then took a train back to Switzerland. Early the next morning I was packing my car rack with a new wing.

July 16th: The Cap444 is back to zero. A new takeoff at noon from Chamonix/Planpraz left me in a liftless sky. Chamonix had me imprisoned for several days. Getting to cloudbase was no problem, but getting out of the valley with the west wind was a big one. Finally, my wife picked me up, treated me to a big spaghetti dinner, and next day I drove to Saint-André-les-Alpes for (another!!) new start with my heart in my boots.

July 20th: The devil of a westerly would not let up. I thought I was going crazy, and became obsessed with time running out. Another failure was out of the question!

After a meagre 40km, I had to deal with the sea breeze which sent me to the floor of the Val in the Gorge of Daluis, the only possible landing place in the area. The wind picked up tremendously and nearly sent my new wing into a tumble at 50m AGL. I just missed the river and miraculously had a gentle touch-down on the large pebbles.

That evening I was coaxed into partying with a band of guys, borrowed a car and had a good time drinking, but on the way back missed a turn and got my car wheels stuck in a sand bank. Disgusted, I jumped straight into the lake and collected myself again.

Was I jinxed?

The next take-off gave me 30 minutes of excellent conditions, then came a large unavoidable cloud cover that put me in stalemate before Cheval Blanc Mountain for over 2h30m.

Back to start!!

Yes, you can say I am persistent. My motivation is still simmering. but the whole adventure seemed like a grand illusion.

July 22nd: Saint-André is one of the best flying sites in the whole of Europe. I flew for 5 hours under 4,000m ceilings over the Aiguille Rouge, Serre-Ponçon Lake, the Queyras, the Ascension Lakes (the most beautiful bivouac between Chamonix and Nice) and Briançon. Mont Blanc beckoned northward, but a wind from Mondane interfered. The Vale de Suza and the plains of Torino were inundated with rain. I settled for the Aiguille Rouge where lived Joseph, a shepherd and his troop of 1,800 sheep I had met last year.

My landing on a steep slope went perfectly well in spite of 20/30kph cross-tail wind. Next I spent a painstaking hour folding my wing, taking every possible precaution.

It had been a great day! July weather at last. Sometimes lift carried me up at 10 m/s (2,000 ft/min). There were a hundred sailplanes and lots of hang gliders and parapentes and eagles around Dormillouse.

July 26th: Within a few peaceful moments the valley widened, sailplanes sniffed for lift over the plains, while I happened upon one nice big gentle elevator.

At sunset I continued under cloudbase and flew over the Vars Pass to land at 8pm. It was freezing. Gisele and her dogs kindly harboured me for the night. The hut was tucked into the Queyras Mountains, with a view of Mount Viso and the Mercantour peaks. Gisele talked for hours about her love for animals and nature and about her solitude. The atmosphere was so gentle. I was like a nursing baby, oblivious to all troubles …

In the morning the donkeys and marmots watched while Gisele doctored her 1,600 sheep. It was like a picture to be framed, with a royal eagle circling above, and a lenticular halo to make it perfect.

With three large steps I was off, rising above Gisele, who was agape. She had never seen such a thing. Within minutes she was only a speck on the hillside and I was heading for the horizon.

July 28th: As the north wind grew quieter, I set my cap for Serre-Ponçon Lake and all went well as far as the Bonette Pass. Above Foux d'Allos I spotted a hang glider in difficulties, about to land, and before long it was my turn, 100m below the Sestriere Pass. I landed with a strong tailwind on a gradual slope with wheels (no use taking chances!). Then I hiked over the pass, thinking that a head wind would greet me on the other side. My hunch was right. An hour later the sun was back. I launched again and crossed the Ubaye Valley to land at the Crete des Aigles (Eagles Crest) above Lake Serre Ponçon.

What a treat to find an old friend! This time it was Philippe, another sheep herder, who invited me in and sat me down to a beer.

'We shepherds are true marginals of society, but you, you are the original vagabond of the skies.'

And so I was baptised.

August 6th: It was only in the heat of the rising sun that I could really catch some sleep. My morale was intact, and yesterday's mistakes were forgiven. After all, not all cumulus clouds that look luscious are necessarily so.

Sure of myself, full of concentration, I launched at 11.30 and clung to a cloud even though the base was relatively low. Every crossing was ensured in this way, and I made headway in spite of the headwind. After Mount Pelat, I circled for 45 minutes over the south faces, waiting for the west face to heat up. I took every precaution necessary. There were less than 60km left to get through my Cap444, including the 10 extra kilometres that I promised myself. There was plenty of time. I lost my way on the map, but kept my heading on the compass.

High in the sky on the horizon a wing was turning, then another and another. The sky was filling up. Sailplanes too. At that point I found the lake at Saint-André-les-Alpes, which I had left 15 days earlier.

The 444 was behind me.

That winter a documentary on Didier Favre's attempts at the Cap 444 won the Grand Prize at the St Hilaire Film Festival.

Judy Leden watched the change from competition pilot to serial vagabond, forging a unique path in the sport of hang gliding. She was flying in the Lariano Triangle Competition in Italy, waiting for the task window to open, when a figure appeared from below, striding purposefully up the slope. Sporting a week's growth of beard and the woolly hat that he was never seen without, Didier was in pursuit of a spare up-right for his glider following a mistimed slope landing. He was in the middle of one of his mega-trips, a grin fixed permanently on his face and an acquisitive light in his eyes.

It was sheer bloody mindedness that won him through the Cap 444, but he formed strong ideas on the sort of equipment a bivouac flyer needed to take with him. Like Pierre Bouilloux, Didier went for the Spartan ideal, though losing his sail the way he did persuaded him to take a sleeping bag, and not content himself with using the glider carry-bag, and leave the glider at risk. He wrote an equipment guide for Cap 444 flyers the following year:

> The flight is not the sole object of worry when bivouac flying. Safety, nourishment, sleep, repairs, carrying one's wing, these are some of the numerous problems to be solved. Safety takes priority.
>
> Thanks to distress signals, smoke bombs and wheels on the A-frame, one can fly away with more confidence than

ever. Bivouac flying is no longer a superhuman feat. Over the years it has been tested and tamed.

Distress signal: Alone, lost at the bottom of a valley or on top of a mountain, if you do have an accident you must have quick access to medical assistance. Experience has proven our radios are too limited to be efficient. There is a solution: distress signals with a life-span of 7/10 years (Locat type), which are lightweight and cost about $100.

In case of an accident, at least in Europe and North America, you can pull a handle and the apparatus will emit a non-stop distress signal for 30 hours, which is picked up by one of two satellites (SARSAT or COSPOS) passing over once every two hours. The signal (in Europe) is then transmitted to a recovery station in Toulouse which organises the appropriate assistance to the country in question. Thanks to the Canadians, French, Americans and Russians, the satellite service is free.

Base-bar wheels: Hail to the inventor of base-bar wheels who undoubtedly did not know the value of his product to hang glider pilots, because no landing is ever 100 per cent sure. Stress, thermals, brush, stones, wind, potholes, these are just some of the obstacles a pilot may encounter.

Also takeoffs on shallow slopes at high altitudes where the air is less dense can cause problems, because you have to run faster to get airborne. If the A-frame touches the ground it can mean damage.

The easiest solution is to fix wheels to the bottom bar. Personally, I opted for small plastic wheels, although I recommend inflatable rubber ones that better absorb frontal and lateral shock. They weigh 450grams per wheel (1 lb), diameter 200 x 50cm (8 x 2 inches). At least the wheels give one the comforting thought that sooner or later they will save a control bar ... if not an arm.

Smoke bomb: Wind conditions on the ground vary, often making their strength and direction difficult to judge. When in doubt, throw a smoke bomb and say bye-bye to stress. Fix a smoke bomb on to your harness (weight 30 grams and as cumbersome as a matchbox). Thrown from a height of 50–150m, it smokes for 30 seconds and gives a clear indication of the wind conditions. I use 5/6 each season.

A-frame: The most vulnerable part of a wing is the A-frame, particularly the base of the control bar, which 9 times out of 10 is the only part of the wing where breakage occurs. Base-bar wheels reduce the consumption of A-frames. I use the simple round bars, rather than air-foiled ones, because they are easier to grip, lighter, cheaper, and they can be bent back into shape more easily. I used to fly with a spare A-frame tucked into the nose of my glider, but now with my new wing I fix it to the cross-boom with two bungees, as close to the keel as possible.

Protection from the elements: In general, there are places to lay one's head, even in the mountains, within a minute to an hour on foot, but occasionally there is nothing. In this case a sleeping bag or warm clothing is vital. My own sleeping bag weighs only 900 grams (2lbs) and rolls up into a neat little ball. For Spartans, a bivouac bag makes a good enough bed, so long as one wears warm clothes. I recommend Polartec thermal underwear, and carry a 900gram set. During the successful 444 I had neither carry bag nor sleeping bag, and the nights were cold but tolerable. But it is true that the better one sleeps, the better one flies.

Miscellaneous: A good pair of shoes or boots is a must and may not only keep one from getting blisters, but could save you from a broken ankle on high mountain pastures. After years of casual consideration to my feet, I finally woke up and got myself an excellent comfortable pair of hiking shoes that cover the ankle and have non-slip soles.

My latest gadget is perhaps the best companion of all. It is a prototype watch by Thomen, with an altimeter and a compass as well, light, compact and reliable!

Of course, conquering the Cap 444 was never going to be enough for Didier, and he lost interest too in a 555. In April 1992, he announced a new task, a Cap 1111, an extraordinary journey he intended to make, by foot and wing from Monaco on the French Riviera, across the entire chain of the Alps to land in Slovenia. He intended to be on his own, flying with the birds or whatever he came across in the sky, but landing so that he could take off the following day, for at least three months. And because he felt he betrayed his own ideals, he failed:

Sospel, Côte d'Azur, June 21: A final wave and my friends' white Toyota disappears. I am alone and it is raining. There isn't a single hope of taking off today. Tomorrow? Surely the day after? Bad weather never lasts on the Côte d'Azur. Without sunshine I am nothing but a land creature crawling among others. When the sun smiles I am capable of lifting off from this miserable 400m mound and going all the way to Slovenia.

Listening to the rain falling on my 14 square metre kite turned umbrella, my optimism is not dampened. I am a 'man of certainty'. If something is theoretically possible inside my head, it is already accomplished. There is only one simple formality left: do it!

For a suitcase, I have only a harness and its few pockets for clothes, food, equipment, spare parts, maps, books, binoculars, flasks and logbook; 6/7 kilos in which to cram the obvious and dismiss the superfluous. With a 30kg hang glider, a few kilos of photographic equipment, parachute and two harmonicas, the total 50kgs is like lead on the ground and straw in the air.

My privilege as a pioneer of 'The Crazy Crossing' is to define the rules and principles by and for myself. The idea is to travel the Alpine arc, nearly 1,200km, with no other means of transport but my wing and legs, managing alone. In case of an accident, I am comforted by the thought of possessing a little 300g beacon which is supposed to communicate with satellites when the pin is pulled, to initiate my rescue.

One rainy day I found myself face to face with the human specimen I once was. Not long ago, at 44 years of age, I burned all the files, business plans and contracts that had enslaved me, to start life from scratch. My stubble, silly red cap, Bermuda shorts, walking boots and a flower between my teeth had nothing in common with his businessman's mask. Poor, hurried prisoner of time …

DIDIER FAVRE – VAGABOND OF THE SKIES

Mount Mournier, July 9th: After 9 days at Sospel, the sky clears long enough to allow a flight to Mt Authion in the National Park of Mercantour, after which another period of bad weather greets me. Rather than sulk, I learn how to make goat's cheese. When another patch of blue sky appears, Melodie (my glider) and I take to the air.

To have such immense space for a playground is simply magic, with clouds, rain, sun, wind, thermals and birds as partners and adversaries, and the Alps and the Gorges de Dalius as a setting. A falcon joins us as we approach Mont Saint-Honorat. Then the rain forces us to land on the roof of a deserted world where we are grounded for 4 days.

After filling my flask with rain water that streams off my battens, I search for the hut I spotted before landing. The rapidly forming fog and slippery slope are against me, but thanks to my new gadget, a watch equipped with an altimeter and compass, I find my way. The door is closed with a string. No one is in, but bags of wood and salt, ample provisions and 4 jerrycans of red wine announce an imminent return. Probably not today in this thick fog. Lying before a wood fire with only my harmonica to break the silence, I think life is grand.

Mont Sangraure, July 11: From Mont Sant-Honorat I go west toward Saint-André-des-Alpes, then north, making a large detour due to the very low clouds that keep me from venturing over the high ridges. River sources spurt out from everywhere, some joining to form beautiful waterfalls. A fox frisks about carelessly, unsuspecting of the two-legged animal doing the same above him. Clouds race southwards as the Mistral (after the rain, Public Enemy No. 2) sets up. Melodie waits patiently in the fog, soaked to the tubes.

We manage to takeoff at 1.30 when a tiny window opens over the valley. Once out of the protected little circus, the serious muscle work begins. The lift is strong, but cut about by the wind. Everything I gain in altitude, I lose in drift. Pushing against the wind, I struggle for 2 hours and 20km to the Montagne des Têtes, where the wind strengthens too much for comfort. I land in front of a refuge which has neither phone nor food, and so decide to go by foot to Mariaud. I had landed next to this hamlet 6 years earlier, and the sole inhabitant, Eudoxie Roux, as friendly as she was old, lent me her telephone.

After hiking for 2 hours through the deserted wilderness of Galèbre, the welcome is rather cold. A bearded hiker begging for a telephone can only arouse distrust. When I ask for Eudoxie, the atmosphere changes. 'She died four years ago,' said her son Yannick, a seasoned shepherd. He offers me the barn for the night, bread, cooked sausages, cheese and eggs. 'They're fresh today. Make a hole each end and suck out the yoke; it's more nourishing than steak!' At the table, my borrowing of Yannick's knife to cut the bread is not appreciated. Knives are personal objects to shepherds, a symbol of their survival.

The Mistral keeps me three days in the area before I fly north in a headwind under a low cloudbase to cross the Serre-Ponçon Lake. If it had not been for the Mistral, I would never have known this fabulous region, except as a black number on a map, indicating kilometres travelled. I owe my best discoveries and experiences to bad weather. Flight is the vehicle which takes me to the essentials – friendship, nature and life.

The charm of bivouac flying is really on the ground.

Le Piolit, July 15: For the first time I have company; four jovial Italian pilots and a little French girl whom I leave behind. Conditions are weak but I am hungry for some flying time. An eagle joins me and soon after his lady; 'Good day, your Majesty'. I accidentally cut into a thermal, forgetting the right of way, 'Excuse me, your Majesty!'

On a hillside is the sanctuary of Notre-Dame de la Salette, which becomes my goal for the day. Instead of finding nuns behind closed doors I discover a booming tourist attraction. Too much for my solitary spirit. Melodie embraces me for the night on a nearby hill top.

Apparently, Our Lady is in no mood for miracles, because bad weather haunts me for another 3 days. At last

DIDIER FAVRE – VAGABOND OF THE SKIES

I manage a few 'flea jumps' and reach les Alpes d'Huez at the same time as the bicycling Tour de France.

Cloudbase at 2,600m does not help matters in the Hautes Alpes. I cast a last nostalgic look at the house of the shepherd who put me up, somewhere in the spider's web of entangled ski-lift cables, and a sad glance at the marvellous lake engulfed by the ski resort.

In my euphoria at climbing to cloudbase, I do not even notice that I am over Glandon Pass, which I had been dreading. But after the Maurienne Valley and the Madeleine Pass, conditions deteriorate. In the Tarentaise the valley wind reverses and there is nowhere to land except on a handkerchief near Hautecour la Basse.

Storms, fog and warm air from the south are on the menu. Everything seems to be a deliberate obstacle to my ambitious project, yet my morale is intact. It takes a long hard struggle to reach La Plagne, but I do finally make it to the Italian side of Mont Blanc via the Petit St Bernard Pass, though not without noticing the barbed wire littering the border between France and Italy. Months before, I initiated a clean-up of these eyesores left over from the war, which, among other things, are a menace to animal life.

Mont Blanc, August 1: At launch I have company again. This time a trespasser that invades my thoughts and increases my doubts. Stress! Where is the lift? Should I go right or left? Will it be deviated by the wind? So many questions that no one can answer. That is the inconvenience of this solitary venture, yet I have all the trump cards in my hand; ideal altitude (2,600m – 8,500ft), a head wind, a ray of sunshine. The west wind is strong but high in altitude and it should not affect me.

One, two, three and up! Melodie and I ride the first serious thermals since our departure, and whiz vertically around a glacier circus in a flurry of rocks and crevices. At 3,900m the view is spectacular, the Vallée Blanche lined with a myriad of peaks and domes in a white wonderland.

Five weeks into my Alpine crossing the conditions finally improve. I leave Italy for the Swiss Valais, home turf.

Kühboden, August 5: Kühboden, above Fiesch, is a Mecca for hang gliding. The higher one goes, the more grand the view becomes. The glaciers, particularly the majestic Aletcher, which bends into the walls of the Eggishorn, are exceptionally beautiful and can only be fully appreciated in flight. I enjoy the festival of the hundred hang gliders and paragliders filling the sky. Flying is easy in such thermic conditions. But to cross the Furka Pass I need height, which is difficult with a low cloudbase. I cross the glacier without hope of finding lift over the hotel roof. Will I make it? Sink drags me helplessly down to land below the pass at 2,400m.

At 6pm I am ready to do a straight glide to a hotel a few hundred metres away, and snap a few shots of the glacier bathed in light. Because it is such a short flight, I equip myself lightly. My mind is elsewhere, with Claude, a friend with whom I had a quick radio interview. There is an article in the newspaper about me which I am anxious to read. I take off, forgetting to clip in! Unforgivable blunder. It is the end – a brutal ending – Melodie took to the air alone and I was left in tears at launch with a broken arm. It was not an accident so much as a lesson I will never forget.

The 'Crazy Crossing' will just have to take a rain cheque.

Didier spent the winter of 1992–93 recovering, repenting and determined to take what happened personally. It was no one's fault but his own, as he instantly knew. But in his mind he had disrespected an Ethical Equation, in effect that what goes around, comes around, for which he had rightfully suffered. So it was the following May that he took a shot at crossing the Pyrenees – between France and Spain, from one end to the other. He left from Pic d'Ohry in France, and managed to do 100km before heavy wind and rain stopped him. Claiming in his own mind that it was just a practice flight anyway, he packed up and went back to Monaco to make a second attempt at the extraordinary crossing of the whole of the Alpine range to Slovenia:

On June 21, 1993, exactly one year after my first attempt at crossing the Alps, I find myself in the same spot in Sospel, inland of Monaco, but conditions are quite different. Last year it took 10 days to leave the area; this time, the thermals are smoking. In fact, there is an elevator just waiting to lift me from takeoff to cloudbase as fast as 8 m/s. My friend Patrick Guerne is filming and not unmoved as he watched me lift off en route to Slovenia.

It is not long before I am faced with my first obstacles. After just 15 kms it is impossible to go further. The Therives Pass is covered in cloud, and my wing is not handling well. Landing is a must.

But the question is, where do I land? Until now, I had not given it much thought. There is no flat ground nor bald hillside. My only option is a tiny field filled with fruit trees and electrical wires, with a fierce tail wind to boot.

I am not ashamed to do my first landing on the wheels of my control bar, and let my body drag over the ground to slow the glider down. My leading edge stops 30cms short of a plum tree. Great start!

While de-rigging, I notice that the nose-cone has been forgotten, which explains the uneasy handling. Obviously, I am not really 'into the Cap' yet. Rather than hike back to take-off with my wing on my shoulders, I call a taxi. It is still my privilege to do so.

June 21: For want of thermals, I am forced to land in the river bed of the Var below the Sausse. It is steamy; storms are about to blast off. Dozing off, I am suddenly awoken by a worker from a nearby quarry who thinks I have had an accident.

'Are you hurt?'

'No. Why? I was just sleeping.'

'What are you going to do now?'

'Take all my equipment up there, to the top of the Tête de Travers.'

'Well, I'll be damned!'

He returns to the hard work and suffocating dust of the quarry. In another 10 years he will still be there, and yet he feels sorry for me having a few hours of gear-lugging ahead of me!

It is pouring rain, thunder is groaning and there is no shelter. Night is coming on. In the distance I can see a stone fence that might surround a cabin. A shepherd's cabin, I hope, not a hunter's. Shepherds never lock their cabins, whereas a hunter's lodge is as tight as a safe.

'Phew, a shepherd's hut!' No one is home. Rarely was a roof so appreciated.

At dawn, while studying a map of the local area at the doorstep, I catch a glimpse of a swallow that swoops down, close to my head and slips through the open door. There is a falcon taking off not far away. Imagine, the swallow seeking refuge in a human home to escape its predator! How gratifying to be trusted by a bird.

June 23 – July 3: Thanks to the Mistral I am able to penetrate rather than draw a flight path over this beautiful region, the Lavecq Valley, where shepherds watch their sheep on horseback. They look proud, especially Marcel, with his authoritative moustache. His son Lionel is clad in a large slicker which covers the back of his white horse. Two other shepherds live on the other side of Sestriere. Lionel says with a 20-year-old's enthusiasm, 'People are surprised I have no electricity or running water; they ask how I'm doing but I'd rather they ask how my sheep are doing.'

Yannick is another shepherd I met in the enchanting region of Calebre during my first attempt to cross the Alps. A real musician, he taught me to play blues on the harmonica. We celebrate our reunion with pastis, the sound of African Djembe drum and a chorus of whining sheep. Yannick is wild, secret, fond of freedom, nature and his job.

What a surprise along the Allos Pass! It is Irek, a great grey-haired Dane with a pony-tail covered by a cowboy hat, who turned a Citroën into a caravan and took to the road with his horses and chickens. Intense reunions between vagabonds. He too intends to cross the Alps, but his aim is to reach Russia within 5 years.

July 20: After a few dismal days, I leave La Plagne like a thief at the first glimpse of the sun to land near the ski resort of Les Arcs, where Jean Pocard, hard-working father of seven and one of the last Beaufort cheese-makers, kindly offers me a place to sleep in the cheese room next to the enormous cauldron.

July 27: The going is slow; over two months into my journey and I am finally leaving France. In a quick glide over the glacier of Mont Pourri, I fly over Lake Chevril, near Val d'Isère. The scenery is magnificent with an intimate view of the seracs and crevasses of the glacier. Once past the ridge, the thermals take me towards a cluster of beautiful lakes at the bottom of the glacier, near a mountain ridge.

On the other side of the Aosta Valley in Italy, three eagles join me and we circle in quartet. One lands on a rock to watch me. It is odd to see a grounded bird watching a man in the air!

In the distance is the Grand St Bernard Pass, bordering Italy and Switzerland, but a north wind keeps me from reaching it. Before losing too much altitude I land on top of Crévacol, but the slope is very steep and a strong tail-wind makes landing difficult. Passing from bright sun to shade is momentarily blinding. A rough landing results in two bent uprights, one of which I manage to straighten. Fortunately, I have two spares.

August 12: The sun is setting; thermals are weakening, and like an eagle in search of prey I am searching for an ideal place to land. I have no more food and have to get some reserves.

Above Flims, I spot a tepee on top of a steep slope, de-rig amidst wonderful white mushrooms that I gobble raw, then I ran down to the huge tent where I am invited to Franzi's birthday party. She tends the cows. Eleven people are housed in the tepee … and me. Watching the fire in the middle draw strange shadows on the white canvas while a peace pipe is passed, I am a happy man!

August 14: Just before Chur in the valley of Vattis, the going is rough. Within seconds, I sink as low as 100m AGL. It would be terrible to end my bivouac journey in these remote parts with rock faces, steep forests and no access to the summits. The only way out is through the narrow end of the valley, but a small 100m mound keeps me from descending. It is a trap. With my heavy load I would not be able to make it out of there on foot.

At one point the valley forms a slight angle, dug by a cascade of rocks. I manage to stop the altitude haemorrhage and zero over a chalet tucked into the trees. Ever so slowly, I gain a few metres in height, and after an hour of concentration and struggle with all my might, I finally reach a more comfortable altitude.

But that little miracle is owed to the strengthening 'Foehn', which will soon turn mean. It is blowing south in gusts, forcing me to keep a firm grip on the control-bar, which drives me to physical and psychological exhaustion. I choose to escape toward the plains near a tiny stream that further on turns into one of the biggest rivers in Europe, the Rhine.

Over Landquart, I drift with the wind, negotiating each puff of air and trying to maintain altitude without losing anything. At the foot of Mt Vilan, it is the same. This is a real test of patience. Don't be hasty, work for every extra metre …in the end I am rewarded. The valley opens up, turbulence diminishes and calm returns. I feel like a contortionist but finally make it upwind to land on Mount Churz at 2,000m. Good God, what a flight!

August 17: Cloudbase is at 2,800m but the lowest mountains going over the pass into Austria are all over 3,000m. Perhaps tomorrow will give higher cloudbases.

I spot Silvretta's cabin at the foot of the glacier, my favourite place to nestle in, but a Swiss flag battered by the wind tells me to be careful landing. With the bar against my stomach, I steam in at full speed toward the slope behind the cabin to make a neat flare, except that the wind lifts my left leading edge and one wing scrapes the ground. I end up caught in one of the cables and cannot manage to undo the caribiner that ties me to it.

Meanwhile, the whole mess is sliding downward and tearing the sail. There is nothing I can do, and nor, apparently, can the five imbeciles watching me just a few steps away.

I decide to carry my wing to the Obstansersee refuge on the Austrian side of the pass. In order to save time I take a short cut used by the lumberjacks, but it is just a dead end. The woods keep getting deeper and darker and my backpack keeps getting heavier. The forest is unwelcoming. Night falls fast so I have to stop because it would be too dangerous to continue on that steep slope. Alas, I forego the comfort of the refuge to face a cold night outdoors, with my polar trousers and 700g sleeping bag for warmth. It is so cold that I have to heat the water in my bottle before I can drink it.

Next day, a huge cliff forces me to descend the valley by working my way, grip by grip, down off steep slopes and a dry waterfall. Thank goodness I didn't try to reach the refuge last night. Bivouac flying is often less risky in the air than on the ground. If I had fallen, no one would have been able to find me. But these complications are part of the game. They mean paying more attention to every step, watching for the slippery stones, or which rock or clump of grass to grip. The time and energy spent here is insignificant compared to all the time in the world I actually have to spend.

August 30: Because I cannot find any flat area to sleep on, I keep slipping downhill throughout the night. Not even tucking myself into my wing can spare me; Dacron sail material is very slippery.

Two conflicting air masses keep me from taking off. On my right, the continental air offers a nice view with a cloudbase of 3,500m. But my direction is left, where the sea air keeps the clouds low. The scenery is such a wondrous spectacle veiled in white that I don't regret not being in the air.

The next day a nasty wind sweeps up my red cap which has been my inseparable companion (night cap, cold cap, sun cap, water cap, radio carrier, good luck hat, eye protection, nose protection, friend and witness to all my adventures). I had laid it on a rock to take a photograph and it flew off like a feather. Bad omen? I won't fly today. Instead I will compose a harmonica requiem for my cap.

WILD ADVENTURES OF THE NEW AVIATORS

September 1: Near the top of Mt Volaia where there are old WWII fortifications, there is an ideal launch but a gusty tailwind. Should I risk a takeoff? I am so close to my goal. I decide to give it a try. I have become so crusty and cautious, yielding to the slightest uncertainty. It is torture to be faced with my own principles when judging risk.

Around 2pm my patient waiting for the right wind to launch is rewarded. I go for it, and takeoff is easy! One hour and 30km later, a wrong decision puts me below a ridge and minutes later I am landing in a mass of thorns in a narrow valley – smiling! Who cares? At least I am safe and closer to goal. Slovenia is only 40kms away. I hear cow bells and bleating goats as I fold my wing. Half an hour later, I am the guest of Italian-speaking Arturo. I am in Italy!

Bianca, the old donkey, has not carried a load in ages, but Arturo insisted. He ties two half-barrel shaped bags on to each side of her and piles on my equipment. We take the road to the Lanza Pass, where there is a lovely little inn. That funny little donkey is the only exception to the Cap's rule of non-assistance. I have refused help at least a hundred times, but Bianca was irresistible!

September 2: Tarvisio is the last Italian town before Slovenia, over which I scrabble with a tiny thermal to get myself towards goal. What if I am forced to land in a hostile region where mountains are so thickly covered with trees that takeoff is impossible? Imagine after such an amazing journey, ending up having to carry my wing across the border? How humiliating! My eyes are already in Slovenia but I am losing altitude. There are no clouds in the last valley I have to cross. I hesitate a moment before going back in search of a thermal near the ridge at tree level.

I've got one! It's taking me up at 5 m/s! I take a few photos to capture this intense moment for eternity, then climb to cloudbase. Crossing the border is a mere formality now, which I do singing at the top of my lungs. Conditions are so good that I glide past Kranjska Gora all the way to Jesenice, where, like a play about to end, a curtain of cirrus invades the sky. It is 5 pm; children rush towards me. It is difficult to communicate so I play a tune on my harmonica that they happen to know, and they accompany me in song, totally unaware of my exhilaration.

There is little doubt that this is the greatest hang glider flight ever made, a physical and spiritual journey that can hold its own against any single-handed journey, by any means of transport, anywhere in world history. The fact that hardly anybody in the world knows about it is more a comment on the world than the journey.

Like all great pilots, Didier was fascinated by new developments in the wings we fly. There is always something new to be tested, and in the years since 1971 hundreds of pilots have stood on top of hills with a new wing above them, and just before the take-off run, wondered if it would fly, and how it would handle.

On 6 May 1994, in the early evening, Didier found himself in such a position. He was set to do a proving flight on a radical new wing called the Delka, designed and built in secret by his friend and fellow Swiss, Laurent 'Lauri' Kalbermatten, who had already made a significant contribution to the designs of paragliders. Didier was not going to test-fly off a small hill, low and slow. They chose instead a launch 1,000m high (3,280ft) in which the early part of his flight would be over Lake Geneva. Like other test pilots, Alvin Russell, John Hudson, Paul Maritos, George Worthington, he did not have a rocket parachute, but he did not think he needed one because of Didier's enthusiasm for the new design:

> The originality of the Delka is that the pilot is integrated with the wing, like a bird [and Lilienthal – BM], rather than suspended underneath as in a classical hang glider. The pilot's head tops out over the wing while his arms direct the aerodynamic controls set in the sail. His legs hang out behind.
>
> The Delka (named for DELta and KAlbermatten) resembles no other aircraft, and definitely marks a giant step in light wings. Many experts have tried, but never succeeded, in conceiving such a wing, where the pilot's integration with the machine makes for obvious advantages in performance. But 38-year-old Laurent Kalbermatten did it, and we should say, again!

For the moment the designer is content to perfect the prototype which he does not expect to sell commercially before 1995, by taking all safety precautions and above all preparing pilots for a new way of flying, which previous flight will not have prepared them for.

By virtue of its compact size – folding down to 2m50 (8 feet 3 inches) – and light weight – 25kg (55lbs) including harness – the Delka is smaller and lighter than a hang glider, but it has an impressive potential for performance. The Delka might well replace the present-day hang glider.

The first flight is preceded neither by models nor tests on hillsides nor computer simulation (writes Didier). I am still fit after my crossing the Alps, and made the inaugural flight without the slightest problem.

Nevertheless, a lot of work remains to be done, 'but there's no hurry' says Kalbermatten, who feels strongly that the exponential popularity of paragliding is actually detrimental to its proper development, which was scarred by too many accidents. For the Delka, he prefers to progress slowly and surely. 'A first flight means nothing more than the thing can fly.'

Flight Log: 6.30am: The mist is fogging my optimism. Lots on my mind today. By noon the low pressure passes and the sun finally imposes itself upon the landscape. Two buzzards let themselves go up in a gentle thermal as if they were totally indifferent to the teeming traffic below. I am below, looking up, but I will be joining them in a few hours, though not with the same peace of mind nor wandering spirit. For once, I will content myself with a short straight flight, and who knows what kind of landing?

Lauri is in the hangar, uncommonly serious as he takes inventory of all the possible hang-ups. We are optimistic. Still, I leave a note for my loved ones on the windscreen of my car … just in case.

At the takeoff site at 6.15 in the evening, Lauri alone rigs the wing, fits me into the harness and checks the slightest details three times. He is tense, to say the least. Not even a little tune on my harmonica loosens him up. Surprisingly enough, I am the one who is serene. In fact, I am determined, motivated, confident. I see this as a fabulous rendezvous with a revolutionary machine that is going to transform our free-flying habits. It is an honour to be here. I am ready.

Conditions are ideal and the light is magic as it dances on the lake 1,000m below.

Roland Delez takes off on his hang glider to photograph the Delka. I follow and keep straight, as instructed, until I am over the lake. At 700m the water is like a blue-tinted mirror. The flight is incredible, because I am actually inside the wing with my head peering over the outer surface, and my legs dangling behind. There are only a few short minutes to grasp as much as possible about the wing's reactions.

Because I am too low to reach the landing area we agreed the night before, I let my pilot's instincts guide me. Approaching the terrain, I give a hearty tug on the controls at the last minute and make a perfect landing in Noville, just 8 minutes and 10 seconds after taking off.

No one dared say it at launch, but the wing is so well-designed that anyone could have flown it.

'I last saw him at Bassano,' Judy Leden wrote. 'As usual he did not waste time with social niceties, getting straight to the point of sharing stories and dreams. He was happier than I had ever seen him. His thickly accented words came out at breakneck speed as he told of the next generation of hang glider – the *Delka*. With the excitement of a schoolboy he produced photographs, beaming with delight in finding people to share his enthusiasm.'

On 5 August 1994, Didier Favre took off on another proving flight (one has to ask why Lauri Kalbermatten did not do his own flying, rather than have someone else risk his neck?) Sherry Thevenot told me that it was not known exactly what happened except that Didier may have confused the controls, which were tip-dragger and weight-shift combined. He could have pushed on a speed stirrup, and when the wing went into a steep dive found that he was not in a physical position to be able to take his feet off the stirrup. In any case, the Delka did not recover. In the same way as Alvin Russell died, and John Hudson, Paul Maritos and George Worthington died, and as so nearly I died, Didier

Favre wanted to prove something new could fly better. He was killed for his opinion.

Like the others he knew the risks, and death was always the alternative if one took one too many risks with life. Death is our unspoken companion, someone quiet who sits by our shoulder like a bandersnatch and more often than not says nothing, leaving us to fly again another day. But sometimes, not just when we risk too much, because Didier took much worse risks than flying the Delka that day, but like throwing a dice, death decides to tap us on the shoulder, and we have to go. One day, of course, the tap comes to all of us. You don't have to take any risks at all. It will just happen one day. It is just a question of when.

Although Didier Favre was the quintessential Western man in all his contradictions, his fierce individualism and his identification with nature, his successful business career that he threw away for a single French franc, his brutal competitiveness and the fact that he would give the shirt off his back if someone needed it, Judy Leden – as good a flyer in the world to write his obituary – felt the words of an Eastern and not a Western poet penned the best epitaph for his life:

> For what is to die but to stand naked in the
> wind and to melt into the sun?
> And what is to cease breathing but to free the
> breath from its restless tides, that may rise and
> expand and seek God unencumbered?
> Only when you drink from the river of silence
> shall you indeed sing.
> And when you have reached the mountain
> top, then shall you begin to climb.
> And when the earth shall claim your limbs,
> then shall you truly dance.
>
> The Prophet: Kahill Gibran

Sources

W   *Wings*, the BHGA magazine, which I edited for a year
XC   *Cross Country Magazine*, then mainly edited by Sherry Thevenot
FL   *Flightline*, the magazine of the British Microlight Aircraft Association
HG *Hang Gliding*, the magazine of the USHGA

Features from various miscellaneous magazines

Reference coding

Wings: W576.15 an article published on p.15 of the May 1976 edition.

Cross Country: SO94 was published in the September–October edition in 1994.

Flightline: FL3/486.8 is an article published in the March–April 1986 edition on p.8.

Hang Gliding: HG991 was published on September 1991.

1. Characters and Other Holy Lunatics

Rich Pfieffer's book *Pfieffer on HG*
W181. AMCUP report on aerobatics
W691.43 Account of Pepe's death
HG392.50/51 Demographics of HG, we're getting older!
W178.17 Welsh KO KO'd, lunatic distance flying and courage
WA585.38/39 Profile of La Mouette @ Gerard Thevenot

XCJJ93.39/40 Gerard Thevenot, Spanish Joe interview
XCDJ94/5.13 Angelo Crapanzano on Thevenot's Fr team exclusion
XCSP89.32 More on soaring bush fires
W977.12/13 Lester Cruise's loop and break-up
W379.14 Dangerous Sport Club leaps off Kilimanjaro
WN379.7 Ashley's reply to Kili criticism
WN379.15 Ashley's article (part 1) on the Kili flight
WN479.10 John Hudson on night flying Winter Hill
WN479.15 Ashley on Kili, part 2
W280.14/15 Midnight flight into the 1980s
W780.12 OAPs HGA
W1084.12 Lovely Jack Donaldson, OAP HGP
HG383.4 Kerfuffle over Rich Pfieffer's Rose Bowl flight 104,000 counts 'assault with deadly weapon'
HG1089.38/40 Good OAP article, 70 yr old on XC
XCWI88.32 Bostik grounded for soaring bush fires XCJJ92.3 Base jumping at Yosemite
XCFM94.9 Base jumping a 5,000' cliff in Norway
XCJJ94.6/10 BASE Jumping, more details, including world record
XCON94.42/45 London–Paris by microlight (and back)
XCAM91.6/7 Girl jumps off wing of HG, often!
W988.17 Owens Valley and broken neck story
XCAU90.23 Bungee jump from balloon, Mark Buscail, with camera
XCJJ92.3 Base jumping pix at Yosemite
XCDJ92/3.44 Bungee jumping from a PG

2. Distances and Heights After 1981

W1080.9 Definitive run-down of world records
W1080.16 Account of Calvert's record 79-mile flight
W1180.8 More new GW records
W681.18 Jim Lee flies 170 miles, between 13,000 & 15,000ft
HG677.11 Account of 38m XC by the young Larry Tudor
HG677.34/36 Account of 44m flight XC on an SST
HG777.12/13 Jeff Scott flies record 72 m
W582.8/9 Calvert beats 100 m (112m) in UK

SOURCES

W1082.19 John Duncker, 19 stone, 225 pounds, climbs 8,500ft
XCAM92.26/27 Soaring dust devils – Jim Lee explores
WW983.12/13, 31 Larry Tudor flies 226m, without oxygen
HG1089.17/21 Kevin Christopherson's 287m flight
XCSU88.28 European official distance record 250kms
XCSU88.30 Larry Tudor's 1987 349 km world record
XCSP89.23 4 XCs from Bruce Goldsmith
XCAU89.30 K Christopherson's 465k Tudor-beating flight
XCAU89.41 UK distance record of 244.7 k
XCWI89.19/21 Detailed account of Christopherson's XC record
XCSU90.17/18 Larry Tudor takes back distance record, 484k
XCSU90.19 Summary of world distance records
XCJJ92.35 Johnny Carr's 45m out and return
XCJJ92.46/47 314 miles in South Africa
XCAM94.14 Drew Cooper sets Oz dis rec of 427 k
XCON94.6/8 Larry Tudor's 307 mile flight
W983. Front C. Lark second to 100 m in England
W9.83.11/13, 31 July 13, Longest day in Owens, all records fall.
W684.18. Pendry flies 130 miles along south coast
W689.11 & 21 Judy gets Brit women's dist record 114m, Wensleydale
W789.17 Very funny Liavan Mallin XC story, 61.5m in Ireland
W1089.19/21 Kevin Christopherson, distance flying & courage

3. Birds and the New Aviation

WN379.27 Flying against a peregrine falcon
XCAU90.5 Mr Elliott, an eagle in Oz
XCDJ93/4.5 Bill Lishman, flying with geese
XCFM94.30/34 Bill Lishman, flying with geese article
XCJJ94.4 Update on the Lishman geese migration
WA486.33 Jo Bathmann's account of an upset eagle
W787.20/5/26 Rob Bailey mixes with eagles in Oz
W1191.27 Crow flies with man at Mam Tor
XCSP88.14 Eagles and HGs in Oz
W880.17 Jeremy Fack flying with vultures in Africa
W884/11/12 Judy Leden flying with condors in Himalayas

4. Paragliding

W1280.31 Brian Gaskin story in Icarus, I was wrong
W581.24 Icarus previews parasails in small para
W986.9 First mention of paragliding
W589.13 History of Paragliding
W1191.24/25 Robbie wins world PG Champs
XCSP88.16 Paragliding early background
XCWI88.33 Jean Marc Boivin paraglides off Everest
XCSP89.24/25 Account, paragliding from Everest
XCSU89.35 New paraglider distance record 49.4k
XCSU90.12 First 100k flight by paraglider
XCSU90.38 Japanese HG schools and stats
XCFM91.6/7 Paragliding dist record to 150k
XCFM91.26/27 Account of flying off Everest by PG
XCFM91.40 Paragliding distance records – the World
XCAM91.46 1-page history of PG
XCFM92.12 Analysis of PG accidents
XCFM92.18/20 Paramountaineering (!)
XCFM92.21/22 New PG distance record of 231k
XCON92.52 Harald Eigner – 152 PG, Euro record
XCDJ93/4.26 Profile, OZ PG Champ, good on Oz stats
XCDJ93/4.30/31 Ex PG account, W height gain Rec in Namibia
XCFM94.20 Nearly falling out of a PG, 'Andy's Fright'
XCAM94.21 Profile, Gin Soek Song, Korean designer of PGs
XCAM94.30/33 Kenyan safari with PGs and corrupt officials
XCJJ94.36/37 Profile of Sadao Hangai, Big Jap PG maker/flyer
XCON94.22 World PG distance record stats, 30 countries
XCAM95.50/51 First 100m PG flight in the UK
XCAM95.64 World PG dist record now 283.5k

5. Women and the New Aviation

W1078.14 G Worthington on woman pilots (Page Pfieffer)
W1080.28/29 Sexist Battles, humour from Rex Grogan
W980.31 Lovely cartoon about naked lady and weather forecast
W283.10 Letter from GHP wife, pro, on first 2-up flt

SOURCES

W1182.15 Debbi Renshaw, first woman in US Masters – came nowhere
W589.53 Kay Simpson on being a woman pilot
W190.25 The Harriet Quimby Trophy
HG789.18/20 Profile, Kris Greblo (Joe's wife, a flyer)
HG989.42/43 Katharine Yardley, new WXC record 164m
XCSP88.25 Women with wings
XCSU88.30 Jenny Ganterton's 68.75k triangle
XCSU88.6 Women fly HGs off Kilimanjaro
XCSU88.28 Three women enter German HG league
XCWI88.11 Beautiful Jap girl int, flew with Tudor
XCWI88.18 Eve Jackson's Segrave gold medal
XCWI88.19 Women's world altitude gain record
XCWI88.33 Girl tows to 15,000ft
XCWI89.8 Harriet Quimby Trophy/background
XCSU90.41/42 Irish girl Liavin Mallin, Owens accident
XCSU90.49 Kari Castle new World distance record of 291k
XCFM91.16/17 Kari Castle's 182 XC, + 3 records
XCFM92.16 Kari Castle on 210m flight
XCJJ92.36/37 Woman (Ally WHO?) wins 1991 British PG Open
XCAS92.52 Sarah Fenwick 63K on PG, new WWR
XCJJ93.5 Astonishing stats from Japan. 20% pilots women!
XCJJ93.26/30 Mickey Mouse Women's Worlds in Japan
XCDJ94/5.16 Nice girlie story following B Goldsmith G XC on a PG
W881.11 Jenny Ganderton's first XC, 20 miles
W784.7 Jenny Ganderton regains Br Dist record, 65.49 miles
GR679.37 Feature on top US female pilots, incl Paige Pfieffer
HGATF.142 Heavy story about Pfieffer flying against his wife
W582.11 First women's Brit league
W1183.17 Judy wins Brit champs, still outside League
W684.7 Sexist invite to Owens for Judy
W894.14/14 Len Hull wins Hungarian Open, Judy third, Brits team gold
W986.9 Short piece on Judy winning Women's Euros (shit mag!)
W1288.13 Judy (middle column) flying with bad arms
W689.6 Brit Ladies champs (Judy) + 1989 Blériot, narrow Brit win
W989.27/29 Lucy McSwiney wins paragliding gold
HG991.13 Rankings at 1991 Women's worlds
W683.7 Judy Leden's account of 49m UK flight
W983.11 Judy Leden takes world dist record 145.6m

W884/11/12 Judy Leden flying with condors in Himalayas
W589.82/85 Judy Leden jumps off Mt Cotopaxi (account)
W1191.22/23 Judy wins world HG Champs
WA486.38 Judy Leden, a brief biog.
XCWI88.8/9 Judy Leden on sponsorship
XCAU89.41 Judy Leden's Channel crossing
XCSU90.27 Judy's Channel Crossing, an account
XCSU90.43/44 Judy Leden, Sarah Fenwick, XCing in Oz
XCAM95.6/7 Judy wins world women's PG title

6. Events After 1980

W180.12/13 John Hudson on Owens Valley
W180.24 Formation of the XC League by Dave Harrison
W480.22/24 Lachens article, incl The Black Death
W880.7 Proposal from us that CIVL do XC worlds
W783.11 Steve Moyes wins worlds (see his Dad)
W883.6/7 Hughes wins Owens Classic
XCSP88.20/21 Joe Bostik profile, single minded
XCSU88.22 Robbie Whittall, short profile
XCAU89.23 Tomas Suchanek, profile
XCSU90.30/31 John Pendry profile
XCAS92.40/42 Profile, Angelo Crapanzano
XCON92.15 Profile, Manfred Ruhmer (Austria)
XCDJ92/3.40/41 Psyching up (and down) how HGP help each other
XCDJ93/4.16 Tomas Suchanek, Twice WC, a profile
XCDJ93/4.20/21 Jap competition, difficult and lucrative
W881.15/17 OV Racing, JH, Brit comes 6th (comp 4 yrs old)
W1181.2. Where the Fosters sponsorship money went
W1181.5/9 Japan worlds, Brit wins team comp, Pepe wins
W682.4/7 Brits win Blériot at Lachens
W682.13 Preview 1982 AmCup
W782.15/21 Account of 1982 AmCup
W982.14/19 Brits win Eu Champs 1,2,3, 5. Hughes Champ
W1182.2 Fosters renew for much less money
W1182.15 Ledford wins US Masters, first woman invite
W1181.25 Stan Abbott blags glider off BHGA

SOURCES

W183.5 Ronnie Faux on luck of English at '82 AmCup
W483.4/5 Roy Hill removed in coup d'état
W683.13/15 Hughes wins 2nd Fosters
W783.7/11 Steve Moyes wins 1983 worlds. Oz wins team prize, Brits second
Note: Blériot in 1978, '79 drawn, lost 80 (I was coach), won in 1981, '82, '83
W783.16/17 Brits win Blériot
W883.6/7 Tony Hughes wins Owens Classic
W582.11 Johnny Carr wins 1st Fosters
W784.18/19 Pendry wins Austrian Masters, preview of Kossen worlds
W984.7 Hughes retains Euro champs, Brits Team 3rd after Germans/French
W1084.14/16 Tudor wins Owens, Pendry 2nd, Hughes 8th
W585.14/15 Pendry wins Oz Buffalo Classic, Carnet 6th
W986.7 Australia wins AmCup, lots of controversy
W986.14/15 Profile, Derek Evans, good bits on comp philosophy
W1186.16/17 John Duncker's AmCup account
W488.15/19 Some stuff on the 1988 worlds ... not very good
W888.20/21 Brits 1, 2, 3 in Euros, Pendry wins
W389.8 Brits 1, 2, 5, 6 in Brazil + Monique's accident (a character)
W4/589.22/25 How Brits win in Brazil, 8 of top 10 on Magic Kisses
W4/589.35 My whinge about lack of Brit recognition
W989.24/25 Robbie's brill win at worlds, Brit gold
W1089.9 More details, including scores, on Robbie's win
W690.6/7 Brazil pre-worlds (won by Brazil)
W890.6 Brits win Euros, team and individual, France 2nd
W990.24/25 Full details on Brit Euro win, 2-wayer with France
W1090.32/33 Veterans Competition in Austria
W1090.38/39 M. Whittall reports on Superleague and sponsorship
W892.18/19 Brits (Pendry) win Euros, and team event too
W892.34 French win Blériot
HG989.24/32 US account of the 1989 Worlds
XCSP88.8/11 Gerard Thevenot on 1988 Oz worlds
XCSU89.8/9 Pendry leads Brits to world domination
XCSU89.14/15 Brazilian Cup, warm up to worlds, Brits dominate
XCSU89.31/32 Bassano, Pendry wins for 4th time
XCSU90.16/18 Alternative Brazil Champs. Paolinho wins

XCSU90.29/30 Bassano, Brits first 4, Whittall wins paras, RMH 2nd
XCAU90.30/31 Pendry's early career (of which I know little)
XCAU90.35/37 Pendry wins 1990 Euros. Brits win team prize
XCAM91.17/20 1991 Worlds, won by Suchanek, Brits win team event
XCJJ92.14/15 Bassano, Alain Chauvet wins, Brits beat French
XCAS92.6/9 Europeans. Pendry wins, as do Brits
XCAS92.26/27 Pre-worlds at Owens. Pendry wins, Sherry hates site
XCAM95.27 Last PIRS before 1995 worlds

7. Deaths, and All That

W1276.20 UK analysis of accidents
W377.4 Analysis of British deaths in 1976
Note: Ten fatalities in 1978 in the UK
WN479.22/25 Accident summary for 1978
W880.9 International accident stats
W481.18/20 1980 accident report
W584.10/12 Summary of UK accidents in 1983 (106, 4 fatal)
HG677.48/49 1976 accident survey, by RV Wills (Bob's Dad)
HG777.44 More analysis of 1976 fatalities
HG977.34/39 1st US Nationals lookback, of 36, 6 are now dead!
HG980.42/45 Summary, 1979 accidents, some of 1980 HG383.35/37 Accident review for 1982
HG389.38/39 Summary of accidents from 1970–88, in USA
HG392.18/20 Summary of 1991 US accidents in HG
W876.16 Accident report, Barbara Jones, Guy Twiss
W777.19 Death of Bob Wills
W678.7 Paul Renouf's accident
W678.20 Accident reports, including Renouf and Nick Lawler
W1280.8 Peter Brown's death
W181.6 Death of Dave Jones in M/L
W281.20 Good Icarus comment on K Cockroft
W481.12 Obit on Dave Jones (see W181.6)
W1281.22/23 Bob Wills, the Tony Fuel one-foot story
W782.26/26 George Worthington on the Wanderer; it killed him
W982.3. Death of George Worthington
W1082.8 Eulogy by John Hudson for GW

SOURCES

W283.5 Death of Ashley Doubtfire (32?)
W383.5 Tribute to Ashley Doubtfire from Gerry Breen
W583.3 Ashley's death prompts club probe
W883.3, 13 Steve Hunt killed on Pathfinder microlight
W883.5 Death of Jim Taggart
W284.7 Chris Bulger already US Masters and Open US Champ
W284.11 Dave Bedding praises the Explorer (killed on one?)
W889.13 Obits to Mark Southall and John Hudson
W889.14/17 The Great Italian killer storm
W1191.9 Death of Andy Napolitan
HG877.18, 51 Bob Wills, Obit from his parents
WA486.9 death of Dan Racanelli
Adventure Sports.39 K. Cockroft on Owens Valley
XCAU89.41 Deaths of John Hudson and Mark Southall
XCSU90.15 Paolo Coelho, a profile (v poor kid, HG saved him)
XCAM91.20 Death of Pepe Lopez
XCAM91.50 Death of Andy Napolitan
XCDJ93/4.18 Death of Paulo Coelho (accident, but how?)
XCJJ94.5 Death of Keith Cockroft – a good poem

8. Migration

W181.5 Milton's Migration Rules
W284.16/17 Mike de Glanville's original migrational therapy
XCFM94.46/47, 55 Mike de Glanville's 1983 migrational therapy
XCJJ92.18/21 Judy Leden and RMH towing HGs in Kenya Rift Valley
XCSU89.17 Regs for 444, especially prize 10 (5 babes)
XCFM92.6/8 Bivouac flying the 222
XCON92.14/15 Cap 333, Pierre Bouilloux
XCFM94.6/8 Scotland is for me, poetic PG by Hubert Aupetit
XCDJ94/95.62/63 XC across the Pyrenees, the eight-year challenge

9. Didier Favre – Vagabond of the Skies

XCSU88.30 Didier Favre's 444, news item
XCAM92.20/22 Didier Favre's 444 journal

WILD ADVENTURES OF THE NEW AVIATORS

XCAM92.48 Didier's 1992 (abortive) Cap 1111
XCON92.30 Didier's equipment tips for Bivouac flying
XCON92.52 Didier breaks arm on 1992 Cap 1111
XCDJ92/3.6/8 Didier on abortive Cap 1111
XCDJ92/3.11 Spanish Joe interviews Didier
XCJJ93.54 More on Didier's Cap 1111
XCDJ93/4, 5 Didier's book on Cap 1111
XCDJ93/4.8/10 Wonderful account of Cap 1111
XCJJ94.16/17 Didier Favre on the Delka, which soon killed him
XCON94.20 Judy Leden's appreciation of Didier Favre's death